Data Mining

with Microsoft® SQL Server™ 2000

Technical Reference

Claude Seidman

PUBLISHED BY
Microsoft Press
A Division of Microsoft Corporation
One Microsoft Way
Redmond, Washington 98052-6399

Library of Congress Cataloging-in-Publication Data
Seidman, Claude, 1964-
     Data Mining with Microsoft SQL Server 2000 Technical Reference / Claude Seidman.
         p. cm.
     Includes index.
     ISBN 0-7356-1271-4
     1. Data mining.   2. SQL server.   I. Title.

     QA76.9.D343 S45 2001
     006.3--dc21   00-069526

Printed and bound in the United States of America.

1 2 3 4 5 6 7 8 9   QWT   6 5 4 3 2 1

Distributed in Canada by Penguin Books Canada Limited.

A CIP catalogue record for this book is available from the British Library.

Microsoft Press books are available through booksellers and distributors worldwide. For further information about international editions, contact your local Microsoft Corporation office or contact Microsoft Press International directly at fax (425) 936-7329. Visit our Web site at mspress.microsoft.com. Send comments to *mspinput@microsoft.com.*

Acquisitions Editor: David Clark
Project Editor: Lynn Finnel
Technical Editor: Jim Fuchs

Body Part No. X08-04138

Contents

Acknowledgments   xi
Introduction   xiii

PART I Introducing Data Mining

1 Understanding Data Mining   3

What Is Data Mining?	3
Why Use Data Mining?	4
How Data Mining Is Currently Used	6
Defining the Terms	7
Data Mining Methodology	9
Analyzing the Problem	10
Extracting and Cleansing the Data	10
Validating the Data	10
Creating and Training the Model	10
Querying the Data Mining Model Data	10
Maintaining the Validity of the Data-Mining Model	10
Overview of Microsoft Data Mining	11
Data Mining vs. OLAP	11
Data-Mining Models	11
Data-Mining Algorithms	12
Using SQL Server Syntax to Data Mine	14
Summary	14

2 Microsoft SQL Server Analysis Services Architecture   15

Introduction to OLAP	16
MOLAP	18
ROLAP	18
HOLAP	19
Server Architecture	20
Data Mining Services Within Analysis Services	20

Client Architecture   21
    PivotTable Service   22
    OLE DB   23
    Decision Support Objects (DSO)   24
    Multidimensional Expressions (MDX)   25
    Prediction Joins   25
Summary   26

3   Data Storage Models   27

Why Data Mining Needs a Data Warehouse   27
    Maintaining Data Integrity   28
Reporting Against OLTP Data
Can Be Hazardous to Your Performance   31
Data Warehousing Architecture for Data Mining   33
    Creating the Warehouse from OLTP Data 33
    Optimizing Data for Mining   36
    Physical Data Mining Structure   42
    Three-Tier Architecture   43
Relational Data Warehouse   43
    Advantages of Relational Data Storage 44
    Building Supporting Tables for Data Mining 45
OLAP cubes   46
    How Data Mining Uses OLAP Structures 46
    Advantages of OLAP Storage   47
    When OLAP Is Not Appropriate for Data Mining 49
Summary   49

4   Approaches to Data Mining   51

Directed Data Mining   51
Undirected Data Mining   52
    Data Mining vs. Statistics   52
    Learning from Historical Data   57
    Predicting the Future   59
Training Data-Mining Models   61
    Evaluating the Models and Avoiding Errors 62
Summary   65

PART II Data-Mining Methods

5   Microsoft Decision Trees   69

Creating the Model	69
Analysis Manager	70
Visualizing the Model	87
Dependency Network Browser	94
Inside the Decision Tree Algorithm	97
How Predictions Are Derived	109
Navigating the Tree	109
Navigation vs. Rules	112
When to Use Decision Trees	113
Summary	114

6   Creating Decision Trees with OLAP   115

Creating the Model	115
Select Source Type	116
Select Source Cube and Data-Mining Technique	116
Select Case	118
Select Predicted Entity	119
Select Training Data	121
Select Dimension and Virtual Cube	121
Completing the Data-Mining Model	123
OLAP Mining Model Editor	125
Content Detail Pane	126
Structure Panel	126
Prediction Tree List	126
Analyzing Data with the OLAP Data-Mining Model	126
Using the Generated Virtual Cube	128
Using the Generated Dimension	129
Summary	133

7   Microsoft Clustering   135

The Search for Order	136
Looking for Ways to Understand Data	136
Clustering as an Undirected Data-Mining Technique	137
How Clustering Works	138
Overview of the Algorithm	138
The K-Means Method Clustering Algorithm	138
What Is Being Measured Exactly?	142
Clustering Factors	142
Measuring "Closeness"	143
When to Use Clustering	146
Visualize Relationships	146
Highlight Anomalies	146
Create Samples for Other Data-Mining Efforts	148
Weaknesses of Clustering	148
Creating a Data-Mining Model Using Clustering	149
Select Source Type	150
Select the Table or Tables for Your Mining Model	150
Select the Data-Mining Technique	151
Edit Joins	152
Select the Case Key Column for Your Mining Model	152
Select the Input and Predictable Columns	152
Viewing the Model	154
Organization of the Cluster Nodes	154
Order of the Cluster Nodes	156
Analyzing the Data	156
Summary	158

PART III Creating Data-Mining Applications with Code

8   Using Microsoft Data Transformation Services (DTS)   161

What Is DTS?	162
DTS Tasks	162
Transform	162
Bulk Insert	163
Data Driven Query	163
Execute Package	164

Connections   167
     Sources   167
     Configuring a Connection   168
DTS Package Workflow   169
     DTS Package Steps   169
     Precedence Constraints   170
DTS Designer   171
     Opening the DTS Designer   171
     Saving a DTS Package   172
dtsrun Utility   174
Using DTS to Create a Data-Mining Model   177
     Preparing the SQL Server Environment   178
     Creating the Package   182
Summary   208

9   Using Decision Support Objects (DSO)   209
Scripting vs. Visual Basic   210
     The *Server* Object   211
     The *Database* Object   219
Creating the Relational Data-Mining Model Using DSO   221
Creating the OLAP Data-Mining Model Using DSO   230
     The *DataSource* Object   232
     Data-Mining Model (Decision Support Objects)   233
Adding a New Data Source   233
Analysis Server Roles   234
     Data-Mining Model Roles   235
Summary   236

10   Understanding Data-Mining Structures   237
The Structure of the Data-Mining Model Case   237
     Data-Mining Models Look Like Tables   237
Using Code to Browse Data-Mining Models   238
Using the Schema Rowsets   243
     MINING_MODELS Schema Rowset   243
     MINING_COLUMNS Schema Rowset   249
     MINING_MODEL_CONTENT Schema Rowset   259
     MINING_SERVICES Schema Rowset   262

SERVICE_PARAMETERS Schema Rowset 266
MODEL_CONTENT_PMML Schema Rowset 268
Summary 269

11 Data Mining Using PivotTable Service 271
Redistributing Components 272
Installing and Registering Components 273
File Locations 274
Installation Registry Settings 275
Redistribution Setup Programs 275
Connecting to the PivotTable Service 276
Connect to Analysis Services Using PivotTable Service 276
Connect to Analysis Services Using HTTP 280
Building a Local Data-Mining Model 280
Storage of Local Mining Models 284
SELECT INTO Statement 286
INSERT INTO Statement 286
OPENROWSET Syntax 287
Nested Tables and the SHAPE Statement 289
Using XML in Data Mining 290
The PMML Standard 290
Summary 296

12 Data-Mining Queries 297
Components of a Prediction Query 297
The Basic Prediction Query 298
Specifying the Test Case Source 298
Specifying Columns 300
The PREDICTION JOIN Clause 300
Using Functions as Columns 304
Using Tabular Values as Columns 304
The WHERE Clause 306
Prediction Functions 307
Predict 307
PredictProbability 308
PredictSupport 308

PredictVariance   309
PredictStdev   310
PredictProbabilityVariance   310
PredictProbabilityStdev   310
PredictHistogram   310
TopCount   313
TopSum   313
TopPercent   314
RangeMin   314
RangeMid   314
RangeMax   314
PredictScore   314
PredictNodeId   315
Prediction Queries with Clustering Models   315
Cluster   315
ClusterProbability   316
ClusterDistance   316
Using DTS to Run Prediction Queries   317
Summary   322

Appendix   325

Glossary   349
Index   359

Acknowledgments

This book was indeed a monumental effort to write—but a fun one as well in large part thanks to Lynn Finnel and Jim Fuchs, who not only provided me with outstanding support but also showed such great interest in the subject matter of the book. Like a kid who falls asleep in the back seat of the car while his parents drive, I felt completely safe in knowing that they were there to make sense out of my endless, twisted technical ramblings, turning them into beautifully coherent sentences. I would also like to thank Rob Nance who is, as far as I'm concerned, a brilliant graphic artist, especially when you consider the scribbled sketches I sent him. Thanks also to Jamie MacLennan, who took the time from his busy schedule whenever he was able to answer some of the trickier questions I had about this product.

It was truly an honor and a pleasure to write this book on such an exciting subject. For this opportunity and the guidance he provided as I went along, I thank David Clark. I really want to thank Santiago Ramirez and Michael Sheinson at Fleet Lease Disposal Inc. who were courageous enough to embark on a large data-mining project with me, which allowed all of us to see the benefits of information discovery when applied to the car business. They provided me the biggest data-mining laboratory any author could hope for!

Last, but certainly not least, I thank Karen, my wife, for taking over all the tasks that were mine before the book started and for putting up with my late nights spent in front of my computer screen. I thank my seven-year-old daughter, Jade, who brought me drinks and food and kept me company in my office while I worked. She also kept my three-year-old son, Nico, busy whenever he showed far too much interest in my work.

Introduction

Today, when we shop for books on amazon.com, click banner ads on the Internet, or receive a preapproved credit card in the mail, we can't help but notice how "personalized" our experience with big companies is becoming. The online book sellers seem to "know" what books I like to read and what music I like to listen to. Their banner ads seem to call out my name, and when I see an ad for scuba gear, I have to wonder how they knew I liked to scuba dive. I mention these examples to illustrate the applications of data-mining technology and to show how widely this relatively new technology is being used. Data mining, now more than ever, is accessible to almost any business that understands its benefits.

If you type "data mining" in your favorite Internet search engine, you'll get more responses than you'll have time to read. Fast computers, cheap and unlimited storage, and better communication has made it easier for companies to access their huge stores of data, pinpoint and gather information, and make sense of it. Businesses are using data mining to look for everything from online buying patterns to credit histories. Clever marketing firms are turning this knowledge into gold.

Microsoft SQL Server 2000, like many other large-scale relational database systems, has benefited from the increased availability of inexpensive storage media along with more and more powerful mainstream servers. Storage in the enterprise is no longer a problem; companies store years of detailed transactions in point-of-sale systems, Web logs, and even audio and video streams.

Automated data mining provides tools with packaged statistical formulas that database experts can use without having to understand the statistics behind the mining efforts. With these tools, a data-mining operator can click on a button and process many gigabytes, if not terabytes, of information about customer demographics, purchasing habits, and economic indicators, and in the time it takes to finish a cup of coffee, answer the question "Who will respond favorably to my telemarketing campaign and why?"

As this book shows, the Microsoft Data Mining tool is almost this easy to use. This technical reference describes data mining and its underlying theories and uses two sample databases to show you how to build your own data-mining model.

Who Should Use This Book

This book is designed for IT workers who design, implement, and use Analysis Services and intend to use Microsoft Data Mining. This book does assume familiarity with relational databases and to a lesser degree, with the online analytical processing (OLAP) database. A system architect can use this book to understand Analysis Services. A database administrator can use this book to understand how to set up the data-mining environment including the relational database sources. An OLAP administrator can use this book to understand how to provide case data to a data-mining model from OLAP and how to use that model to enhance the analytical capabilities in already existing OLAP cubes. Finally, application developers will be able to use this book to write front-end applications that perform administrative tasks as well as prediction queries.

What Is in This Book

Part I, "Introducing Data Mining," outlines the approaches that lead to a successful data-mining campaign and shows why data mining is so important. Data mining is a subject rich in theories and processes, and many introductory books have been written on the subject. This first few chapters of this book are also a practical and theoretical introduction to data mining. Part I discusses the crucial elements that underlie the logical and statistical foundations behind the data-mining tools included with Microsoft Analysis Services. It also discusses why we use data mining and how the data-mining process works.

Part II, "Data-Mining Methods," looks at data mining from a more technical and product-specific perspective. We show you how to use all the Microsoft wizards and other interactive tools to design and create data-mining models. You will learn how to create "ready-to-mine" tables and efficient data-mining models. You will also learn how to "train" models and interpret the results to gain a deeper understanding of your data.

Part III, "Creating Data-Mining Applications with Code," is the reference for those developers who will be creating applications that use the Analysis Services engine or PivotTable Service to manage the data-mining models. For administrative applications, developers will learn how to create applications with the same functionality as Analysis Manager if they so choose. For applications that rely on existing models to make predictions, developers will learn how to issue prediction queries using code. This is one of the most exciting aspects of Microsoft Data Mining because it gives you the ability to create sophisticated front-ends to data-mining applications using Microsoft Visual Basic, Microsoft Visual C++, Microsoft C#, or ASP pages.

With that, let's get on to learning about data mining.

Part I
Introducing Data Mining

Turn computers loose on your data, and you don't know what they'll come up with—that's the whole point

Edmund X. DeJesus, Senior Editor, BYTE Magazine

Data mining, also known as Knowledge Discovery (KD), is the computer-assisted process of digging through and analyzing enormous sets of data, finding previously undiscovered patterns, and then deriving some meaning from them. Data mining involves both describing the past and predicting future trends.

In this section, I'll discuss data mining in general—what it is and what it isn't. I'll go over many of the important principles and definitions behind the data-mining methodologies, including the role of data-mining models, statistics, and algorithms. I'll also explain how data mining fits within the Analysis Services architecture and how it interacts with the Microsoft SQL Server 2000 relational database engine and the OLAP engine.

Chapter 1
Understanding Data Mining

Recently I spoke with the CEO and CIO of a major auto sales company about their databases. Among other things, we were trying to find the most optimal way of storing their massive quantities of sales data and other important corporate information. As we scanned the millions of rows in the databases, the CEO said in awe, "I bet there's a ton of information in here worth lots of money—if only we had a thousand years to make sense of it all." This comment very much sums up the typical reaction of many a corporate head, astronomer, doctor, and financial trader with stores of potentially valuable data but no way to make it work for them. Data mining leverages the computing power of today's servers to transform mountains of raw data into useful information.

The ever-increasing physical storage capacity of computers, coupled with easy access to powerful processing muscle, makes sophisticated data analysis possible in ways that were unimaginable only a few years ago. Until very recently, only large corporations and universities with access to super computers and mainframes could perform useful data-mining tasks. As powerful servers become available and more affordable—as compared with the price of a super computer—smaller companies are able to harness this server power to mine their stored data in order to gain a competitive advantage in the marketplace. To mine data in ways that are innovative, and at times seemingly surreal, we must first understand the technologies available, and then how to apply them to a particular data cache (see "Your Life On Disk" on the next page).

What Is Data Mining?

Data mining is the process of discovering meaningful patterns and relationships that lie hidden within very large databases. Because browsing through tables and records rarely leads to discovery of useful patterns, data is typically analyzed by an automated process, commonly referred to in data-mining lingo as Knowledge Discovery (KD). *Knowledge Discovery* is a component of data mining that uses the power of the computer combined with a human operator's innate ability to zero in on visually apparent patterns. By automating data mining, computers discover the patterns and trends present in the data while the person in charge of making use of these discoveries decides which patterns are truly relevant.

Data mining can find descriptive and predictive information. Which type of information you choose to discover depends largely on what you want to accomplish with the results. When *predictive information* is sought, the goal is to derive information that offers clues about a future event. For example, if a car dealer wants to know what she can get for a 1998 Ford Mustang with 68,000 miles on it, she's looking for predictive information. Assuming the dealer has kept a few years worth of sales history, this warehouse of data can be mined and then used to assign an asking price and predict the selling price. Variables such as a car's year and model are fed into the computer, and a price prediction is derived from previous sales.

If the same car dealer wants to give a first-prize trip to Hawaii to the most profitable salesperson of the year (note that I say most profitable, not the one with the highest gross sales), she would want descriptive information about her employees' sales histories. Many factors other than total sales influence profitability, such as the number of referrals a sales person gets from her regular customers. This kind of information has no predictive value per se, but it does accurately describe past events in a manner that may have been difficult to see by normal means, thus offering the opportunity to make decisions based on newly discovered relationships.

Why Use Data Mining?

Data mining is an activity that offers business advantages, as well as solutions to some mounting problems associated with exploiting the knowledge embedded within corporate databases:

- Growing disk space capabilities
- Improvements over relational database management system (RDBMS) engines
- Enhancements to online analytical processing (OLAP)

It's no surprise to anyone in the information technology field that disk space is becoming cheaper as it becomes more abundant.

Your Life on Disk

British Telecom is exploring the idea of storing everything a person sees and hears on disk! "Over an 80-year life we process 10 terabytes of data …", to quote Ian Pearson, the official Futurologist at British Telecom. As surreal as this may sound, it does show that disk storage capability isn't a concern for data miners.

Disk space is becoming cheap enough that data storage is no longer as much of a concern as is making sense of the data stored. For more everyday examples, you only need to look at banks and credit card companies. They commonly store and archive every single customer transaction that occurs for the life of an account. Obviously, these companies hope to use this data to find out more about their customers and to discover the characteristics of an ideal member. Given that many major credit card companies print nearly half a billion statements a month, automated data mining is the only hope of finding any meaning in the mass of information housed on their hard disks.

In response to this explosion of data on corporate hard disks, great strides have been made to improve the response time of RDBMS engines to queries issued against them. However, once data has been stored for long periods of time, it becomes more useful to query data based on aggregated information rather than individual line items. For instance, a large retail chain will be more interested in sums of sales per region and per product type than in an analysis of the individual sales themselves. Aggregating data at this level, although possible with most SQL-compliant RDBMS engines, isn't the most easily optimized process for these engines. When it comes to queries, these engines are specifically optimized to find sets of data by responding to given criteria, not necessarily to continually perform mathematical calculations.

The OLAP database was created specifically to alleviate the problem of calculating aggregations on the fly. Unlike RDBMS engines, OLAP is designed to precalculate aggregates and store them in a manner that permits queries to simply return results from preprocessed tables. This takes advantage of the abundant availability of disk space while eliminating the need for expensive processing power.

In addition to the storage benefits provided by these OLAP systems, special storage and display features allow users access to vast data archives by using rolled up views of aggregates. While OLAP certainly gives many companies a better means of handling their information, it does not tell these companies what to look for. For instance, large auto dealerships spend a great deal of time analyzing the profit margin of each make and model of car they sell. The bottom line dictates next year's showroom. Dealerships analyze most of the obvious factors such as price, odometer reading (if it's a used car), model, and make, but the most successful dealerships employ experienced staff who are able to identify other less obvious but equally significant factors such as the color, engine size, and transmission type.

Even the most experienced dealers still make a few mistakes simply because many hidden factors, which are hard to account for, come into play. These can include the amount of time a car sits on the lot, its location on the lot in relation to other makes of cars (if you park sports cars next to trucks, the cars may be less visible), the weather, the time of year, and the Dow Jones Industrial average. The list, as you can see, is almost endless. The fact is that taking all factors into account would require a staff the size of the government's Economic Forecasting Team, which would be enough to deter most dealers from delving this deeply into their data.

Despite its strengths as a data-mining tool, OLAP still requires an initial hypothesis to give direction to the effort of navigating the data. The data is then used to prove or disprove the theory behind the effort. In databases containing a large number of tables and columns, using OLAP often results in trial-and-error approaches, which take large amounts of time and tend to produce mediocre results. As with manual relational database mining, the discovery of patterns and meaningful relationships using OLAP is limited by the person who writes the hypothesis and by the time allotted to explore the data.

The advantage data mining has over OLAP is that it allows the computer to examine every conceivable factor that might affect an outcome and to draw conclusions from that analysis. This process is essentially about finding relationships between attributes of a case—what those attributes that describe the case have in common. If we were to apply the data-mining process to the earlier example of the car dealership, every attribute or variable of the cases involving the sale of a car, such as the color or the model, would be analyzed and taken into account when predicting an outcome such as the price range, which could be inferred as a result of examining the relationship between the attributes of each car and its price.

To be of any use, the automated process needs to provide the dealer with any and all situations that might affect the outcomes, even if they might not seem to make sense at first glance. For instance, based on the data, the dealer might find that pink Ford trucks sell better when placed in the corner of the lot along side used Yugos, but only on Wednesdays, except for Wednesdays in November. Because of the sheer number of factors involved, and because of a natural inclination to preemptively dismiss the improbable, this kind of relationship would likely go unnoticed by a human. Not so for the computer.

How Data Mining Is Currently Used

Data mining is particularly valuable for organizations that collect large quantities of historical information. Banks, insurance companies, credit card companies, and even astronomers use this technology to derive critical information from large, unwieldy data samples. One of the best known applications of data mining is individual credit risk assessment. When applicants fill out loan applications, they're often asked to provide social security numbers, addresses, and the usual identifying information—but they're also required to give other bits of information that say something about them. There are questions about whether the applicant is a renter or a home owner, how long he or she has lived at a current address and been with a given employer, his or her marital status and educational level, and the list goes on and on.

Because financial institutions have a large customer base to draw data from, they are prime candidates for data-mining technology, which can analyze the data and discover the correlations between applicants' personal characteristics and the probability of loan default.

Needless to say, allowing the computer to evaluate and examine all the variables that affect this outcome enables financial institutions to process hundreds of thousands of loan applications at one time with a fraction of the manpower needed in the past.

Data-mining techniques are also widely used in the retail industry to determine the best floor arrangement for products. For instance, a retail store might want to find a way to maximize sales of golf equipment. By examining sales transactions of golf equipment that go back four years or more, one might observe that customers who buy golf equipment often buy a pair of men's shoes at the same time. Armed with this knowledge, the retail store might decide to place golf clubs next to the men's shoe department to maximize the sales opportunity that their proximity offers.

Bar coding has made it possible for grocery chains to identify each item included in a purchase. This data can then be studied and conclusions drawn about purchase relationships. For example, if a store wants to find out how to sell more beer, the grocery chain can retrospectively examine all the beer purchases to find out what else the beer customer puts in their grocery cart. If it's found that customers who buy beer also buy diapers, the store might increase beer sales by running a special on diapers.

Note   This beer and diaper example is not my own invention. For some odd reason—perhaps because of the seeming ludicrous image that it conjures up—it happens to be a classic example used in data-mining literature to discuss certain types of data-mining algorithms.

Interestingly, data mining is used in many fields, such as medical diagnosis and meteorology. These disciplines, like their profit-oriented counterparts, confront the challenge of making sense out of mind-boggling stacks of data. In short, any business or academic pursuit that collects and studies large quantities of data is a candidate for data mining.

Defining the Terms

Data mining is often associated with other data storage and data manipulation techniques such as data warehousing and online transaction processing (OLTP). These techniques share terminology, and some terms are used interchangeably. In the interest of clarity, I'd like to define each of these techniques, the terms they share, and those terms that relate specifically to data mining.

- **Data Mining**   In a nutshell, *data mining* is the process of discovering meaningful patterns and relationships through the automated analysis and classification of large stores of historical data.

- **Data Warehousing**   A *data warehouse* is a central store of data that has been extracted from the operational data in an OLTP database. Unlike data warehouses, OLTP systems are designed to store operational data for efficient processing of transactions. Because the structures of the data in these databases are hard for the end user to understand, these systems are somewhat difficult to report from. Transferring the data to a data warehouse allows the information to be placed in a structure more convenient for reporting from. Unlike the OLTP systems, a data warehouse will accept new data without changing existing data. As a result, the storage structures are designed to house huge quantities of information in structures that favor fast retrieval over efficient transaction processing.

- **Mining models** A *mining model* is the physical structure of a subset of data compiled from a data-mining algorithm, along with the description of the original data set. Data mining needs a structure that contains the patterns present in the underlying databases. This structure is then used as a basis from which to make predictions based on new data by "filling in the blanks" left by the missing values. By gathering information from the original data sets, the data-mining application builds a subset of data that is compiled using a data mining algorithm. This result set can then be used to make predictions against sample data.

- **Patterns** A *pattern* is a set of events that occur with enough frequency in the dataset to reveal a relationship between them. Revealing the relationship is usually an inductive reasoning process. For example, you might learn from a data set that every time a customer buys beer, she also buys diapers. If this event occurs with enough frequency, the data-mining algorithms will identify it as a predictable pattern that needs to be stored in a model. In this way, an operator who browses the data-mining model will clearly see that people who buy beer have a high probability of also buying diapers.

- **Cases** Each item of historical data that's used as a source for a data-mining model is a *case*. For example, if a mining model describes customer purchases at a grocery store, every single purchase would be a unique case that contributes to the "experience" of the data-mining model.

- **Data-mining algorithms** A *data-mining algorithm* is the mathematical and statistical algorithms that transform the cases in the original data source into the data-mining model. How the model looks depends largely on the data-mining algorithm applied to the data. As you'll discover later, there are many algorithms that can be added, but Microsoft Data Mining Services, introduced in Microsoft SQL Server 2000, provides decision tree and clustering algorithms right out of the box.

Data Mining Methodology

As with any discipline involving information systems, data mining requires that a plan be devised and followed to get from the idea to the final implementation. The components of a data-mining plan are listed below and illustrated in Figure 1.1.

- Analyzing the problem
- Extracting and cleansing the data
- Validating the data
- Creating and training the model
- Querying the data model data
- Maintaining the validity of the data-mining model

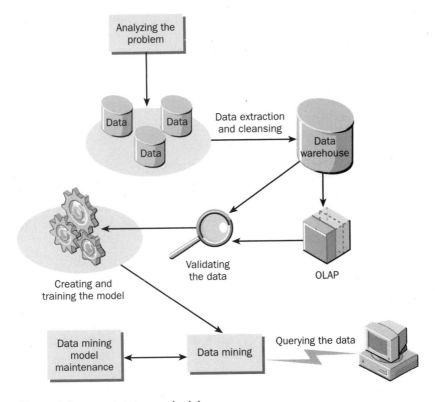

Figure 1-1. *Data-mining methodology.*

Analyzing the Problem

The source databases have to be assessed to see whether they meet the criteria for data mining. The quality and abundance of the data are the primary factors in deciding whether the data is at all suitable. In addition, the expected results of the data-mining effort have to be carefully understood to be sure that the existing data contains the right kind of extractable information. For instance, there's no point in pursuing a data-mining project for a grocery store chain if the data gathered from the cash register does not identify items for each shopping cart. Once the expected results are determined, the best algorithm for the job is chosen.

Extracting and Cleansing the Data

The data is first extracted from its native sources, such as OLTP databases, text files, Microsoft Access databases, and even spreadsheets. This data is then placed in a data warehouse that has a structure compatible with the data model. Typically, Data Transformation Services (DTS) is used to extract and then cleanse the data of any inconsistencies or incompatibilities with a uniform format.

Validating the Data

Once the data has been extracted and cleansed, it's a good practice to scroll through the model that you've created to make sure that all the data is present and complete.

Creating and Training the Model

When an algorithm is applied to a model, a structure is generated. It's important at this point to browse the generated data to make sure that it accurately resembles the facts in the source data. This can't be done in any great detail, but any serious idiosyncrasies can be easily discovered just by looking at the generated model. This process is covered in greater detail in Chapter 9, "Using Code to Interact with Data Mining."

Querying the Data Mining Model Data

Once the proper model is created and generated, the data is made available for decision support. This usually involves writing front-end query applications with Microsoft Visual Basic (VB) or Active Server Pages (ASP) through the OLE DB for Data Mining provider. Third-party reporting tools that understand OLE DB for Data Mining are also an option at this point.

Maintaining the Validity of the Data-Mining Model

As the data-mining model is populated, over time initial data characteristics such as granularity or validity might change. For instance, after six months of populating our grocery chain model, we discover that fresh fish has been taken out of the meat section and placed in its own seafood section and that sliced cheese has been moved from the dairy section to the deli section. Even something as small as classifying a six-pack of Coke as a single item instead of six individual items has a dramatic impact on the accuracy of future predictions because it changes the attributes that the original models were based on.

Overview of Microsoft Data Mining

Data mining is a decision support tool that stands on its own when it comes to analyzing large databases. It has its own unique features which are designed to address unique decision support problems that cannot be solved by other data analysis tools. Data mining is sometimes confused with other tools such as OLAP. This section will describe the basic components and features of data mining.

Data Mining vs. OLAP

Both data mining and OLAP are components of Microsoft Analysis Services. Both serve as decision support tools, but each is designed for a different use. OLAP is primarily designed to store data in summarized tables to facilitate retrieval and navigation of this data by end users. Many vendors claim, however, that this is a data-mining solution because the user can discover information about the data by browsing summarized information, which can then be analyzed to find more causal relationships. However, in most cases, the user is navigating through dimensions that contain meaning and relationships that are already well known. As a result, an interactive display or report showing the breakdown of auto sales by year, make, model, and region is intuitive for the user. If the dealership sells different cars and trucks in different parts of the county, translating a display of this information into a relevant understanding of business activity is a simple matter. OLAP could be used to try to discover new data, but since the data discovery is really being done by the end user, with the assistance of an OLAP tool, the data discovery is bound to be haphazard and incomplete. Data mining is less concerned with allowing an end user to easily browse summary data as it is with automatically discovering new patterns and rules that can be applied to get future results. As a result of this difference, OLAP is an efficient storage and retrieval mechanism and data mining is a knowledge discovery tool.

Data-Mining Models

Source data needs to be structured in a way that optimizes predictions that are based on established variables. As I mentioned earlier, these structures are created by algorithms. When an algorithm is applied to a data structure, the structure is populated with data in a manner that reflects the existence of relationships and patterns of the original data set, thus allowing predictions based on that data to be made easily. Microsoft uses special data structures to store the data-mining models, which can then be browsed using Microsoft Analysis Manager, applications that use the OLE DB for Data Mining Services, or Component Object Model (COM) interfaces such as Decision Support Objects (DSO). All these tools allow new data models to be created, copied, altered, and deleted. Through OLE DB, it's possible to establish direct data connections to various sources, such as Microsoft SQL Server, text files, Microsoft Access, Microsoft Excel, or even Oracle and DB2.

Models vs. Patterns

It's easy to confuse patterns with models; Webster's Dictionary considers them synonymous, but in the context of data mining the two concepts are not interchangeable. *Patterns* are recurring sets of data such as 111211121112111.... The repetition in this example allows us to predict with some accuracy that the next number will be "2." A *model*, in the world of data mining, is a special data structure that stores the cases that have been processed by an algorithm in such a manner that the model contains the same patterns found in the raw databases. The model stores the patterns and thus makes it possible for us to predict what number will follow the third number one in the example above.

Data-Mining Algorithms

Chapter 6, "Microsoft Clustering," and Chapter 7, "Third Party Algorithms," discuss data-mining algorithms in greater detail. Some of these algorithms are natively supported by Data Mining Services, and others are integrated into Data Mining Services by third-party vendors. For the most part, the choice of algorithm is based on the type of model you want to wind up with; therefore, my descriptions focus on the goal of the data-mining process, as opposed to the technical details behind the algorithm.

Decision Trees

A *decision tree algorithm* analyzes the data and creates a repeating series of branches until no more relevant branches can be made. The end result is a binary tree structure where the splits in the branches can be followed along specific criteria to find the most desired result.

Clustering

A *cluster algorithm*, unlike a decision tree, does not split data along any lines but rather groups data in clusters. As can be seen in Figure 1.1, clustering is most useful for visual representations because the data is grouped around common criteria. Many front-end tools display these groups as bullet holes in a target. As with any target that's been shot at for a while, the entire surface is scattered with holes, but some areas will have higher concentrations, or clusters, of holes. If the bullet holes represent sales data, the groups or clusters would represent sales cases that have a lot in common. By looking at the intersections of the data points (or bullet holes) we can see what the sales do have in common.

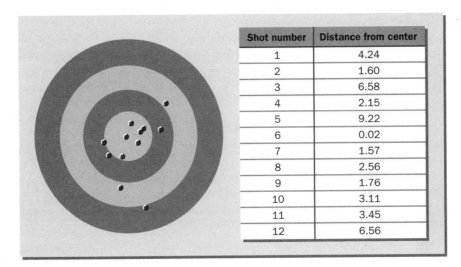

Shot number	Distance from center
1	4.24
2	1.60
3	6.58
4	2.15
5	9.22
6	0.02
7	1.57
8	2.56
9	1.76
10	3.11
11	3.45
12	6.56

Figure 1-2. *Representation of clustering data.*

Association

In order to effectively do market-basket analysis or cross-selling, users need to know what factors "associate" with each other. The typical problem the *association algorithm* solves is to find out what items in a store are bought together—such as the classic example mentioned earlier of beer and diapers. This algorithm is not provided natively by data mining; it's one of the algorithms provided either by third-party vendors or by your own programming efforts.

Regression Analysis or Sequencing

The *regression analysis algorithm* is used to find the relationship between a predicted outcome and several or all of the possible variables that can influence the outcome. Regression methods have their roots in statistical analysis and are similar to linear regression, logistic regression, and nonlinear regression methods. As is the case with association algorithms, regression analysis is not provided natively by Data Mining Services, but can be added by third-party vendors.

OLE DB for Data Mining

This new SQL Server 2000–based protocol is designed to simplify communication and to provide better integration of data-mining tools with data storage and management applications, especially SQL Server. Although OLE DB for Data Mining is a recent arrival, there are quite a few third-party vendors who now provide support for this standard in their products.

Using SQL Server Syntax to Data Mine

When it comes to data extraction, the idea behind OLE DB for Data Mining is to extend the SQL Server syntax with provisions specific to data mining. This is very similar in philosophy to the multidimensional expressions (MDX) extensions that were added to the SQL Server language and designed to facilitate the extraction of OLAP data using the OLE DB for OLAP provider.

One of the new additions is the PREDICTION JOIN clause, which is similar to the join operation in standard SQL syntax. Essentially, its function is to create a join between a populated data-mining model and another table that contains the variables needed to predict the outcomes in a prediction result set. What makes this clause particularly useful is that the output can be returned in the form of an OLE DB or ActiveX Data Objects (ADO) result set. This goes a long way toward making data-mining features available to developers without having to first build the fundamental mathematical algorithms from scratch. This level of access creates and allows this process to be used to enhance decision support systems for risk analysis, market-basket analysis, and so on.

Summary

Data mining is a brand new addition to the SQL Server suite of data management tools. This first chapter introduces Data Mining Services and the concepts and terms associated with it such as data warehousing, mining models, patterns, cases, and data-mining algorithms. I've also spent some time differentiating data mining from other processes such as OLAP and SQL.

Data mining is specifically designed to address the needs of those who are faced with gathering meaningful trends and patterns from very large quantities of data. As my examples show, the practical applications of data mining are endless.

Any data-mining solution involves the use of cases, which come from raw data usually stored in a data warehouse of some sort. The quantity of data is usually far too large to be analyzed as is, so a data-mining model is created and an appropriate algorithm is chosen. The data-mining model is then populated, or "trained," with these cases using a data-mining algorithm, resulting in a logical data structure that represents a condensed version of all the patterns and relationships present in the original data set. The data-mining models and the data contained in them can be accessed using various methods detailed in the OLE DB for Data Mining Specification, available at *http://www.microsoft.com/data/oledb/dm.htm*.

Chapter 2
Microsoft SQL Server Analysis Services Architecture

Microsoft SQL Server 2000 Analysis Services is a suite of decision support engines and tools.

Analysis Services is accessed through a graphical user interface tool which is implemented as a snap-in within Microsoft Management Console (MMC). This tool lets an administrator easily manage various decision-support tasks. As of this writing, Analysis Services provides access to two forms of decision support mechanisms: data mining and OLAP. Although both data mining and OLAP are crucial elements to any decision-support effort, they perform very different duties, as we'll soon see.

> **Note** Analysis Services is the name for the decision support tools included in SQL Server 2000 which includes both OLAP and data-mining functionality. In SQL Server 7.0, Analysis Services was called OLAP Services and as the name implies, it included only the OLAP functionality.

Analysis Services' architecture can be divided into the client portion, used for providing interfaces to front-end applications, and the server portion, which houses the engines that provide the functionality and power to these services. The client and server portions have separate components that are accessed in different ways. For example, client services provide the functionality needed to create local components that are subsets of the server components. Client services are used to create local cubes from server-side online analytical processing (OLAP) cubes. The server components provide the core data and services needed to support Analysis server tasks.

> **Note** OLAP and data mining can easily use data contained in formats other than SQL Server 2000, such as text, Microsoft Excel spreadsheets, or any other OLE DB source.

Introduction to OLAP

Online analytical processing (OLAP) is a technology that allows users to analyze a large database to gain insight on the information it contains. The database for an OLAP system is structured for efficient storage of static data. The storage structure is designed to efficiently retrieve data, particularly aggregated data such as summed totals and counts. Because the OLAP storage unit is multidimensional, it's called a *cube* as opposed to a table. What makes OLAP unique is its ability to store the aggregated data hierarchically, allowing the user to drill down and roll up aggregates by dimensional traits. Dimensions give contextual information to the numerical figures, or *measures*, that you're examining. For example, if you're looking at sales figures generally you would be interested in regional, quarterly, and product sales; OLAP calls each of these a *dimension*. If you wanted to look at one sales region that had a particularly good quarter, OLAP's structure allows you to expand the quarterly view to see each month or day of the quarter. At the same time, you can also drill down into the data on the region with the highest sales to find the cities responsible for the increase in sales. As Figure 2-1 shows, OLAP is a great tool for understanding how measures relate to dimensions. Because the measures are precalculated, OLAP makes navigation through the data almost instantaneous.

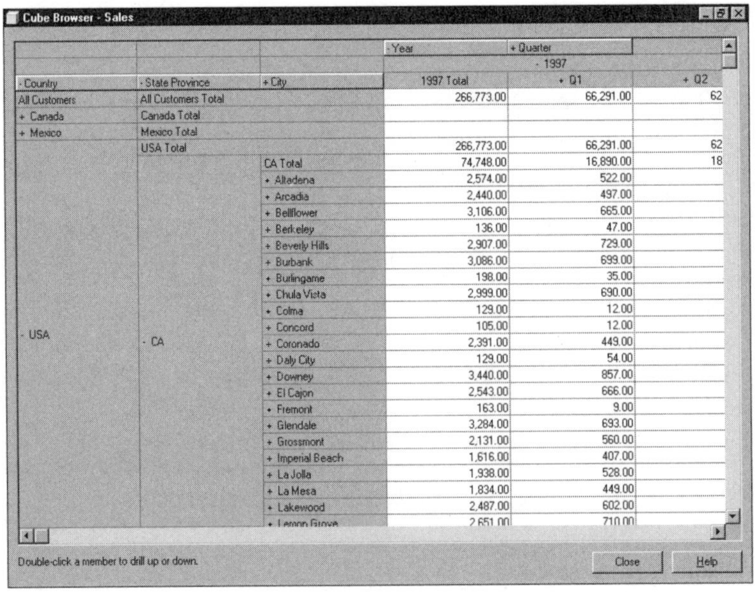

Figure 2-1. *Contents of an OLAP cube.*

OLAP vs. Data Mining

This chapter introduces the concepts and workings of OLAP. This knowledge is important for various reasons, not the least of which is that OLAP is one of the data sources available to you in a data mining scenario. OLAP is also a storage option for data mining models. The data mining process is often confused with OLAP cube navigation, so it's crucial that you understand the capabilities of each process. This book doesn't provide you with enough knowledge to do any significant work with OLAP, but there are some good books dedicated to this subject that are well worth reading such as:

- Peterson, Tim, et al. *Microsoft OLAP Unleashed*. Indianapolis: SAMS, 1999.
- Thomsen, Erik, George Spofford, and Dick Chase. *Microsoft OLAP Solutions*. New York: Wiley & Sons, 1998.
- Kimball, Ralph, et al. *The Data Warehouse Lifecycle Toolkit: Expert Methods for Designing, Developing, and Deploying Data Warehouses*. New York: Wiley & Sons, 1998.

There are two main points I'd like to make about relational data and OLAP. The first is that OLAP tends to remove any levels of granularity in the data. If you were using OLAP to aggregate, individual line items for sales would be disconnected from the OLAP aggregates. The individual line items get lost in aggregates because all of the relevant records get merged into one, which causes the numerical measures to become the summed values while the unique identifiers get discarded. Analysis Services does allow you to drill through to the underlying source data, but only if when you build the cube you choose the option that allows the user to perform drill throughs. The second point to note about OLAP is that it tends to require a more rigid definition of the data structures than a relational database does. Typically, OLAP's information comes from a data warehouse that's been structured specifically for query and analysis. This structure requires tighter design work up front, but the extra work pays off in the end with well-defined data relationships, hierarchies, and definitions.

From a reporting perspective, OLAP exposes its data in the same way regardless of the internal storage options chosen when building the cube. From a structural perspective, OLAP provides these various storage options to optimize data retrieval. These structural differences are completely hidden from the reporting functions. The three storage options available in OLAP are multidimensional online analytical processing (MOLAP), relational online analytical processing (ROLAP), and hybrid online analytical processing (HOLAP).

MOLAP

Multidimensional online analytical processing (MOLAP) is used to build multidimensional cubes from data stored in a data warehouse. Analysis Services uses the MOLAP cube to respond to a predefined range of inquiries, as shown in Figure 2-2. The MOLAP method is often chosen if the initial data sets are so large that the processing of the cube from the original warehouse data requires a batch process. The data is aggregated and processed using a set of predefined calculations. The resulting cube can be queried in much the same way as any other database is queried.

The main reason for using this method is that the MOLAP storage mechanisms are especially effective in retrieving data quickly. Unlike a relational database, which has to build a result set on the fly to answer queries, MOLAP simply identifies the location, or cell, where the precalculated elements reside and returns data to the respondent.

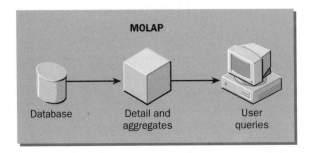

Figure 2-2. *MOLAP structure.*

The downside to this approach is that the cube is disconnected from the warehouse, which makes the process of updating the cube complex. Batch routines that compare cube data to warehouse data and update the cube data as necessary have to be put in place.

Corrections to mistakes found in the original data, once caught and corrected, also have to be made to the aggregated data in the cube. Cube corrections can be made in a number of ways; sometimes the best method is to create reverse records in the warehouse. For example, if you need to correct the dollar amount on a set of invoices you can cancel the incorrect invoices by creating a set of matching invoices and enter negative dollar amounts. Other times, the best—but more time-consuming—solution is to rebuild the entire cube from the corrected warehouse data. MOLAP can store only basic data types, such as text and integers. This creates an important limitation if you need to keep other types of information in the underlying data.

ROLAP

Most of the disadvantages associated with MOLAP are addressed with *relational online analytical processing* (ROLAP). ROLAP also has the advantage of being able to query preaggregated data. ROLAP's storage mechanism uses the original RDBMS, such as SQL

Server 2000, to store the aggregates in tabular form, which can then be used by the OLAP engine, as shown in Figure 2-3. Because of this storage mechanism, the RDBMS engine can be used to manage the generated aggregates. The engine can make corrections and inserts on the individual line items and on the aggregates themselves. Reports can, if they need to, query aggregate tables directly without having to go through the OLAP querying mechanisms, such as OLE DB for OLAP, PivotTable Service, or multidimensional expressions (MDX).

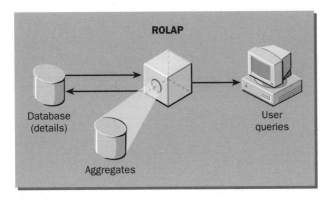

Figure 2-3. *ROLAP structure.*

This storage mechanism does have a downside. The tabular structure of ROLAP, as opposed to the multidimensional structure of a MOLAP cube, is not as efficient for the OLAP engine to query. This inefficiency leads to a performance strain on the system, especially if the data sets are larger than average for a MOLAP storage mechanism. To correct this performance deficiency, you'll need to delve into the myriad complexities of aggregate ROLAP tables and attempt to index them properly. This leads to further limitations because the nature of this type of index tuning task invariably favors some types of queries to the detriment of others, thus creating a need for more specialization of the ROLAP structures than would otherwise be necessary. The facility that the MOLAP cubes provide for ad hoc querying almost seems like a luxury in ROLAP.

HOLAP

Sometimes it happens that 80 percent of the queries concern high-level aggregates, and the remaining 20 percent need access to the low-level line items in the source data. *Hybrid online analytical processing* (HOLAP) was designed to address this need. Essentially, HOLAP combines the advantages of MOLAP with those of ROLAP by storing the high-level aggregates in a MOLAP cube and keeping the low-level aggregates and line items in the relational database tables, as shown in Figure 2-4. The OLAP interface remains unchanged, but the engine is able to selectively choose data from different storage mechanisms based on the given query. Because information stored in the relational portion contains fewer, if any, levels of aggregation, some of the disadvantages of ROLAP can be avoided with HOLAP. Because HOLAP makes the tables far less complex to manage on the relational database side, the data is more easily optimized through indexing. The MOLAP portion of the cube provides fast retrieval for the aggregated portion of the queries without having to expose a developer or administrator to the details of summarized structures.

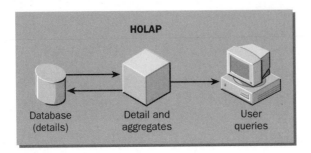

Figure 2-4. *HOLAP structure.*

Server Architecture

Analysis Services' architecture on the server side provides core facilities to create and manipulate OLAP cubes and data mining models. Connections to the original data sources as well as local security access is also managed by the server. The server manages the mechanics of data storage as the cubes and models are being processed. It also maintains the metadata repositories stored and used by Microsoft SQL Server 2000 Meta Data Services.

The user interface provided by Analysis Manager contains *Data Transformation Services* (DTS), which is a SQL Server 2000 service that cleans and transfers data as it moves between data sources. Analysis Manager is the main user interface for Analysis Services, but there are other programming interfaces that enable custom front-end applications to interact with the COM object model that controls the interface to the server. The Microsoft SQL Server 2000 Analysis Services server architecture is shown in Figure 2-5.

Data Mining Services Within Analysis Services

Although Analysis Server has many functions that are used by OLAP and data mining, as shown in Figure 2-5, some of the server features are specifically designed for data mining. For example, data mining uses a storage option that places data mining models in multidimensional structures, in relational database tables, or in *Predictive Model Markup Language* (PMML), which is a standardized Extensible Markup Language (XML) format specifically designed for data mining models.

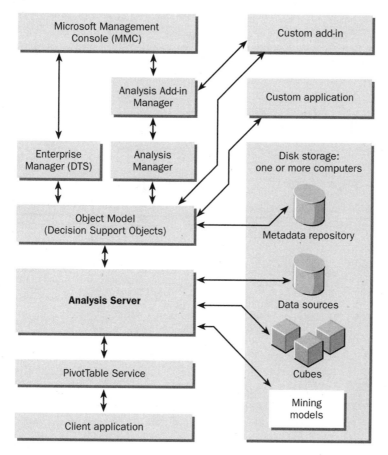

Figure 2-5. *Analysis Services server architecture.*

Note   Security access roles are used by Analysis Services in order to limit access to various objects including cubes and data mining models. These roles function almost identically as SQL Server roles.

Client Architecture

The client side is primarily designed to provide a bridge, or interface, between the server functions and the custom applications. (See Figure 2-6.) PivotTable Service manages the crux of this interaction and also provides interfaces to OLE DB for Data Mining, which in turn either provides connectivity directly to Microsoft Visual C++ applications or to ActiveX Data Objects (ADO).

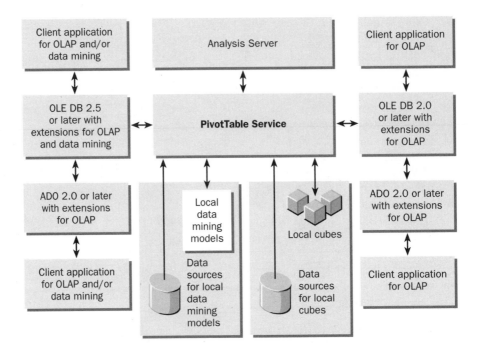

Figure 2-6. *Analysis Services client architecture.*

PivotTable Service

PivotTable Service is a built-in Analysis Server client that acts as an OLE DB provider for multidimensional data and data mining operations. It's positioned between the server engine and other client applications. As such, it provides OLE DB access to applications that need access to multidimensional data and data mining services from a client application. The data returned is generally in the form of tabular data, which can then be manipulated by traditional means using ADO record sets, Excel spreadsheets, or FoxPro tables. In both Data Mining Services and OLAP, PivotTable Service provides an extended SQL syntax that uses *Data Definition Language* (DDL), a language that allows clients to create and update local cubes or data mining models on the fly. These local structures can then be taken offline and used for queries and temporary updates in the pursuit of answers to "What if?" scenarios. PivotTable Service uses this specialized syntax to provide sophisticated query features to the client applications. The data can then be displayed, analyzed with data mining algorithms, or even changed.

Just about any client capable of communicating through OLE DB interface can access PivotTable Service. Clients using C++ can use special PivotTable Service interfaces with COM and OLE DB to create highly specialized custom front-end applications.

The role of the PivotTable Service is to provide access to the Analysis Services' functions through DDL syntax. Since this syntax is primarily designed for queries, the administrative functionality in the language is somewhat limited. Data mining models and cubes can indeed be created, but maintaining these structures is extremely code-intensive and rather impractical.

OLE DB

In order to provide a standard way to access disparate forms of data, whether they come from RDBMSs or Microsoft Outlook folders, and convert them to tabular result sets, Microsoft created OLE DB. OLE DB is designed to provide a common interface to these different data sources in the form of *providers*. For example, there are OLE DB providers for SQL Server, OLE DB providers for Oracle, and even OLE DB providers for comma-delimited text. Providers make it possible for an application to access these different data sources using the same calling methods, while letting the OLE DB provider handle the logistics of converting that data source into a usable table format. Analysis Services uses OLE DB for Data Mining and OLE DB for OLAP.

OLE DB for OLAP

The OLE DB for OLAP provider, shown in Figure 2-7, contains features that allow access to special OLAP structures. OLAP is unique, in part, because of its ability to store data in multidimensional structures. As was mentioned earlier, this multidimensional structure doesn't easily translate to simple tabular formats. To address this problem, Microsoft developed ActiveX Data Objects (Multidimensional) (ADO MD), which is a subset of the familiar ADO COM interface. ADO MD provides the same connection and querying facilities as ADO, but it also includes a record set with cells instead of rows and columns. A set of coordinates is needed to retrieve the cells.

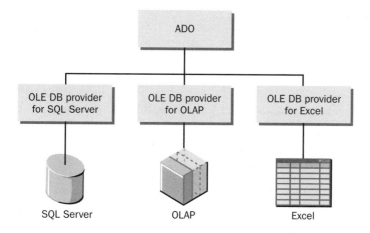

Figure 2-7. *OLE DB for OLAP access.*

OLE DB for Data Mining

OLE DB for Data Mining exposes the data mining model object in the form of a table. It also provides a series of statements that allow an application to manipulate this object. This OLE DB provider supplies virtual table objects that can be created with a form of the SQL CREATE syntax; they can be populated with INSERT and queried with SELECT.

The data in the data mining model is structured as it would be in a database that contains a group of related tables. An auto dealer database might contain data about car sales made by auto salespersons along with information about the year, make, and model of the cars. This information might have a Salesperson table as a parent table for the Sales table, and the Sales table might have foreign key relationships to the actual car data. In a relational structure, a join between the Salesperson table and the Sales table will most likely cause the salesperson information to be repeated as many times as there are sales for each one of the salespersons. This is because for every record in the Salesperson table there might be more than one sales item record. Since the data mining model doesn't actually store data in relation tables, it simulates that functionality by creating *nested tables*, as shown in Figure 2-8. In the example shown, if the salesperson is the focus of the data mining prediction, each salesperson's record represents a *case*. Once the records from the sale are nested with the salesperson's record, it becomes a *case set*.

CustomerID	Age	Gender	Name	OrderItems				
				OrderItemID	OrderID	ProductID	Cost	ProductType

Figure 2-8. *OLE DB nested table.*

Inserting cases into the data mining model causes the OLE DB provider to launch a process that first applies the algorithm to the data and then stores patterns in the model. The stored patterns can be used with PREDICTION JOIN statements to compare a table with variable fields to the patterns in the model. Since the data mining model actually contains every combination of cases learned from the original data source, and statistical information about the number of cases used to create the distinct combination, this model and the original variables are used to make predictions.

Decision Support Objects (DSO)

Analysis Services exposes much of the functionality of the engine; it allows you to create cubes, databases, and data mining models and manage server functions. These functions are exposed through a series of well-defined COM interfaces. These interfaces also provide access to the properties of almost all the objects available in the server, such as roles, dimensions, and partitions. The conjunction of this set of COM interfaces is called *Decision Support Objects* (DSO). Using DSO bypasses the PivotTable Service entirely because it provides a direct interface to the engine. This direct interface limits the functions of DSO from performing queries in the same way that PivotTable Service does.

DSO is implemented in the form of a hierarchy of objects and collections that map to the functions and components in Analysis Services. This allows applications to easily integrate with the underlying engine without having to understand the complexities inside.

Generally DSO is used to programmatically perform administrative tasks that would otherwise have to be performed interactively with Analysis Manager. Entire front-end applications similar to Analysis Manager can be written by anyone who knows DSO and can instantiate COM objects using Microsoft Visual Basic or Visual C++. DSO is also used to allow batch routines to perform routine, scheduled administrative tasks such as updating cubes or adding new cases to a data mining model.

Multidimensional Expressions (MDX)

Because of the unique structure of OLAP cubes, a specialized subset of the SQL Server language called *Multidimensional expressions* (MDX) exists specifically to query it. Although the syntax of the query resembles a standard SQL Server query and uses syntax such as SELECT, WHERE, and FROM, the differences become quite apparent when a query of any degree of complexity is attempted. Observe the following query provided in the *SQL Server Books Online:*

```
WITH MEMBER All_Countries.USA_and_Japan AS 'SUM({USA, Japan})'
SELECT CROSSJOIN({Smith, Jones},
    {USA_North.CHILDREN, USA_South, Japan,
        USA_and_Japan}) ON COLUMNS,
    {Qtr1.CHILDREN, Qtr2, Qtr3, Qtr4.CHILDREN} ON ROWS
FROM SalesCube
WHERE (Sales, [1997], Products.All)
```

This kind of syntax is needed because OLAP is less concerned with retrieving data from sets of records than it is with pinpointing the coordinate position where the aggregated data is located, a task comparable to searching for a particular apartment in a building. To find the apartment, you need not only the building address, but also the building number, floor number, and apartment number. With this information you can walk straight up to the door and avoid searching every building on the block to find one apartment. Using MDX, you can formulate requests using specific coordinates that take you directly to your data.

Prediction Joins

Much like MDX, Data Mining Services uses its own subset of the SQL syntax. This functionality is provided to allow front-end applications to make predictions based on data in the data mining models. This syntax will be examined in detail in Chapter 12, "Data-Mining Queries."

Summary

Analysis Services, although included with SQL Server 2000, is actually an independent set of services that combines OLAP functionality with data mining facilities. Both have a server architecture that shares features used for decision support services. OLAP and data mining also have unique features, some of which have been discussed in this chapter. The server components perform the fundamental, core engine–level functions of those services while exposing their interfaces through PivotTable Service.

PivotTable Service serves as a client to the server components of Analysis Services and acts as a bridge to applications that need to access objects through an OLE DB provider. It provides language extensions that create server side and local, offline data mining and OLAP structures and the syntax to create queries. MDX is the specialized language extension for OLAP and PREDICTION JOIN is the SQL subset used to make predictions from data mining models.

As an alternative to PivotTable Services, most Analysis Services administrative tasks can be performed more directly through the use of DSO—a set of COM interfaces that expose their functionality to ActiveX client applications.

OLE DB is the mechanism provided by Microsoft to allow clients or ActiveX wrappers such as ADO to access many different types of data through essentially the same programming interface. OLE DB interfaces with the PivotTable Service to communicate with server-side Analysis Services structures.

Chapter 3
Data Storage Models

The physical efficiency and usefulness of the data-mining process depends in large part on the underlying *data model*—the physical structure of a subset of data compiled from a data-mining algorithm, along with the description of the original data set—you use. Depending on the type and quantity of data you have and the results you are looking for, you can create a mining model directly from live OLTP data, which ensures your data is current, or from batches of data, which are extracted into specially enhanced reporting structures and kept for future use. As we'll discover in this chapter, the data model design has a big impact on the responsiveness of the server and the quality of the information mined.

Why Data Mining Needs a Data Warehouse

A data warehouse provides a repository for an organization's data. This repository is located in a central storage facility from which users can retrieve data whenever they need it. Using a single and centralized data warehouse as a data source increases the quality and consistency of an organization's data because the final data validation procedures are almost always handled by one team. Most major institutions and corporations (as well as many small ones) with high volume data processing tasks use a data warehouse model.

Organizations that manage data in warehouses often find that their data is too general and unmanageable to base specific and specialized decisions on. Although data warehouses do a good job of structuring data, you need data mining to extract useful information from the underlying data. Before you can begin the process of data mining, you have to store and structure the data in some type of warehouse.

One great virtue of data warehousing is that it can separate the reporting data (the data on which data mining is performed) from the OLTP data (the data structured for efficient transaction processing). It's very important to keep these processes separate, particularly when the data is being mined. Both processes begin with the same data, but in most cases they use different data structures to get different results. The structure affects how easily the data can be extracted and how the queries are formulated. In the right structure, simple queries can answer complex questions. Besides ease and simplicity, another consideration when deciding how data is going to be structured to meet reporting needs is server performance and resources.

Although data warehousing and data mining are closely related and interrelated processes, data mining requires different structures for its data, uses different algorithms, and, as we've discussed, is designed to accomplish different objectives.

Maintaining Data Integrity

The differences in these processes are reflected by their almost opposite objectives. OLTP is used to enter raw data and transactions from sources such as

- Mail order sales
- Cash registers
- Measuring instruments such as those used in nuclear power plants
- Mainframe file imports
- Web server logs

Regardless of the source, what's important is that the process guarantees that the integrity of the data is maintained and that nonsensical data never gets into any of the tables. One way to guarantee this integrity is to use relational database management system (RDBMS) features to enforce rules that block the entry of bad data. Another way to guarantee the integrity of the data is to create data structures that don't require the same data to be entered multiple times. A classic example of a data structure built to support customer invoicing has a Customer table, an Invoice-header table, and a Line-items table. These tables are structured so that a customer name and address is entered only into the Customer table. The Invoice-header table contains all the information needed to identify an invoice such as the invoice number, date, shipping address, and so on, and a reference to the customer that placed the order. The Line-items table contains quantities, discounts, and references to the Invoice-header table. The items purchased are represented with product codes. Each code refers to products in the Product table. The intelligent use of references reduces redundant data entry and makes the model efficient. Figure 3-1 shows how the efficiency of this model also increases its complexity, making it somewhat more difficult for users to understand.

The main goals of an RDBMS engine such as Microsoft SQL Server are efficient management of information and the maintenance of data integrity. *Normalization* is the process that minimizes redundant information in a database, establishes efficient relationships among the database's tables, and ensures data integrity. One side effect of a normalized database is complex queries. Let's say that we want to use a SQL query to retrieve all the names of customers who purchased tofu in April, 1998, along with the quantity and date of each purchase. The query would look something like this:

```
SELECT
    cst.CompanyName,
    ord.ShippedDate,
    prd.ProductName,
    COUNT(1) AS qty
FROM customers cst
    JOIN [orders] ord
        ON cst.CustomerId = ord.CustomerId
    JOIN [order details] det
        ON det.orderid = ord.orderid
    JOIN [products] prd
        ON det.productid = det.productid
```

```
WHERE ord.ShippedDate BETWEEN '4/1/1998' AND '5/1/1998'
AND prd.productname = 'TOFU'
GROUP BY
    cst.CompanyName,
    ord.ShippedDate,
    prd.ProductName
```

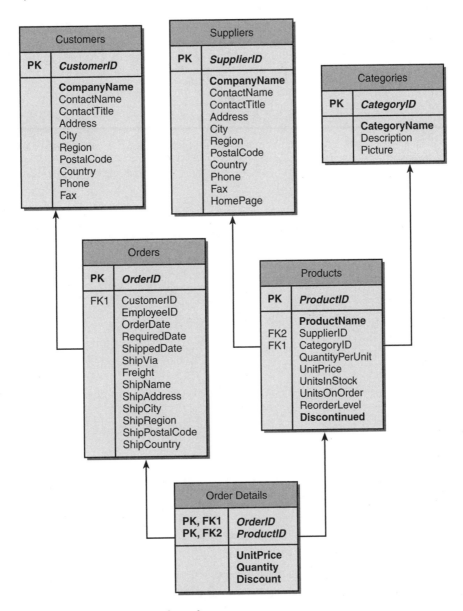

Figure 3-1. *Relational database diagram.*

Note If you want, you can run this very same query in the sample Northwind data-base included with SQL Server 2000.

Although this is hardly one of the most complicated queries you can come up with, it does seem like a lot of work for little information. To make this query, I had to join four tables together in order to get three fields. If I wanted to include regional and territorial information in my query, I would have had to join six or seven tables together! Fundamentally, there's nothing wrong with this way of querying data—as a matter of fact, SQL is a highly evolved language that is able to handle far more complex queries than this. To understand the underlying data and simplify the extractions, let's consider other methods of structuring the data.

For argument's sake, let's assume that all we want is to report and extract data from our structure. We don't care about data integrity or efficient use of structures for OLTP. We could then change our structures to look something like the one shown in Figure 3-2.

Figure 3-2. *Denormalized data structures.*

The process of melding multiple tables into one is known as *denormalizing*. Although I would not advise applying this process to a OLTP system, it does make the job of simplifying queries easier.

When the database is denormalized, the query shown in the earlier example looks like this.

```
SELECT
    CompanyName,
    ShippedDate,
    ProductName,
    count(1) AS qty
FROM ProductPurchases
    WHERE ShippedDate BETWEEN '4/1/1998' AND '5/1/1998'
    AND productname = 'TOFU'
GROUP BY
    CompanyName,
    ShippedDate,
    ProductName
```

By denormalizing the tables, we eliminated the complexities associated with joins. The downside to this process is that it increases data redundancy, and more data requires more disk space. Filtering a denormalized database is inherently slower than filtering a normalized database. Finally, we also made data entry a more cumbersome process because data elements such as the customer name and invoice number, which are referenced in a normalized structure, have to be entered for every item the customer purchases.

Reporting Against OLTP Data
Can Be Hazardous to Your Performance

Because many reports are more informative when they are created from the latest data, it might seem reasonable to sacrifice simplicity for current data. In the interests of getting the most current information, we could make a case for investing in more powerful machines to process our more complex queries. There are, however, other reasons besides the complexity of queries to avoid reporting against live OLTP data. For one thing, in OLTP environments RDBMS engines are already using valuable machine power to maintain security, indexes, data pages, memory, and other critical resources without having to drain more power to answer large queries.

Having to share machine power is a common problem associated with the mixing of reporting with OLTP, but another phenomena called *locking contention* actually presents a greater threat to performance. A mechanism in the RDBMS engines is specifically designed to lock records before updating them in order to avoid data anomalies created when two or more users attempt to update data records at the same time or when one user reads a record as it is being updated. While OLTP databases insert, delete, and update records, reporting processes read or select data. To ensure that a report does not output incongruous results, the RDBMS engine will refuse to change a record that's being read by a report. To generate an accurate quarterly accounts closing report, the engine has to use static data. If there was no locking mechanism in place, it's possible that some of the totaled items on the first page could change without that change being reflected in totals on the subsequent pages. In this case, a manual tally of the figures would reveal the discrepancy. The locking mechanism makes sure everyone takes their turn to access the data for reading and writing.

Caution Locking doesn't prevent proper functioning of a database, but it does force transactions to "wait" until the resource is released. A locked database most often acts like a system slowdown and causes some front-end applications to time out. One of the most misunderstood and overlooked locking problems is referred to as the *deadlock*. A deadlock occurs when two connections attempt to access and lock the same two resources at the same time. The first connection might succeed in locking the first resource but not the second resource, which has been locked by the second connection. The second connection is in the same situation as its rival, except that is has successfully placed a lock on the second resource and is waiting on the first resource. Each connection will hold to their positions like dueling partners, each waiting for the other to "blink." SQL Server recognizes a deadlock and kills the connection with the least amount of CPU cycles invested, thus turning the user into a *deadlock victim*. In most cases, the deadlock victim's applications will crash.

Many reporting-tool vendors tout the flexibility of their ad hoc querying interfaces for end users as one of the most powerful features of their products. While these reporting tools that only read data seem harmless, they too can be hazardous. If the data to be reported on is on the OLTP server, great care has to be taken to ensure that runaway ad hoc queries can't be made because you will have little control over what users might try to do on the production servers. Sometimes the RDBMS engine needs to create temporary work spaces for internal sorting and hashing needs. If a user creates and runs a query that turns out to be missing join predicates, the RDBMS engine could attempt to build a result set large enough to prevent core business transactions from accessing needed disk, memory, or processor resources.

The process of building new data models is even more intrusive than building reporting functions because unlike most reports, a data model's exhaustive search for patterns requires it to read as much data as possible to create the information that gets stored in the model. The nature of the data-mining process is such that very large quantities of data need to be analyzed at once in order to derive accurate patterns and new trends. Because of the extensive scope of this data analysis, Data Mining Services would most certainly find itself competing directly for resources with line-of-business transactions if Data Mining Services was getting its data from the OLTP server.

Tip The best way to avoid poor performance and to optimize OLTP and data mining is to create a data warehouse on a separate database from the OLTP database or on a separate server, and use that data exclusively for extraction and querying. In this way, the core line-of-business applications can be isolated from the model-building processes of data mining while still permitting flexibility for users who need to construct reports for their own needs. If the data-mining process slows the server temporarily, it becomes more of an annoyance to any other reporting process instead of causing problems for critical customer service processes.

Data Warehousing Architecture for Data Mining

Data Mining Services does not have access to higher-level data structures and models. It has no semantic structure to check facts. The data-mining model assumes that the data is factual and uses it to provide the resulting predictions. It's crucial that you take the necessary precautions to ensure that the data you start with is accurate. Assuring accurate data may require significant analysis of the attribute values inserted into the data-mining tools. To ensure that the conclusions drawn from past events are indeed valid, the team responsible for the data intelligence tools needs to implement a good process that cleans data as it goes into a data warehouse. The first step in the process of mining data is to find out whether you actually have the right data in your database. Deriving new patterns and rules not only requires specific data to be available, but also requires this data to be in granular form. If granular data is not available, you run the risk of missing certain meaningful information. For example, if the car dealership discussed in the previous chapter wanted to discover information about related sales, including the sale of car accessories, loans, or insurance, it would only get access to part of this information if related sales are not tied to vehicle sales. To apply data mining, you must first understand your data. Ask yourself the following questions:

- What data is available?
- How granular can we make the information?
- How useful is the data?
- What is the quality of the validation process?

Once the quality of this data has been validated, your next concern is how to move the OLTP data into a warehouse.

Creating the Warehouse from OLTP Data

The process of extracting data from an OLTP system for a data warehouse is complex, time-consuming, error-prone, and probably about as glamorous a task as peeling potatoes. Unfortunately, there is no way around this step in the process. The quality and usability of the resulting predictions makes this step a crucial part of the data-mining process.

Note   Data warehousing uncovers most of the problems that exist within the production systems. Any errors that don't get resolved at this point will surely show up in the form of bad results in the subsequent data-mining process that uses the warehoused data simply because those processes are the most visible components of the system.

Ensuring Data Quality

Most large databases are full of errors, sloppy entries, and missing data. Errors usually go unnoticed because people assume that if large amounts of data have been collected without causing the shutdown of the system, the data must be OK. This assumption is proven false the minute the extracted OLTP data is applied to a well-designed data warehouse.

Many organizations, particularly some of the large companies that house enough data to consider data mining, often use many different data-capturing systems that define and describe transactions, entities, and relationships between tables in different ways. Some systems use multiple naming conventions, incompatible or hidden encoding structures, or historical summary information, which is kept for only a limited time. Here's a non-exhaustive list of problems encountered when creating a data warehouse.

- **Hard-coded names** Programs that rely on the file or table names to access data. These present a problem because the logic applied to retrieve the data is too closely coupled with the logic present in the code.

- **Inconsistent field lengths** Field lengths may differ for the very same attribute in different tables. For instance, a company name might be allowed 50 characters in one table and only 35 in another. This is a problem only if entries with field lengths of 35 or more are present in one system and end up truncated when merged with the tables that have entries with smaller fields.

- **Missing values** The tables might contain missing values in certain fields, or numerical fields might have 0 instead of NULL values for unknown amounts. This can cause serious problems when performing summary aggregates and averaging. This is even more detrimental to the data-mining process simply because of the potential a 0 value has for predicting future behavior.

- **Inconsistent values** These occur when two departments enter the same conceptual entity but give it two different names. For example, if different operators enter the values of "Green," "GRN," "GR," and "Forest Green" to describe green automobiles, the data-mining model will create four classifications for the same color car. Inconsistent values are also created when values such as the area code of a phone number or a name without a title is entered.

- **Inconsistent field types** This problem occurs when values for the same type of item are kept in different data types. For example, it's possible to have zip codes kept in an integer-type field in one table and in a character-type field in another table. This inconsistency makes it very difficult to automatically merge these values into one table. Program code or conversion functions are required to integrate them.

- **Inconsistent entity handling** When different departments within the same company take charge of their own data, each department might have different levels of tolerance for sloppy data entry. For example, if a table contains only one field for both first and last names of individuals, the names can be entered in multiple ways. If data can't be parsed into first and last names, the records can't be automatically merged with records in other tables with the same names. Inconsistent handling of entities can even make it difficult to separate the names into two or more fields.

Storing redundant data on *data islands*, or unique data repositories, located throughout the company also leads to problems. Islands of data, illustrated in Figure 3-3, are especially difficult to handle because the context in which the data was entered each time has to be known in order to accurately house the data.

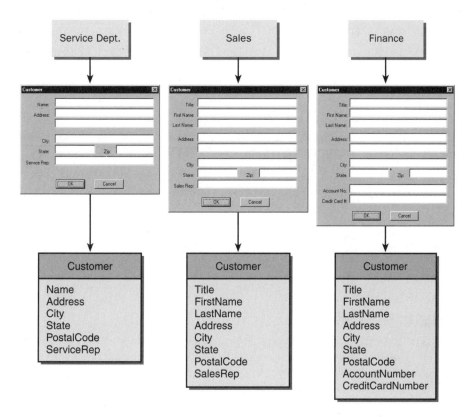

Figure 3-3. *Data islands managed by individual departments.*

Data Warehousing Nightmare

One cable television and Internet service provider I did OLAP consulting work for ran into problems when it tried to build its first data warehouse by combining subscriber information taken from various departments and each department used a different system to record subscriber information. Each department gave subscribers unique customer entities with specific attributes that resulted in duplicate and triplicate entries. Because deriving conclusions about individual customers was crucial to the data-mining process, a huge amount of work had to be done to "clean" this data and combine the records so that each subscriber had only one record that could then be housed in a table within the data warehouse.

When to Discard Data from the Warehouse

Once the data is cleaned and stored, some warehouse records may still be useless. It's difficult to know which records to discard and when. Often, the best solution is to remove some records entirely from the source data before using it for data mining. Remove records that don't represent the reality of the transactions or the current state of the business. These records only cause false predictions about future results and include the following:

- **Test data** Developers and systems administrators are often surprised by the quantity of test-related data that resides in production environments. Test data is made up of bogus clients and fictitious transactions and therefore is not to be used as source data.

- **Data that represents exceptional circumstances** For example, if a grocery store had increased sales of batteries and canned foods after a hurricane, these sales should be discarded. The numbers would do nothing to help predict trends, unless, of course, hurricanes were a frequent occurrence in the area.

- **Artificial data such as dummy refunds made to rectify erroneous sales** For instance, if an accountant discovers that the previous month's sales figures included some double entries from a faulty application, he might enter equal negative amounts or create fake refund entries to rectify the data. The entry of artificial data rectifies reporting totals and keeps accounting applications running smoothly. Unfortunately, any phantom sales and refunds must be removed from the data source, or the predictions will also be illusory.

Optimizing Data for Mining

Optimally (and optimistically speaking), the data sources used to create data-mining models are contained in one simple table of columns and rows. Of course most data sources are quite different, even those that come from a warehouse. Often data is stored in multiple tables (perhaps even in multiple formats), and the tables are related in all sorts of explicit and not-so-explicit ways. For the best predictions and performance, keep your source data organized in as simple a format as possible.

Data Structures

When a data-mining model is made, it is the data-mining algorithms that extract the data from a *flattened table*, which is a single table or view that contains all the necessary rows and columns from the data source. Once this has been managed, the important decision of how to manage the columns and rows has to be made.

Choosing Columns

Columns, or fields, are the units that contain a particular kind of data in a given data type. When used for data mining, the column type is of little concern. It doesn't matter whether the column contains a number, a character, or a data field; what is important, however, is the distribution of the contents of that field.

When identifying the columns you want to use to create your data-mining models, keep in mind what role those fields will play in determining how the data-mining model will be constructed. The following are roles that a given column can have in this process:

- Input column
- Target column
- Key column
- Value column

Input columns

Input columns are used to create the original patterns. They include the attributes of a given case that describe the characteristics that influence an outcome. The following is a list of attributes included in the case of a car. Each one would be an input column.

- Year
- Make
- Model
- Body Type
- Color
- Engine Type
- Mileage

It's a given that some cars will sell for a higher price than others based on the combinations of their attributes. Data mining investigates patterns based on attributes as it creates a model.

Target columns

These are the outcomes that you want predicted. A car dealer's target columns could include

- Average age of customers
- Average annual income of customers
- Predicted sales of those cars priced at 10 percent over blue book value

Results are expressed in these target columns. If you examine the column inputs, you can determine the value of the targets. In this example, after examining the patterns, the car dealer could discover that 25-year-old males with average incomes of $75, 000 buy red Corvette sports cars if they have less than 20,000 miles on them.

Key columns

Key columns are not used for deriving data-mining patterns but are used to correlate data in a model to prediction cases in a table. The use of key columns will become clear in Chapter 12, "Data-Mining Queries," in which queries are discussed in depth.

Value columns

Value columns contain specific numerical values, such as the price of a particular item associated with each row. In this case, values help predict the future price of the items.

Columns to Avoid

If a table has columns that contain the same values, these values can't be used for data mining. Sometimes values are repeated if a subset of data from the data warehouses is used to create a mining model, and if that subset, by definition, refers to a certain type of case. For example, if a car dealer wants predictions only about Ford vehicles, the Make column in the table should contain only "FORD" as the value.

The value of "0" would show up in every row if, for example, the dealer had a RUSTPROOFING column to input the cost of rust proofing a new automobile, but as it happened, no one ever had his or her car rust proofed. Obviously this column would be completely useless for making predictions.

It's also a good idea to check for columns with oddball cases, which if included might skew results. For instance, if only four out of 112,000 customers bought leather headlight covers, the LEATHER_HEADLIGHT_COVERS column should be ignored since it's unlikely that such a miniscule deviation from the norm would be of any use for modeling purposes. This is not to say that the causes for this lack of headlight-cover sales shouldn't be examined—but it seems evident that those leather headlight covers should be either marked down or removed from the shelves. Generally speaking, if 97 percent (or more) of a column's data is identical, then chances are slim that you can use that field to discover any meaningful patterns.

When columns are unique (instead of too similar) to one another, their value also diminishes. Every database has dissimilar input columns such as:

- Social security numbers
- Vehicle identification numbers
- Primary key values
- System-generated passwords
- Names
- Telephone numbers
- IP addresses

A pattern cannot be derived from this list of attributes because the values only occur once. There are also no meaningful similarities to be found in the values in a given column. A pattern can exist only when a value repeats over and over under similar circumstances.

There is no question that some of these unique columns with unique values contain valuable information. For example, social security numbers can be parsed to show where and when they were issued; and vehicle identification numbers are encoded with the year, make, and model information. However, to make use of this information, those columns would have to be split into two or more columns. Each new column would have information grouped together and these groups would be used to derive predictions. In this example, the original fields would be ignored or discarded.

Some columns add no predictive value because their value is constant in relation to other values in other columns. For example, if all BMWs come with air conditioning, the relationship between AIR_CONDITIONING = YES and MAKE = BMW has no predictive value. It has no predictive value not only because one condition always exists with the other, but also because the condition exists in the first place because the dealership decided to make AC standard fare in BMWs.

Selecting Rows

Rows represent individual cases that are used to create the model (see Figure 3-4). Check that the data in each row is accurate; valid predictions depend on it. The cases in the rows themselves can be represented by a *view* made by joining two or more tables together. Regardless of how rows are represented, care must be taken to understand the granularity and accuracy of their content.

	Customer ID	Company Name	Contact Name	Contact Title	Address	City	Region	Postal Code	Country
+	ALFKI	Alfreds Futterkiste	Maria Anders	Sales Represent	Obere Str. 5	Berlin		12209	Germany
+	ANATR	Ana Trujillo Empa	Ana Trujillo	Owner	Avda. de la	México D.F		05021	Mexico
+	ANTON	Antonio Moreno T	Antonio Moreno	Owner	Mataderos	México D.F		05023	Mexico
+	AROUT	Around the Horn	Thomas Hardy	Sales Represent	120 Hanover	London		WA1 1DP	UK
+	BERGS	Berglunds snabbk	Christina Berglu	Order Administra	Berguvsväge	Luleå		S-958 22	Sweden
+	BLAUS	Blauer See Delika	Hanna Moos	Sales Represent	Forsterstr. 5	Mannheim		68306	Germany
+	BLONP	Blondel père et fil:	Frédérique Citea	Marketing Mana(	24, place Kl	Strasbourg		67000	France
+	BOLID	Bólido Comidas p	Martín Sommer	Owner	C/ Araquil, E	Madrid		28023	Spain
+	BONAP	Bon app'	Laurence Lebiha	Owner	12, rue des	Marseille		13008	France
+	BOTTM	Bottom-Dollar Mar	Elizabeth Lincol	Accounting Man:	23 Tsawass	Tsawasser	BC	T2F 8M4	Canada
+	BSBEV	B's Beverages	Victoria Ashwor	Sales Represent	Fauntleroy (	London		EC2 5NT	UK
+	CACTU	Cactus Comidas	Patricio Simpso	Sales Agent	Cerrito 333	Buenos Air		1010	Argentina
+	CENTC	Centro comercial	Francisco Chan(	Marketing Mana(	Sierras de C	México D.F		05022	Mexico
+	CHOPS	Chop-suey Chines	Yang Wang	Owner	Hauptstr. 29	Bern		3012	Switzerlar
+	COMMI	Comércio Mineiro	Pedro Afonso·	Sales Associate	Av. dos Lus	São Paulo	SP	05432-043	Brazil
+	CONSH	Consolidated Holc	Elizabeth Brown	Sales Represent	Berkeley Ga	London		WX1 6LT	UK
+	DRACD	Drachenblut Delik	Sven Ottlieb	Order Administra	Walserweg	Aachen		52066	Germany
+	DUMON	Du monde entier	Janine Labrune	Owner	67, rue des	Nantes		44000	France
+	EASTC	Eastern Connecti(	Ann Devon	Sales Agent	35 King Geo	London		WX3 6FW	UK
+	ERNSH	Ernst Handel	Roland Mendel	Sales Manager	Kirchgasse	Graz		8010	Austria

Record: 14 | 1 ▶ ▶I ▶* of 91

Figure 3-4. *Data rows and columns in a table.*

Calculated and Derived Data

In addition to rows of raw data, you can also add columns and use them to enhance the value of the data in the rows. If the car dealer wants more information, he performs calculations on the row values. Some vehicle-related samples of calculations include:

- Mileage / Number of owners
- Mileage / Price
- Blue book value – Sale price
- Number of prospects / Number of sales
- Sale price – Trade-in value
- Sale price – (Transportation cost + Inventory cost)
- Sticker price – Sale price

If a data-model builder is sufficiently knowledgeable about the business or subject being studied, there is no limit to the relationships she might look for. The first list of calculations are straightforward; in the interest of discovering new patterns, let's derive more imaginative values such as these:

- **Sale price / Age of car**   To find price patterns.
- **Age of salesperson – Age of customer**   A long shot, but generation gaps shouldn't be discounted.
- **Miles per gallon / Annual income of customer**   Are customers with high annual incomes as concerned with fuel efficiency as those with average annual incomes?

Certain fields contain hidden information that can flag important values. If a retail store combines date values (and these days are related to sales values) with a holiday database, the retailer could discover which items sell best on holidays. Other values related to dates include:

- Weekday versus weekend sales
- Month of the year
- Season of the year
- End of month versus beginning of month
- Tax-refund time

As mentioned earlier, other data items can be parsed to extract more valuable data. These include:

- **Vehicle identification numbers**   Used to derive various fields about the year, make, model, and manufacturer.
- **Zip codes**   Each code is specific to a geographic location.
- **Telephone numbers**   Area codes are also specific to a geographic region.
- **IP Addresses**   Networks are identified by portions of the IP address. This address tells the owner of a Web site what provider a visitor to his site uses.

One thing that makes data mining such a labor of skill and imagination is its capacity to make optimal use of derived variables. Valuable information can be extrapolated from seemingly mundane data by using derived data, variables, and simple calculations.

Determining Data Granularity

Ideally, the data used for mining should be of the same granular level as the case level of the predictions you're seeking. Let me explain. If your vehicle sales predictions are based on individual cars, it makes sense to base the data-mining model on individual car sales. On the other hand, if you want to predict which makes and models will sell best in 500 nationwide dealerships, it makes more sense to summarize the vehicle data by make and model characteristics, thereby reducing the level of granularity. If you wanted to predict total yearly sales of cars per state, the granularity of the source data would be more effective if set at the state-level of granularity.

Besides reducing the granularity of your data, summarizing allows you to create variables derived vertically instead of horizontally. For example, a column containing the total costs grouped by car make can be materialized through aggregation in a way that isn't otherwise possible.

When creating a flattened view of a data source, it's sometimes advantageous to combine both detail-level data with summarized data, as shown in Figure 3-5.

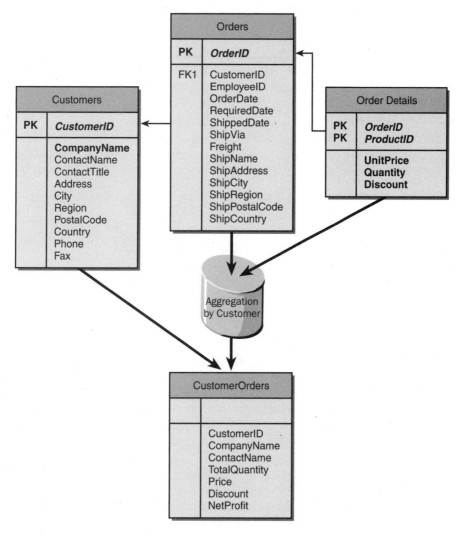

Figure 3-5. *Join of detail level data and summarized data.*

A way to see the advantage of combining detail and summarized data, is to create a data source with customer information and an assortment of invoices for each customer. If you are interested in the type of items the customer purchased per invoice, group the individual line items of the invoice by item type. Figure 3-5 shows a series of invoices from customers of a local computer store. The predictions that result from this data source are based on types of components, not on the individual components purchased by each customer, so the line items are grouped by fixed disks, memory, processors, and so on.

Physical Data Mining Structure

Now that I've described the implementation of the data structures, it's worth looking at a few examples of the most recognized architectural models. Although these architectures are not concerned with the data sources, or even with the models themselves, they do describe how the client applications interact with the data-mining models. An architecture is chosen by the size of the data source that will be mined and by the frequency with which the prediction queries will be issued against the data mining models.

Client (Single-Tier) Architecture

In the scenario illustrated in Figure 3-6, a client machine contains the engine that performs the actual data mining. The data stored in a warehouse is downloaded, stored on the client machine, and all the data preparation and mining is carried out on the client machine.

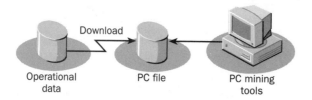

Download

Operational   PC file   PC mining
data   tools

Figure 3-6. *Single-tier architecture.*

As client machines become more powerful, so do servers, which means that networks used to download the data source to the client machine could soon be drowning in monster-size data files. Networks should be used for this purpose only when the amount of data to be mined is small and the process is infrequent enough to allow the client machine enough time to process tasks without exhausting its resources and those of the network to which it's connected.

Two-Tier Architecture

Two-tier architecture, as illustrated in Figure 3-7, can mine millions of records on reasonably high-performance servers without a very complex physical architecture. The server houses the data-mining engine as well as the data warehouse and runs all the processes locally. The client machines, through an OLE DB connection, simply call the engine to perform all the necessary data-mining processes and when applicable, receive prediction result sets.

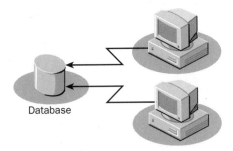

Figure 3-7. *Two-tier architecture.*

Three-Tier Architecture

This architecture generally requires a dedicated high-performance server to run the data-mining engine on the middle tier and an equally high-end server to run the database engine on the back end.

In the example shown in Figure 3-8, the data warehouse resides on the back end while the middle tier is responsible for mining that data. The middle tier loads the data from the back end and mines it, and the results are passed on to the data-mining client machine. To the client machine, the process is identical to the two-tier model.

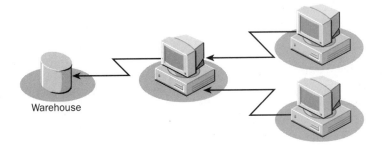

Figure 3-8. *Three-tier architecture.*

Relational Data Warehouse

The relational data warehouse is, as the name implies, a storage structure that uses the same relational engine as an OLTP database. The warehouse uses the same engine, but stores the data in a separate location from the OLTP data such as another physical server or database. Even though maintaining data integrity and optimal normalization are not top priorities for the relational data warehouse, it does need to use the unique querying powers of the RDBMS to retrieve data according to the specifications of any given SELECT statement.

Advantages of Relational Data Storage

Using relational data storage as the source for data mining is one of the best options available for designing the architecture of a corporate intelligence system. There are some tradeoffs, but consider the advantages described in the following sections.

Flexibility

When both the OLTP data and the data warehouse share the same engine, there's a very good chance that the inter-server or inter-database data transfers are especially favored by the seamless communications structures that usually exist between the RDBMS implementations. When these engines use the same version and are made by the same vendor, as is the case if both database engines are SQL Server 2000, then the data transfers are perfectly seamless.

> **Note** If you decide to use OLAP, a special communication bridge has to be built between the OLAP engine and the RDBMS to facilitate the movement of data from the relational structures into the cubes. Although there are specific advantages to proceeding in this way—for example, the interfaces to the cube are standardized—special care has to be taken to understand the inner workings of both relational and OLAP structures to ensure that the cube really does reflect the state of the data in the OLTP system. In other words, you should understand how to get information from the cube and from the relational database so that you know which rows in the database are processed and in the cube and which ones still await processing.

Relational Databases Use Standards

Database designers and system administrators find relational databases easy to understand because they share standards with OLTP systems. There are plenty of OLAP vendors with unique storage implementations and querying rules, but the science and structural philosophy of relational data is common to most RDBMS engines. The warehouses are better built because the standards are familiar to more people; for example, terms such as primary keys, foreign keys, rules, and special data types are second nature to most engineers working in the field. Because the two structures can be directly compared, the OLTP data is easy to test and validate. Because the metadata is easily accessible, the database permits the use of indexes, which are beneficial and easily applied to the data-mining process.

Easy Access to Lowest Level of Granularity

One of the most important steps in the data-mining process is the comparison of test cases to real cases.

> **Note**   Test cases are cases that were not used to build the original data-mining model, but which are kept in order to measure the effectiveness of the model. These cases are used as inputs as if they were new data that had unknown values that need to be predicted. Since you already know what the real values are, the outputs from the model can be tested for accuracy against them.

If the input cases are of the same granular level as the transactions used to create the data warehouse, it's also crucial that the model contains that same level of granularity. For example, if you wish to create a data-mining function that lets you input an automobile's characteristics and then guess its price and customer profile, you would need a data-mining model that contains individual cases at a granular level including sales and customer information.

OLAP optimizes the use of aggregated information by sacrificing convenient and intuitive access to the detail level of data that is used to populate the cube. Naturally there are ways to work around this problem such as using the drill-through functions in Analysis Services, but these functions often require the use of other special functions that in turn refer back to the underlying data source in a somewhat disjointed manner. Even with this disadvantage, OLAP is still used for many data-mining scenarios.

Building Supporting Tables for Data Mining

The main source component of the relational data-mining process is the *case table,* which contains the raw data the computer must "learn" from. Out of this table, you have to create the following columns:

- **Case key column**   This is the column that uniquely identifies the case you want to model such as the make of car or the name of a bank customer.

- **Input columns**   These are the columns that contain the known attributes that describe the case. For instance, the car, color, and make are known attributes that go into a case record and later serve to facilitate predictions using similar attributes in test sets.

- **Predictable columns**   Predictable columns contain the expected values for predictions, which are based on the attributes in the input columns.

Case tables contain all the columns needed to establish the cases set for a data-mining model. There are times when the cases can be derived directly from a single table in a relational database. This is a simple matter to set up because all the relevant columns are kept in one place. If the source is in multiple tables, joining the tables to make them appear as one will make this task a bit more complex. When you select a data-mining method, whether it's clustering or decision trees, you must choose an algorithm to use with the relational data-mining model, which then automatically attaches you to a specific data-mining algorithm provider. The data-mining algorithm provider presents the choices of data-mining algorithms and defines the physical structure for the data-mining model.

OLAP cubes

OLAP cubes are an important part of data mining not only as a source of data for creating data-mining models, but also as a structure for storing data-mining models themselves.

How Data Mining Uses OLAP Structures

Instead of using a traditional flattened table, OLAP provides a cube's dimensions as the input source. With this cube's dimensions, the data-mining service creates the cases needed for the data-mining model.

The columns in an OLAP data-mining model are constructed from visible levels in the OLAP cube. To create an OLAP data-mining model, the Mining Model wizard requires a cube whose dimensions contain at least one visible level.

Once the model is created, it can be stored in a *virtual cube,* or a dimension of the original source cube. OLAP data-mining models cannot be created directly from relational data sources or virtual cubes that contain a data-mining dimension.

The outputs or prediction results can come in various forms depending on how the results are going to be used. These forms include:

- One of the measures of the source cube
- Member property of the chosen dimension and level member

In the beginning of this chapter, we looked at some basic differences between data warehousing structures and OLTP data. We denormalized, or flattened, table structures to reduce table joins. If we really want to take this process one step further and eliminate the need to filter data altogether, we can create structures that are not only denormalized, but horizontally and vertically partitioned as shown in Figure 3-9.

These tables are almost completely useless for an OLTP database. Instead of rows containing attributes that can be filtered through a WHERE clause, multiple tables of the same exact structures are created. These contain a reduced set of fields used to answer more specific questions. They also contain only rows that belong to a category, such as a Products category or a Date-of-Purchase category. On the other hand, a query, like the one shown below, is easy to construct not only because the tables contain less rows, but also because the WHERE clause is unnecessary.

```
SELECT
    CompanyName,
    ShippedDate,
    ProductName,
    count(1) AS qty
FROM Tofu_Purchases_April_1998
GROUP BY
    CompanyName
    ShippedDate
```

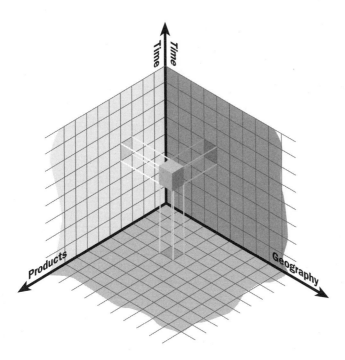

Figure 3-9. *Cubed structures.*

Advantages of OLAP Storage

An OLAP cube is designed to rigidly structure data to make it easy for us to examine aggregates. This aggregation, because it's precalculated, offers a unique opportunity to create derived fields that can exist because there is only aggregated data and no detailed-level data. These fields include:

- Sums
- Averages
- Standard deviations
- Ranks
- Counts
- Mathematical functions
- Financial functions

Speed

Data in OLAP cubes is preaggregated and stored in cells that require a querying engine to define the cell coordinates. OLAP data is radically different from relational data. OLAP cube data takes longer to prepare and is used only once. However, one of the big advantages of OLAP technology, regardless of how it's ultimately used, is the speed by which an operator can navigate sums and averages across dimensions. If the cases that feed the model are contained in a very large data warehouse and if the data-mining process is able to dispense with the need for detailed-level data, then the models can be built in a fraction of the time required to build a similar model using relational data.

Easy Navigation

To fit into a cube, data must be precisely structured to meet the cube's requirements. The cube's structure is exposed to outside reporting tools and OLE DB wrappers such as ADO MD, so you can determine the cube's dimensions. After you know the cube's dimensions you can surf the cube's data to quickly examine aggregates through various dimensional levels. This is possible because dynamic aggregates conform to the framework provided by the relatively static dimensions.

> **More Info** Because Data Mining doesn't need to navigate data like a human operator does, easy navigation is a relatively unimportant feature. On the other hand, the results of data-mining queries are automatically placed in dimensions that are stored in OLAP structures and those dimensions, when applied to aggregates, let you quickly review some what-if scenarios.

OLAP Storage Requires Highly-Structured Dimensions

In order to make the aggregates consistent across dimensions, the dimensions and measures themselves must be clearly defined. Many dimensions contain information that, when processed, exists in a hierarchical structure. For example, if a Car information dimension is created with Year as the top dimension and Car Make as a low dimension, the OLAP engine will usually show a warning message or not create the dimension if there are more distinct Year values than there are Car Make values because this can be a violation of the intended structure of the cube. OLAP's fact checking ability prevents the storing of faulty or irrelevant aggregates in the cube.

Semantic rigor on the part of OLAP makes for more accurate data-mining models because the algorithms assume that the attributes of those individual cases actually mean something. Because nothing at the engine level or conceptual level of the relational model really prevents inaccurate hierarchies from existing, the model is more prone to error. A false hierarchy, for example, might create models that place too little, or too much, emphasis on certain attributes because they seem to belong to a certain level in a given dimension. This inaccurate level assignment could result in false predictions.

Flat Tables vs. Multidimensional OLAP Tables

While flat table structures are fine for simple data-mining projects, they present several problems for more complex projects. Flat tables are difficult to analyze, they contain lower grained information, and when they are used for complex projects so many rules are needed to maintain the integrity of the data that the model becomes overly complex and unwieldy. On the other hand, an OLAP data-mining system analyzes data across multiple dimensions and takes full advantage of the patterns along these dimensions. The patterns are merged, conclusions are drawn, and predictions are made based on summarized groups of data. In the end, our fictitious data-mining car dealer discovers trends such as "Red trucks are profitable overall, but much of the profit comes from dealerships in the southern United States" and "Blue trucks are profitable too, but mostly in the northeast United States."

When you think about it, data analysis, in almost all cases, involves a certain degree of analysis of cumulative figures. Most companies with large data warehouses rarely analyze an individual case. It's the cumulative data such as sales per month or sales by store that most interests the business analyst. Data mining analyzes and makes predictions based on this type of cumulative data.

When OLAP Is Not Appropriate for Data Mining

As wonderful as OLAP is, there are some important limitations to consider when using it as a source for data mining. The most important limitation of OLAP is that it does not provide data granularity. As mentioned earlier, OLAP is great when it comes to aggregation; unfortunately, it completely fails when the data mining model is required to represent individual line items such as Sales. If a marketing department wanted to use data mining to predict the sales potential of a certain make of automobile, regardless of the individual features and condition of the vehicle, it would make sense to use sales summaries of the car make and not the individual sales for each car. An OLAP structure would work perfectly for this job. On the other hand, if your predictions need to be based on individual cases (such as on the customer case, in order to make predictions about individual customer behavior), the OLAP structures would be incapable of providing such input.

Summary

As discussed, the data-mining models are ultimately fed with data from OLTP systems, which are most often kept in relational database structures. Although there's little doubt this OLTP data should be moved to a data warehouse more conducive to the process of data mining, one of the first things to determine is whether this new structure is going to be another relational system or an OLAP system.

Relational systems offer a bit more flexibility and are easier for people to build. It also is the only storage mechanism that seamlessly preserves the original granular levels present in the original OLTP systems.

OLAP offers an enhanced storage mechanism that optimizes data retrieval, enforces rigid semantic structures, and facilitates intuitive navigational features. As a source for building data-mining models, it offers a wider array of storage options for the predictions and the models themselves, including other OLAP structures. Although OLAP doesn't store low-level granular data, it's the ideal source of summarized data about groups.

When deciding on a physical architecture on which to implement your data-mining operation, the size of the data models and the frequency of the prediction queries must be taken into account. The three-tiered architectural model is ideal when there is an exceptional amount of data to be mined. Three-tier models require two high-end servers that divide up the task of serving the data from the model. The most common architecture is the two-tier model; one tier is for the clients who query the model and the second tier is for the server that processes the requests. The single-tier model is designed for light-weight data-mining processes that can be executed on client machines without having an adverse affect on network bandwidth or exhausting the relatively weaker resources in the client machines.

Chapter 4
Approaches to Data Mining

Organizations apply data-mining technology to their stores of data for two reasons: to make sense of their past and to make predictions about their future. Ultimately, they use the information taken from this computerized fortuneteller to make decisions about their futures. As we'll see shortly, the kind of information an organization wants determines the kind of model it builds and the algorithms applied to the structured data.

Real World   Fortune Telling for the Real World

Predictive, as opposed to descriptive, data modeling derives future results from theoretical data sets. These results are used by organizations and companies to determine what actions to take. For instance, we could build a model that would provide data that predicts the price range for a new Lincoln Continental. The model could also yield data that predicts how long the car would sit on the lot at a given price. Based on these two predictions, the dealer could determine the optimal selling price and how long he could expect this model of car to sit on the lot at this price. The dealer might also use the data to attract a certain clientele. If queried correctly, the data could tell the dealer what kind of customer buys what kind of car. The resulting model would provide a list of car makes and models that appeal to wealthy retirees. Another list would tell the dealer the average income of SUV drivers. Although this data analysis doesn't require target variables to work, actions can still be taken based on the data. For instance, based on past sales data and demographics, a dealership located in West Palm Beach, Florida, an area with a large population of retired folks, might decide to fill their lot with Cadillacs and Lincoln sedans.

Directed Data Mining

In order to perform a directed data-mining operation, all the known factors, or input variables, need to be given so that the data-mining engine can find the best correlations of those attributes to a rule within the data-mining model. The prediction is based on unknown values or target variables, meaning that the data-mining engine will find the most likely value for those missing values based on the known values provided with the input variables.

Directed data mining uses the most popular data-mining techniques and algorithms, such as decision trees. It classifies data for use in making predictions or estimates with the goal of deriving target values—in fact, it's the request for target values that gives directed data mining its "direction." A wide range of businesses use it. Banks use it to predict who is most likely to default on a loan, retail chains use it to decide whom to market their products to, and pharmaceutical companies use it to predict new prescription drug sales.

Undirected Data Mining

Because undirected data mining isn't used to make predictions, target values aren't required. Instead, the data is placed in a format that makes it easier for us to make sense of. For example, an online bookseller could organize past sales data to discover the common characteristics of genre readers from the United States. The data could reveal (as unlikely as it seems) that readers of murder mysteries are predominantly women from Maine and upstate New York and readers of science fiction are predominantly Generation-X men living in Washington and Oregon. Clustering is the algorithm commonly used for mining historical data. As the name implies, clustering clumps data together in groups based on common characteristics. The bookseller's marketing department could use these revelations to direct the company's advertisements for sci-fi books to men's magazines.

Another way to treat this data is to take one of the derived clusters and apply the decision trees algorithm to it. This allows you to focus on a particular segment of the cluster. In fact, clustering is often the first step in the process used to define broad groups. Once groups are established, directed data mining is used on groups that are of particular interest to the company.

Data Mining vs. Statistics

Newcomers to data mining naturally tend to think of the term as a new way to say statistics. Hard-core cynics even refer to data mining as "statistics + marketing." Nothing could be further from the truth, but since many of the data-mining algorithms were indeed defined by statisticians, it's no wonder that some of the terminology and techniques are suspiciously similar, such as probability, distribution, regression, and so on. Data mining as a process is influenced by several disciplines, including statistics, machine learning, and high-performance computing. If you examine how quantitative information is analyzed, you'll find that data mining and statistics are concerned with many of the same problems and use many of the same functions. Data mining and statistics both use

- Uniformly stored and relevant data
- Input values
- Target values
- Models

OK—so why then should you read this book instead of *Advanced Statistics for Data Base Queries*? (I don't know if this book exists, but if it does—buy it!) This question doesn't have a simple answer, but an understanding of basic statistical principles will certainly help you appreciate the differences. Data mining is different from pure statistics in several ways.

First, data mining is a data-driven process that discovers meaningful patterns previously unseen or otherwise prone to be overlooked, while statistical inference begins with a hypothesis conceived by a person, who then applies statistical methods to prove or disprove the thesis. Data mining also differs from statistics in that the objective is to derive predictive models that can easily be translated into new business rules.

The defining feature of data mining is that the machine, not the operator, does the complex mathematics used to build the predictive model. Computers do the high-level inductive reasoning required to analyze large quantities of raw data and can then output the results in a format that the owner of the data—whether she be a nuclear physicist or a cattle rancher—can understand.

Only by analyzing large sets of cases can accurate predictions be made. Pure statistical analysis requires the statistician to perform a high degree of directed interaction with the data sets, which interferes with the potential for making new discoveries. Discovery, in the world of data mining, is the process of looking at a database to find hidden patterns in the data. The process does not take preconceived ideas or even a hypothesis to the data. In other words, the program uses its own computational ability to find patterns, without any user direction. The computer is also able to find many more patterns than a human could imagine. What distinguishes data mining from the science of statistics is the machine.

This said, data mining's roots are revealed in the language it shares with statistics. Some common terms that are important to know are discussed here.

Population

Population is the group that comprises the cases that are included in the data-mining model. In order for the data-mining effort to be successful, the characteristics common to this group must be clearly defined. As obvious as this might seem, the task of creating a well-defined population is more challenging than you might guess. If you're studying customer-buying habits in one store, the population is clearly defined; anyone who made the cash register ring is part of that population. To study that population, all you need to do is mine the data gathered from the point-of-sale machines.

However, if your population is created by asking residents of a specified geographical area to fill out a questionnaire about their shopping habits, you have to take into account the margin of error created by the data collection method and by the questions asked. This population is better defined as residents of a neighborhood who were willing to answer the questionnaire. If your questionnaire was returned by 20 percent of the residents, your data isn't an accurate representation of the neighborhood or its shopping habits.

Sample

If a data set contains an unmanageable number of cases, a smaller, random subset of the larger data set, or *sample*, is extracted and mined. The assumption is that because the sample is randomly selected, it represents the same data distributions as the larger set. There are no hard and fast rules, but experience and knowledge about the data dictate the size of the smaller sample. Too small of a sample might contain cases with too many exceptions that would then be overrepresented in the resulting patterns. A sample needs to be large enough to absorb the impact of exceptions in the same way as the larger data set would.

Range

A *range* includes the extreme exceptions in a data set. For instance, cases for automobile sales might show that most autos cost between $10,000 and $30,000. The cars in one example might include a car that sold for $100 and another that sold for a whopping $300,000. These two fringe figures are valuable in that they help define the boundaries. In statistical terms, the range in this case is said to be $299,900 ($300,000 – $100).

Bias

When you extract a sample of data for analysis, the method you use to choose the data could *bias*, or skew, the results. A biased extraction can misrepresent the entire population it came from. For instance, let's say you want to measure the purchasing habits of the population of Minnesota. Because this data set is uncommonly large, you decide to extract a sample of the residents of Minneapolis and Saint Paul. The fact that the entire sample population is urban in a predominantly rural state would bias the results. The results of this data-mining effort would fail if you tried to apply the resulting predictions to data that came from Albert Lea, Minnesota. Attributes particular to Minneapolis-Saint Paul would not describe the small town of Albert Lea.

When you extract a sample from a data set using nonrandom methods, take great care to ensure that the methods you use do not inject bias into the data set—or if you can't completely avoid the bias, at least understand it and take it into account when making decisions based on your results.

Mean

Mean is another word for average. To calculate the mean, add up the results of a column and divide the result by the number of instances as shown in Table 4-1. Averages are heavily affected by extreme values, especially if the total number of instances is few. For example, if nine persons have annual incomes of $100,000, $50,000, $50,000, $15,000, $15,000, $15,000, $15,000, $9000, and $9000, their average income is $30,889—this average isn't representative of any one person's annual income, but is an average nonetheless. If a new value of $100,000 is added, the average jumps to $37,800. Averages for very large data sets are more accurate provided there isn't a large gap between high and low values.

Table 4-1. Calculating the Mean

Wage earner	Annual Income
Mary	$100,000
John	$50,000
Jim	$50,000
Fred	$15,000
Jean	$15,000
Bill	$15,000
Kim	$15,000
Ron	$9,000
Lea	$9,000
Total	$278,000
Average (Total/9)	$30,889

Median

A *median* is the middle value in a data set as shown in Table 4-2. In this example, the middle value is $15,000. Median values are less affected by extreme values. They come in handy when determining an average in a data set that might have some data that is too loosely defined. For instance, it's conceivable that in our example incomes over $100,000 are simply assigned a value of Income Over $100,000. Without specific values over $100,000, it's impossible to calculate a mean but easy to determine a median.

Table 4-2. Determining the Median

Wage earner	Annual Income
Mary	$100,000
John	$50,000
Jim	$50,000
Fred	$15,000
Jean	$15,000
Bill [MEDIAN]	**$15,000**
Kim	$15,000
Ron	$9,000
Lea	$9,000
Total	$278,000
Mean	$15,000

Distribution

The position, arrangement, and frequency of the differences in a set of data is known as *distribution*. When you create a model, it's important to understand how many different values exist in a column. A column with only one state name such as CA in it is a poor candidate for data mining because there's no distribution in the data. On the other hand, if six states are represented in that column, the distribution of data is measured across six different values. The values are then weighed to determine how many occurrences of each state exist in the model. The best way to view the distribution is with a graph with the states plotted on an x-axis and the number of occurrences plotted along the y-axis as shown in Figure 4-1.

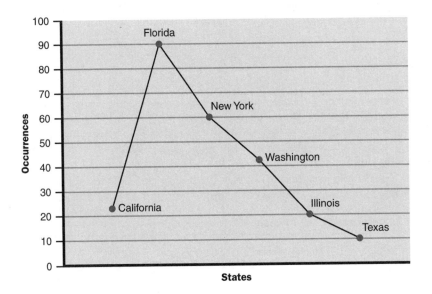

Figure 4-1. *Distribution across six states.*

At times, the column is populated with an either/or value such as Male or Female and TRUE or FALSE. This kind of distribution is known as a *binomial distribution*.

Mode

Mode refers to the most frequently occurring value in a distribution (15,000 in the previous example).

Variance

Unlike a range, which only measures the values on the extremities of a spectrum, *variance* is the sum of the differences between each value in a data set and the mean of that data set divided by one less than the number of values in the data set. For example, the variance of the salary data in Table 4-1 is

$$((100{,}000 - 30{,}888)^2 + (50{,}000 - 30{,}888)^2 + \ldots + (9000 - 30{,}888)^2) / 8$$

Variance is used to determine how far off the mark the extreme values are from the expected values.

Standard Deviation

Standard deviation is the square root of the variance. Like the variance, the standard deviation calculates the dispersion between a given value and the mean. The differences from the mean are easier to express with standard deviation than with variance because standard deviation is expressed in specific measurement units that are organized in tiers. The values, expressed as two standard deviations or one standard deviation, tell how far from the mean these values are.

Correlation

When a variable changes as a result of a change to another variable, the two variables are said to *correlate*. For example, there is a correlation between income and taxation. Generally, the more money we make, the more taxes we pay.

Caution   It is extremely important to understand correlation as it relates to data mining not only because of its predictive value, but also because correlated attributes can actually appear to be predictions. For instance, your data-mining model can predict with 100 percent accuracy that whenever the month is December, the season is winter in the Northern Hemisphere. This simple example shows that if the data was less obviously correlated, you might think you had built an especially accurate predictive model. Generally, if you begin to notice that your predictions are 100 percent on target all the time—you've probably discovered a correlation and not a pattern.

Regression

After you find a correlation, it's important to measure the rate of change between one variable and another. *Regression* tries to find the pattern of change between one variable and another in order to make accurate predictions based on the change in the values of a given variable. For example, there could be a direct correlation between the miles driven with a given car and the amount of gas it consumed for every mile on that trip. By understanding the ratio of miles per gallon, it's possible to predict how much gas a car will consume in 30 miles.

Learning from Historical Data

Data mining predicts future results, but it also draws conclusions about past events. When drawing conclusions about past data, the goal of the data-mining process isn't to make predictions but to understand the cause and effect relationships between elements of data.

There are six ways to use data mining to gain knowledge about past events.

Influence Analysis

An *influence analysis* determines how factors and variables impact an important measure such as performance. For instance, a manager of a telephone call center that handles credit card collections might want to know what factors contribute to the success ratio of collections to calls. There are many variables that can affect a call's success, such as:

- Call frequency
- Time spent per call
- Type of call—inbound vs. outbound
- Sex of the person speaking to the customer
- Sex of customer
- Time of day call was made

The manager's goal might be to understand the environment and conditions that affect successful call outcomes, not to make predictions based on new data sets. Based on the mining of this data, she might find that it behooves the call center to encourage employees to spend less time on inbound calls and more time on outbound calls, except in the evenings after 6 P.M. Even though the data might influence the center's policies, the analysis isn't really predictive. It's simply understanding the causal relationships hidden inside the historical data.

Variation Analysis

A *variation analysis* looks for variations in a set of data and attempts to isolate any one factor that might influence a given measurement. Finding variations in data is important when you need to discover what factors cause cube dimensions to differ. For instance, it might be useful to see the differences in call efficiency by location, by time of day, and by manager. A variation analysis might provide the following analysis, "Call centers in large cities have lower call efficiency than call centers in small towns."

Comparison Analysis

Using the preceding example, *comparison analysis* could be used to compare the efficiency of calls made in two call centers in two different locations to help decide which one should be expanded. This comparison is difficult to do with the standard SQL language constructs but is relatively easy with data mining and OLAP because of the built-in ability of these tools to display measures according to dimensional splits.

Cause and Effect Analysis

A *cause and effect analysis* determines the effects of a given event, something that data mining is perfectly equipped to handle. For instance, it's no surprise that a 50 percent increase in calls per hour to a given center severely reduces call efficiency, but a less obvious insight is that fewer fraudulent calls are caught by the overworked operators when calls increase by one-half. A cause and effect analysis would reveal that increased calls also increase losses due to fraud.

Trend Analysis

A *trend analysis* looks for changes in the value of a measure over specific periods of time. The data is measured in terms of direction of movement rather than quantitative expressions. For instance, trends are almost always used to describe the state of the stock market, as in "The market is up" or "The market is down." These statements express the difference between the current valuation and previous valuations of the market.

Deviation Analysis

Deviation analysis identifies data that falls outside the norm of expected value. Fraud detection uses deviation analysis to spot data that seems suspiciously different from the norm. One way credit card companies discover credit card thefts is by tracking charge trends over time so that they can immediately identify unusually high expenditures placed on a given card.

Deviation analysis is also applied to Web page navigation. For most commercial Web pages there is a logical path for the user to follow to purchase products, browse items, track orders, and so on. One indication of hacker activity or Web security holes is whether a user deviates from the logical path. An analysis of user activity notes abnormal user activity such as attempts to access a given page directly or repeated attempts to log on to the site. Of course, the key to identifying unusual data is to have an established baseline of normal activity. What's needed is a mining model that accurately represents a normal set of cases to compare other data against.

Predicting the Future

You can predict the future by allowing the data-mining engine to compare a set of inputs to the existing patterns in the database. The data-mining engine can use predictive modeling to predict the values of blank records in the database based on the patterns discovered from the database and stored in the model. Unlike pattern discovery, which is designed to find patterns and help understand data, predictive modeling uses the patterns to make a best guess on the values for new data sets.

Determining Probabilities

If derived models from an auto dealership database show that a person who buys a two-seat sports car is almost always a single male under 40, you can predict with a good deal of accuracy that the owner of a two-seat sports car is single, male, and under 40 years old. Given that there are always exceptions, your prediction can be expressed as a probability; therefore, we might actually find that the owner of a two-seat sports car is 80 percent likely to be a single male under 40, 5 percent likely to be female, 10 percent likely to be married, and so on.

Real World Looking for a Few Good Customers

Not everyone is concerned with predicting probabilities. Loan and credit card companies do try to use their data to profile customers; however, they also need to process applications quickly. To speed up the application process, many financial institutions use a point system, which comes from a data analysis of their customer base, to approve or reject an application. All application criteria are allocated points, and if the sums of an application's points meet or exceed a predetermined threshold, the application is approved. The point system is used to streamline the decision-making process by eliminating the need to assess the value of a customer based on probabilities of default each time. The point system's design is based heavily on probabilities when it's initially created but is then used to avoid having a loan officer decide each time whether an applicant who has a 65 percent chance of repaying a large, profitable loan is a better risk than an applicant with an 85 percent chance of repaying a small loan. The point system simply translates all the probabilities into a set of rules that return a "Yes" or "No" for the approval status.

You can create a data-mining model that emulates this point system. When you create the model, you analyze the loan history collected over years. The history will include examples of customers who have paid on time, others who were sent late payment notifications or visited by collection agents, and a minority who defaulted and did not pay all or part of the loan back.

In order to best take advantage of this model, input all the data collected from the applicant, including:

- Address
- Age
- Income
- Homeowner or renter
- Outstanding debt
- Educational level
- Marital status
- Number of children
- Sex

After the application is compared to the performance histories of past and current clients, the output is either Approved or Rejected. Unless a credit board wants to evaluate borderline applicants on a case-by-case basis, raw probabilities do little to speed up the approval process. By specifying the exact result that will be acceptable for approval, you can create a basic "fill in the blank" functionality for your model.

Simulations and What-if Scenarios

When models are generated from more inputs than can be checked by a human, it becomes difficult to understand the model's description of the original data set and important to test the model with data that you understand. Testing the model with well-known data has two benefits: you can identify any anomalies in the rules present within the model and correct them, and you can change the values of the model to see how the predictions are affected, which helps you to understand and perhaps improve the model.

Making predictions based on simulated data sets is one of the best ways to validate the model. To discover the factors that affect acceptance rates, a user can apply test loan applications to the model. A user could also take a failing loan application and change one of the inputs such as annual income to see whether the change results in an acceptance. If that doesn't work, the user could change the age or the sex. Tweaking input parameters tells us what kind of loan application will generally be accepted. You can also validate the model's usefulness in the real world by feeding it applications of rejected candidates. Conversely, you can test it with applications of approved candidates—even fictitious ones—to make sure the model doesn't reject applications for extraneous reasons.

Another, more unorthodox validation method is to create a number of "What if?" data-mining models to discover how a fixed set of inputs works against a given algorithm. For instance, you can create and apply an algorithm to a data set to determine causal purchase patterns. The example mentioned earlier in this book found that those folks who purchase beer often also purchase diapers. You can create models using test data sets to see whether the algorithm correctly identifies obvious inventory trends present in a given warehouse. Using this method, the "What if?" scenarios are created with the models, not with the input cases. You can create a set of cases that obviously confirm the validity of the beer and diapers trend to make sure that the inputs correctly generate the desired predictions.

Training Data-Mining Models

Training data is a term commonly used to refer to the process of analyzing known input cases and deriving patterns from them. These discovered patterns are then put into a form that can be used to construct models. This model training is part of a process known as "machine learning," in which algorithms are automatically adapted to improve based on the experience the computer has gained from analyzing historical data, creating patterns, and validating the patterns against new data.

Data training in Microsoft Analysis Services is accomplished either with data-mining wizards in the Analysis Services Manager or by using PivotTable services and the OLE DB for Data Mining specification. In both methods, a basic model structure is built and the cases are inserted into the model in accordance with the algorithm used by the OLE DB for Data Mining provider to define the model. These options will be discussed in further detail in Chapters 8 and 9.

Evaluating the Models and Avoiding Errors

Because data mining uses a set of data to create a representation of the real world, the model is only as good as the training data. As long as the attributes in the cases contain the same level of distribution as in the real world, the model will be useful to predict future events. For this reason, it's crucial to make sure that the initial data accurately represents real-world data.

Overfitting

One of the great benefits of data mining is the ability to discover patterns in data that you would not otherwise notice. This ability brings with it the potential of finding patterns that may seem logical within the confines of the universe the cases reside in, but completely coincidental in relation to the real world. This problem is called *overfitting* the data.

Real World   The Dangers of Overfitting

There are well-publicized cases of data-mining processes that found, as in the claim made by a French bank, that people with red cars had higher loan-default rates than owners of non-red cars. These patterns were actually present in the database, but obviously have no real value for the bank. Scenarios prone to overfitting are those that contain a large set of hypotheses and a data set too small to represent the real world. Under these conditions, data-mining algorithms find meaningless patterns such as the one that discovered Bentley buyers usually have a first name of John.

There are three ways to solve the problem of overfitting: pruning, chi-squared analysis, and cross validation.

Pruning

When you use the decision trees algorithm you can solve overfitting with decision-trees pruning. *Pruning* is a process of evaluating the information contained in an attribute. Pruning involves modifying the generated model after the fact.

Chi-Squared Analysis

The method most commonly used to determine the relevance of a given attribute is the *chi-squared analysis* method. The formula for this form of analysis is much less intimidating than the name of the statistical test suggests:

```
c2 = Sum[(Expected Value - Obtained Value)^2] / Expected Value
```

If you had 25 different automobile models and 250 different buyers (all with the first name of John) in the database, it's fair to assume that all other factors being equal, each automobile model has ten buyers. The expected value for the Bentley should be ten for the expected number of occurrences. The actual value might be 30, which indicates a high variation from the norm. If 30 is the actual value, the formula looks like this:

```
c2 =  ((10 - 30)^2) / 10
c2 = (-20^2) / 10
c2 = (400) / 10
c2 = 40
```

Now that you have the chi-squared value for an individual case, how do you determine whether that computation is completely out of line? First establish a baseline, or norm, for name distributions. The best way to establish such a norm is to gather data containing first names from a completely unrelated source and run the chi-squared formula against it to build a table much like Table 4-3.

Table 4-3. Chi-Squared Results from a Random Source

Name	Expected	Actual	Difference	Difference ^2	C2
Mary	10	12	-2	4	0.4
John	10	8	2	4	0.4
Fred	10	11	-1	1	0.1
Jill	10	7	3	9	0.9
Larry	10	9	1	1	0.1
Henry	10	13	-3	9	0.9
Bill	10	12	-2	4	0.4
Janet	10	8	2	4	0.4
Roger	10	6	4	16	1.6
Kate	10	14	-4	16	1.6
Total					**6.8**

Now take the data from the data set that will be used for training and apply the chi-square formula to it, as shown in Table 4-4.

Table 4-4. Chi-Squared Results for the Training Set

Name	Expected	Actual	Difference	Difference ^2	C2
Mary	10	20	-10	100	10
John	10	30	-20	400	40
Fred	10	8	2	4	0.4
Jill	10	2	8	64	6.4
Larry	10	1	9	81	8.1
Henry	10	1	9	81	8.1
Bill	10	7	3	9	0.9
Janet	10	0	10	100	10
Roger	10	10	0	0	0
Kate	10	21	-11	121	12.1
Total					**96**

The sum of the chi-squared values was 6.8 in the control data set but a whopping 96.0 in the real data set. What does this difference mean? Such a large difference indicates that the data set used for the auto sales has an unusually high degree of deviation from an expected name distribution. This difference is because of many factors. Perhaps the sample used for the cases was extracted in a first name order, which would explain a high frequency of one name over another. In any case, this test indicates that the name attribute only appears to have an effect on Bentley sales because that attribute happens to have a disproportional distribution in the database, which doesn't reflect the distribution in the real world. In fact, comparing the occurrences of the name John shows to what degree the data set is skewed.

Cross Validation

A third approach is to use *cross validation*, a technique that tests subsets of the known data to see how well the model correctly predicts values based on that data. The model can then be tweaked and retried until the predictions generated match real events.

Underfitting

Another common problem that causes skewed predictions is known as *underfitting*, which happens when the data-mining model isn't provided with enough attributes to discover important patterns. Underfitting is caused when attributes that have high predictive importance are removed from the model because they seemed unimportant initially. A large bank once created a loan application model using every attribute related to loan risk except for a few. One of the attributes taken out of consideration was pet ownership. As it turned out, upon much closer examination of the loan applications, the bank found that pet owners, particularly cat owners, seemed to be much safer customers to lend money to than non-cat owners.

Preparing Data Models for Testing

In order to ensure that the mining models will reflect real trends, some data must be prepared to test the validity of the models. To accomplish this, three different sets of data need to be used.

- **Training set**   A training set is used to build the initial data-mining model. You might find that this set has some bias or idiosyncrasies, but it does reflect the sample used for data mining.

- **Test set**   When the training set is corrected, a test set is created. In other words, once you're sure that your set of cases will build an accurate model, they can be kept for the purpose of using them as inputs for predictions against other models to test their accuracy. The process of correcting this set may be an iterative one, until you are satisfied that the test set will build a model that accurately reflects the real data.

- **Evaluation set**   An evaluation set is data taken from the same population as the test set, but it must consist of different records. This set is used to see whether it can cause the data-mining model created with the first two sets to predict the correct outcomes when provided the attributes from the evaluation sample.

Summary

Predictive, as opposed to descriptive, data modeling derives future results from theoretical data sets. Both models analyze data but descriptive data modeling doesn't produce a model that can be used to derive any predictive results, only an analysis of what has been. Depending on your goals, there are two ways to go about the task of mining data. One is to use directed data mining, which uses known attributes that direct the model to come up with predictive outcomes based on the patterns suggested by attributes present in the model. The second method is undirected data mining, which makes use of attributes only to discover patterns and trends, but not to affect the direction of a predictive data-mining effort.

Although statistics form the foundation of data-mining theory, a statistical approach to discovering patterns and analyzing data has little in common with data-mining methods and processes. Because data-mining algorithms often use statistical formulas as part of the model building process, it's useful to understand statistical principles to understand how these algorithms operate.

For a data-mining model to be reliable, it must be tested. The cases used to create the model should be put to a series of statistical tests to determine whether the data used to build the models needs to be tweaked. After the model is built, it's also a good practice to test it against a set of data where the predictive outcome is already known in order to see whether the model really functions properly as a predictive tool.

Part II, "Data Mining Methods," looks more closely at the methods described in these early chapters. After reading this section, you should have a good understanding of the steps that Analysis Services takes to build data-mining models based on the algorithms chosen. In addition, you will know how to create data-mining models based on your own algorithms or based on those from third-party vendors.

Part II
Data-Mining Methods

The objective in data mining is to find comprehensible rules and relations in case sets. These rules can then be used to predict future trends, to profile customers, to assess risk, or simply to describe and explain the contents of a given database. Because of the preparation needed, data mining is not a completely automated process. Data mining won't ever be a canned application that requires you only to remove the shrink-wrap, install, and press GO. The process requires you to take a whole slew of factors into consideration about the data and its intended use and then to apply the best data-mining methods.

Part II covers decision trees, clustering, and third-party algorithms and uses sample databases to show the data-mining process. The chapters in Part II are important because there is no such thing as a superior data-mining method. In the data-mining world, it's generally accepted that no matter which method you choose, there are going to be trade-offs. Experience and the examples shown here will help you choose the best method for the job. In data mining, there is no such thing as a free lunch; no single method works for everyone.

Chapter 5
Microsoft Decision Trees

In this chapter, we'll see how Microsoft Analysis Services is used to implement decision tree models. As we go over the steps in this process, I'll explain the statistical principles behind the algorithm and how the model is used to make predictions.

Decision trees is a very well known algorithm used in one form or another by almost all commercially available data-mining tools. This umbrella term describes a number of specific algorithms, such as Chi-squared Automatic Interaction Detector (CHAID) and C4.5 and the algorithm process they share, which results in models that look like trees. Decision tree algorithms are recommended for predictive tasks that require a classification-oriented model, and as such they are designed for problems best solved by segregating cases into discrete groups. For example, decision trees are often used to predict those customers most likely to respond to direct-mail marketing or those likely to be approved for loans.

One advantage of this method is that this way of describing nodes with rules is intuitive and easily understood by any operator. However, weighing the significance of a found rule can be a very serious problem for the decision tree approach. The problem originates from the fact that as the tree expands down the levels, there are fewer records left at the nodes of those levels of the classification tree that is being built. A decision tree splits data into a larger number of sets that become smaller as they get more specific. The larger the number of different cases to examine, the smaller is each next separate set of training examples, which because of the dwindling numbers, inspires less confidence that correct further classification can be accurately performed. If the tree becomes overbuilt with a large number of small branches, then there's a good chance that the rules inside those nodes won't stand up to any justifiable statistical scrutiny, mostly because each of the nodes stemming from those branches will generally contain such a suspiciously small percentage of the overall cases. This often leads to the problem of overfitting, described in Chapter 4 and discussed later in this chapter as well.

Creating the Model

The first step in any data-mining operation is to create the model. The data-mining model is generated from cases contained in a data source. Any data source that can be connected to through OLE DB can be used to create a model. These sources include relational databases, OLAP cubes, FoxPro tables, text files, or even Microsoft Excel spreadsheets.

In this section, we'll create two decision tree models—one using standard relational tables from Microsoft SQL Server 2000 as a source and another using OLAP cubes. We'll also look at how to use those data sources to store the test cases used to make predictions and how to store the results of those predictions.

Analysis Manager

The starting point to create a data-mining model is with Analysis Manager included in the Analysis Services Installation package on the SQL Server 2000 CD-ROM.

Before anything can begin, you must register the analysis server that you wish to connect to by right-clicking on the Analysis Servers folder and choosing Register Server, as shown in Figure 5-1.

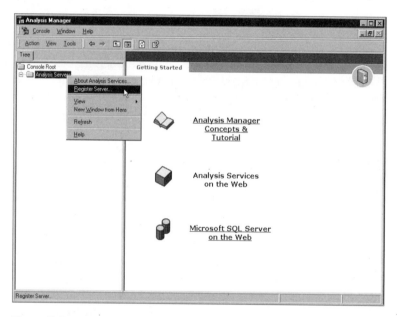

Figure 5-1. *Microsoft Analysis Manager.*

The Register Analysis Server dialog box appears on the screen. The server name requested is the same as the Microsoft Windows server it resides on. Once the server is created, you'll see the FoodMart 2000 sample analysis server database if you chose it as an option during the installation of Analysis Services. (See Figure 5-2.)

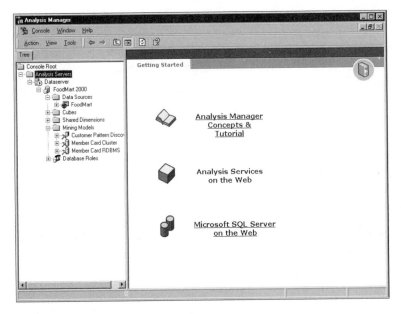

Figure 5-2. *FoodMart 2000 sample database.*

You'll notice that there are several Analysis Manager folders that contain the elements needed to create OLAP cubes and data-mining models. Analysis Server includes the following components:

- **Databases**   Each Analysis Server contains one or more databases; an icon represents each database. There are four folders and an icon beneath each database icon.

- **Data Sources**   The Data Sources folder contains the data sources specified in the database. A data source maintains OLE DB provider information, server connection information, network settings, connection time-out, and access permissions. A database can contain multiple data sources in its Data Sources folder.

- **Cubes**   The Cubes folder contains the cubes in the database. An icon represents each cube. Three varieties of cubes are depicted in the Analysis Manager Tree pane: Regular, Linked, and Virtual.

  In a Cubes folder, an icon represents each cube variety. Beneath each Cube icon is a Partitions folder that contains an icon for each partition in the cube and a Cube Roles icon that represents all the cube roles for the cube.

  To see the dimensions, measures, and other components in the Regular, Linked, or Virtual cube, right-click the appropriate icon and then choose Edit.

- **Partitions** A cube's Partitions folder contains an icon for each partition in the cube. There are two types of partitions depicted in the Analysis Manager Tree pane: Local and Remote.

  In a Partitions folder, an icon represents each Local partition and each Remote partition. To access the settings for a partition, right-click the appropriate icon and then click Edit.

- **Cube Roles** Beneath a cube, a single Cube Roles icon represents all the cube's roles. To access the roles, right-click the icon and then choose Manage Roles.

- **Shared Dimensions** The Shared Dimensions folder contains an icon for each shared dimension in the database. These dimensions can be included in any cube in the database. Four varieties of shared dimensions are depicted in the Analysis Manager Tree pane: Regular, Virtual, Parent-Child, and Data-Mining.

  In a Shared Dimensions folder, an icon represents each of these four dimensions. To see the levels, members, and other components in a dimension, right-click the appropriate icon and then choose Edit.

- **Mining Models** The Mining Models folder contains an icon for each mining model in the database. You'll notice that two icons represent the two types of data-mining models. The small cube icon indicates that the data source for this data-mining model is an OLAP cube, while the cylinder icon indicates that the data source for this data-mining model uses a relational database.

  To view or modify the structure of the relational or OLAP mining models, right-click the appropriate icon and then choose Edit. To view the contents of a mining model, right-click its icon and then choose Browse.

  Beneath a mining model, a single Mining Model Roles icon represents all the roles for the mining model. To access the roles, right-click the icon and then choose Manage Roles.

- **Database Roles** The Database Roles icon represents all the database roles in the database. These roles can be assigned to any cube or any data-mining model in the database. To access the roles, right-click the icon and then choose Manage Roles.

Mushrooms Data-Mining Model

To illustrate the step-by-step process of using decision trees, we'll create a mining model using cases from a SQL Server database about mushrooms. The model will indicate whether a mushroom is edible.

Note This data comes from one of the many "data-mining ready" databases in the University of California, Irvine, Machine Learning Repository. UC of Irvine's Department of Information and Computer Science graciously offers their data at no cost on the Web. For more information, visit their Web site at *http://www.ics.uci.edu/~mlearn/MLRepository.html*.

This Mushrooms database contains over 8000 cases of mushrooms and field descriptions. Table 5-1 lists the field descriptions.

Table 5-1. Fields in the Mushrooms Database

Field Name	Source
ID	Primary Key ID generated by SQL Server
edibility	Target and input field
cap_shape	Input
cap_surface	Input
cap_color	Input
bruises	Input
odor	Input
gill_attachment	Input
gill_spacing	Input
gill_size	Input
gill_color	Input
stalk_shape	Input
stalk_root	Input
stalk_surface_above_ring	Input
stalk_surface_below_ring	Input
stalk_color_above_ring	Input
stalk_color_below_ring	Input
veil_type	Input
veil_color	Input
ring_number	Input
ring_type	Input
spore_print_color	Input
population	Input
habitat	Target and Input

Creating the Database

Creating the database is simple. You only need to right-click on the server and choose New Database. The Database dialog box, shown in Figure 5-3, prompts you for the name of the database, which in this example is Mushrooms. Optionally, you can enter a description of the database.

Note   To create a data-mining model using DTS, see Chapter 8, "Using Microsoft Data Transformation Serivces (DTS)."

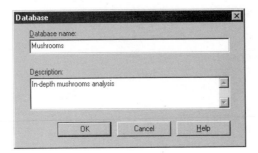

Figure 5-3. *Choosing a database.*

As you can see in Figure 5-4, a database with a folder for each type of component needed to manage your analysis tasks has been created. Some of these folders are optional. For example, if you are mining a relational database, you won't use the Cubes folder.

Figure 5-4. *Data analysis database folder structure.*

To create a new mining model, right-click on the Mining Models folder and then choose New Mining Model to open the Mining Model Wizard.

Mining Model Wizard

Microsoft products use wizards to accomplish certain tasks in a limited and predictable number of steps. The Mining Model Wizard walks you through the following steps to create a model:

1. Select source.
2. Select the case table or tables for the data-mining model.
3. Select data-mining technique (algorithm).
4. Edit joins if multiple tables were chosen as the source in the previous step.
5. Select Case Key column.
6. Select Input and Prediction columns.
7. Finish.

Select source

You have the choice of creating data-mining models, which contain cases located either in relational tables or in OLAP cubes. For this exercise, choose the relational data type to use cases from the SQL Server 2000 database.

Select case tables

As Figure 5-5 illustrates, the connections used with a relational model are created and displayed in the Select Case Tables screen. Also provided here is the option of creating a new connection by clicking on the New Data Source button. You can also specify the number of tables you would like your cases contained in. In this case, we only need one table.

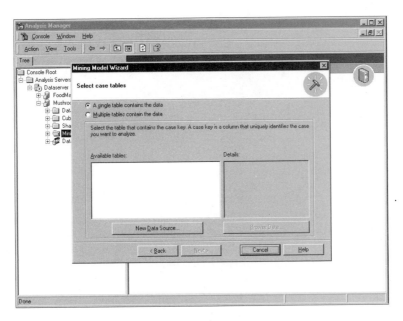

Figure 5-5. *Select Case Tables screen.*

To get a data source, click the New Data Source button to bring up the Data Link Properties dialog box, shown in Figure 5-6. On the Provider tab is a list of all the OLE DB drivers installed on the server where the Analysis Services server is installed. In this case, we pick the Microsoft OLE DB provider for SQL Server to get access to the Mushrooms table on the SQL Server 2000 server, which contains all the cases we need.

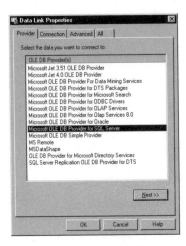

Figure 5-6. *Data Link Properties dialog box.*

To connect to a specific server and database, enter the name of the SQL Server and, optionally, the name of the database on the Connection tab in the Data Link Properties dialog box. (See Figure 5-7.) If you don't provide the name of a specific database, you'll be connected to the designated default database for your server. Supply the logon credentials you'll use to connect. Because of its simplicity, you'll be tempted to use the Integrated Security option to allow SQL Server to make use of the credentials supplied by Microsoft Windows NT and Windows 2000 based on your Windows NT or Windows 2000 user name and password without needing to use a SQL Server user name and password. Be forewarned that using it opens the door for hard-to-find errors to enter because the security context will be associated to the logon credentials of the user currently logged on to the server where Analysis Services resides. For added safety, you can click on the Test Connection button to check the connection parameters you supplied.

Note The database structure information is cached on the Analysis Manager client to save on bandwidth requirements. As a result, whenever you change or add fields to the tables that you use to build the models, you must remember to right-click on the connection and then choose Refresh Connection. This causes Analysis Manager to query the SQL Server to reload the database schema information so that you can see the changes in the list of fields you pick from when creating the data-mining model.

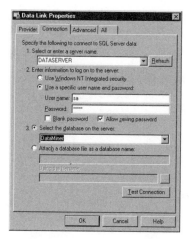

Figure 5-7. *Selecting a database.*

As soon as you close the Data Links Properties dialog box, the Select Case Tables screen has the table information. As shown in Figure 5-8, you select your tables from an Available Tables pane in the Select Case Tables screen. The Details pane gives you a list of the field names available in the table.

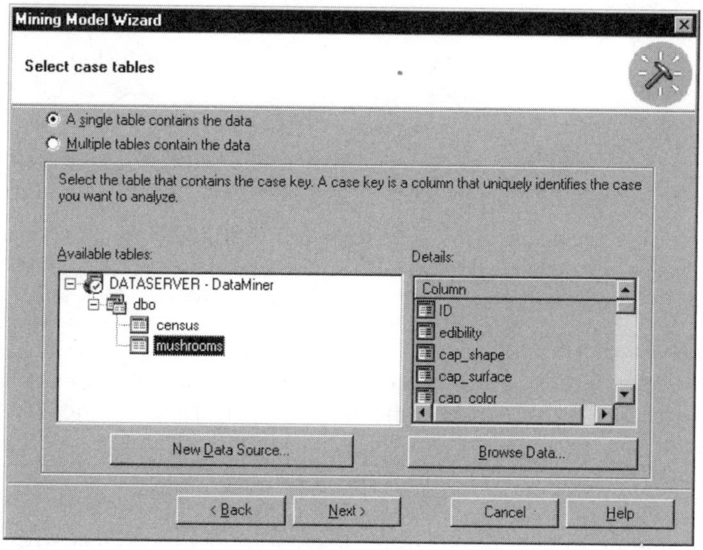

Figure 5-8. *Selecting a case table.*

Before committing the table to the mining model, you can click the Browse Data button to preview the first 1000 rows of data, as displayed in Figure 5-9, to make sure that the contents correspond to your expectations.

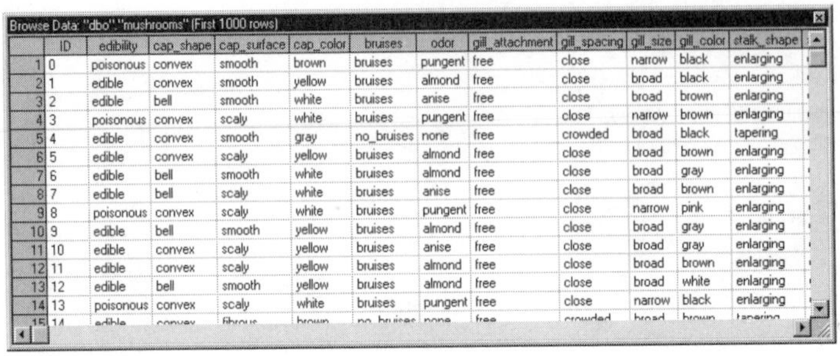
Browse Data: "dbo"."mushrooms" (First 1000 rows)

	ID	edibility	cap_shape	cap_surface	cap_color	bruises	odor	gill_attachment	gill_spacing	gill_size	gill_color	stalk_shape
1	0	poisonous	convex	smooth	brown	bruises	pungent	free	close	narrow	black	enlarging
2	1	edible	convex	smooth	yellow	bruises	almond	free	close	broad	black	enlarging
3	2	edible	bell	smooth	white	bruises	anise	free	close	broad	brown	enlarging
4	3	poisonous	convex	scaly	white	bruises	pungent	free	close	narrow	brown	enlarging
5	4	edible	convex	smooth	gray	no_bruises	none	free	crowded	broad	black	tapering
6	5	edible	convex	scaly	yellow	bruises	almond	free	close	broad	brown	enlarging
7	6	edible	bell	smooth	white	bruises	almond	free	close	broad	gray	enlarging
8	7	edible	bell	scaly	white	bruises	anise	free	close	broad	brown	enlarging
9	8	poisonous	convex	scaly	white	bruises	pungent	free	close	narrow	pink	enlarging
10	9	edible	bell	smooth	yellow	bruises	almond	free	close	broad	gray	enlarging
11	10	edible	convex	scaly	yellow	bruises	anise	free	close	broad	gray	enlarging
12	11	edible	convex	scaly	yellow	bruises	almond	free	close	broad	brown	enlarging
13	12	edible	bell	smooth	yellow	bruises	almond	free	close	broad	white	enlarging
14	13	poisonous	convex	scaly	white	bruises	pungent	free	close	narrow	black	enlarging
15	14	edible	convex	fibrous	brown	no_bruises	none	free	crowded	broad	brown	tapering

Figure 5-9. *Preview of a Mushrooms table.*

Select a data-mining technique

The Mining Model Wizard offers two data-mining algorithms, or "techniques" as they're called in the wizard, for you to select from. For our purposes, we'll select Microsoft Decision Trees in the Select Data Mining Techniques screen.

Create and edit joins

If you selected multiple cases tables in the previous steps, then the Create And Edit Joins screen will appear next. This screen lets you graphically join tables by dragging the Key columns from the parent tables to the children. If you chose only a single table, this step is skipped.

Select the Key column

The next step is to select ID as the Case Key column. The choice of ID has a very important effect on the output of the decision tree because this Key is what the engine uses to uniquely identify a case. Choosing a Key is mandatory, so it's very important to create a Key in the SQL Server database if one does not exist already, especially since a Case Key is not an option for use as either a target or an input value.

Select Input and Prediction columns

In the Select Input And Prediction Column screen, pick at least one Input column for the mining model from the available columns in the list on the left pane. *Input columns* represent actual data that is used to train the mining model. If you selected Microsoft Decision Trees in the Select Case Tables screen, also select at least one Predictable column. *Predictable columns* are fields identified as being used to provide the output predicted from the mining model. If you want to use a model to predict whether a given mushroom is edible, the edible column would be the Predictable column because that would presumably be the one thing we don't know about a given mushroom but that the model can tell us based on all the other attributes of that mushroom. For convenience, these columns are also used as Input columns, and later in this chapter we'll see how we can make the column a Predictable column only. For the purposes of this chapter, we'll select both Edibility and Habitat as the Predictable columns.

Shown in Figure 5-10 are three panes to work with:

- **Available columns**   Select columns from the tree view. Use the buttons provided to move columns to either the Predictable Columns pane or the Input Columns pane or to remove columns from the selection. You cannot use the ID column you selected in the Select The Key Column dialog box as an Input column because it's a key field. Select all the columns besides Habitat and Edibility as Input columns.

- **Predictable columns**   View the selected Predictable columns. This pane is displayed only if you selected Microsoft Decision Trees in the Select Case Tables dialog box. For this exercise, select Edibility and Habitat as Predictable columns.

- **Input columns**   View the selected Input columns.

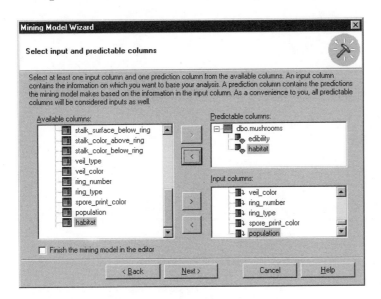

Figure 5-10. *Select Input and Predictable columns.*

If you select the Finish This Mining Model In The Editor check box, you'll bypass selection of Input and Predictable columns and finish working with the mining model in the Relational Mining Model Editor. If you select this option, you cannot process the mining model in the last step of the wizard—instead, you'll need to explicitly select the option in the Editor. Leave the check box clear for this exercise, and click Next.

Finish

Now that the mining-model parameters have been defined, you have to enter the name of the data-mining model—Mushroom Analysis RDBMS for this exercise. If you select the Save, But Don't Process Now option, the data-mining model will be saved but will still need processing to be trained. Choosing the Save And Process Now option (the option you should select for this exercise) saves and trains the model at the same time.

As the model is trained, the various training steps are detailed as they occur. The starting time of the process is recorded, and a progress bar in the bottom of the screen reflects the stage of processing during each step, as shown in Figure 5-11.

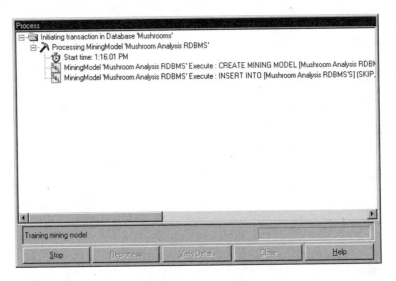

Figure 5-11. *Processing the model.*

Once the processing is complete and you click the Close button, the Relational Mining Model Editor appears, as shown in Figure 5-12. Here you can make modifications to the mining model and reprocess the model as needed.

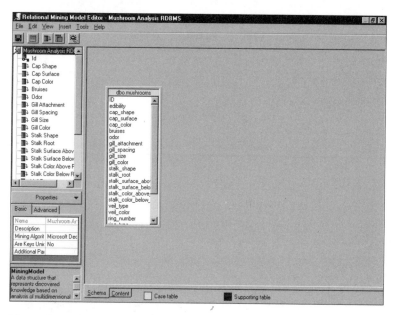

Figure 5-12. *Relational Mining Model Editor.*

Relational Mining Model Editor

As convenient as wizards are in applications, they do limit your flexibility in each step because to maintain simplicity, the wizard must use default values and implicit decisions to accomplish a task. By using the Relational Mining Model Editor, you can dispense with the wizard, at least in part, and make some design decisions that you would not otherwise have the chance to make. To illustrate, create another data-mining model and make the same choices you made before until you reach the Select Input And Predictable Columns screen shown again in Figure 5-13. For this model, select to continue to build the mining model without the Mining Model Wizard.

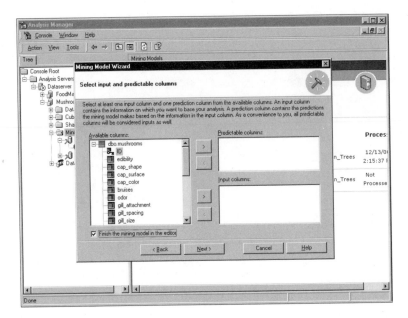

Figure 5-13. *Select Input and Predictable columns.*

As you can see, you did have to use part of the wizard to get to this point, but thus far you have only designated the source type, the source table, the case key, and the mining technique. By selecting the Finish The Mining Model In The Editor check box and then clicking Next, the Finish The Mining Model screen appears prompting you for a name. After you enter a name (Mushrooms DBMS for this example) and click Finish, the main editing canvas of the Relational Mining Model Editor appears.

The editor contains many components that are worth examining. On the upper left of the editing canvas, you'll find the Editor toolbar, shown in Figure 5-14.

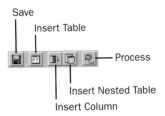

Figure 5-14. *The Editor toolbar.*

Table 5-2 describes the Editor toolbar buttons.

Table 5-2. Editor Toolbar

Button	Description
Save	Saves the relational data-mining model.
Insert Table	Adds a new table to the schema of the relational data-mining model.
Insert Column	Adds a new column to the structure of the relational data-mining model.
Insert Nested Table	Adds a new nested table to the structure of the relational data-mining model.
Process Mining Model	Displays the Process A Mining Model dialog box, where you can select the processing method for the relational data-mining model.

As you can see in Figure 5-15, the Mushrooms DBMS mining model is rather sparsely populated, containing only the case key. You must now add the columns to the model one by one.

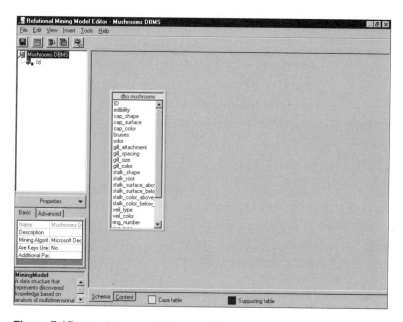

Figure 5-15. *Mushrooms mining model.*

To add a Predictable column, right-click on the column you wish to add and then choose Insert As Column. For this exercise, add the Edibility column as a Predictable column.

Before continuing, let's take a quick look at portions of the Relational Mining Model Editor window. The lower-left pane is the Properties pane, which displays the properties of either the mining model or the individual columns, depending on which one is highlighted in the Structure pane above.

Table 5-3 describes the features of the Properties pane.

Table 5-3. Properties Pane

Feature	Description
Properties button	Shows or hides the Properties pane
Basic tab	Shows the most commonly-used properties, such as Name and Description, for the mining model and mining-model columns
Advanced tab	Displays Advanced properties, such as Distribution and Content Type, used to further define the mining-model columns
Description	Displays the name and a brief explanation of the property selected in the Properties pane

The Basic tab is used to display and, optionally, edit the most commonly viewed properties for data-mining models and data-mining columns. Table 5-4 describes the properties displayed in the Basic tab in more detail and indicates the data-mining object (data-mining model or data-mining column) to which the property applies.

Table 5-4. Basic Tab Properties

Property	Description	Applicable objects
Name	The name of the selected data-mining model or column. This property is read-only for data-mining models.	Both
Description	The description of the selected data-mining model or column.	Both
Mining Algorithm	The data-mining algorithm provider for the selected data-mining model. By default, the available models are limited to Decision Trees and Clustering, but would also display any others for which there would be a provider installed.	Data-mining model
Are Keys Unique	Whether the Key columns in the data-mining model uniquely identify records in the source case table.	Data-mining model
Is Case Key	Whether the data-mining column is used as a Key column in the data-mining model. This property must be set to False before you can delete the column.	Data-mining column
IsNestedKey	Whether the data-mining column is used as a Key column for a nested table in the data-mining model. This property must be set to False before you can delete the column.	Data-mining nested table column
Source Column	The name of the source column in the case or supporting table.	Data-mining column

Table 5-4. *(continued)*

Property	Description	Applicable objects
Data Type	The data type of the data-mining column. This setting must be compatible with the data-mining algorithm provider that is being used. The data types and algorithms that Microsoft SQL Server 2000 Analysis Services supports are documented in the OLE DB for Data Mining specification. For more information about the OLE DB for Data Mining specification, see the Microsoft OLE DB Web page at *http://www.microsoft.com/data/oledb/default.htm*. For data types supported by data-mining algorithm providers, see the data-mining algorithm provider documentation.	Data-mining column
Usage	Whether the data-mining column is used as an Input column, a Predictable column, or both. This property is read-only for Key columns.	Data-mining column
Additional Parameters	A comma-delimited list of provider-specific mining parameter names and values. For mining parameters supported by data-mining algorithm providers, see the data-mining algorithm provider documentation.	Data-mining model

The Advanced tab displays Advanced properties for data-mining models and data-mining columns, such as Relation column information and distribution. Table 5-5 describes these Advanced properties in more detail.

Table 5-5. Advanced Tab Properties

Property	Description	Applicable Objects
Related To	For Relation columns, when multiple tables are being used for case data. This is the name of the column to which the selected data-mining column is related. It is read-only for Key columns. When this property is set for a column, the Usage property is changed to match the value of the related column.	Data-mining column
Distribution	The distribution flag, such as NORMAL or UNIFORM, of the data-mining column. It is read-only for Key columns.	Data-mining column
Content Type	The Content type, such as DISCRETE or ORDERED, for the data-mining column. It is read-only for Key columns.	Data-mining column
Data Options	The model flag, such as MODEL_EXISTENCE_ONLY or NOT NULL, of the data-mining column. It is read-only for Key columns.	Data-mining column

Notice that the column you just added is by default an Input column. To make it a Predictable column, click on the Usage field of the Basic tab and then select Input And Predictable or Predictable, a choice that insures that this value is not used to train the model. For now, select Input And Predictable. After you make this change, you'll see a diamond-shaped icon appear next to the column in the Structure pane. (Yes, we're mining for diamonds of information.)

> **Note** Selecting Predictable is possible only through the Relational Data Mining Model Editor. The wizard offers only Input And Predictable as a Predictable Column option.

On the Advanced tab for the column, you can select the type of data this column represents. Select DISCRETE for descriptive data such as names or types, and select ORDERED for sequential values such as age or years. Add all the other database columns, and make them Input columns. Now you're ready to begin processing, but before you do so be sure to save the new model changes.

To process the model, click the Process Mining Model button (it looks like a set of gears) or choose Process Mining Model from the Tools menu. Whenever you process a new model or a model with a changed structure, the model must be rebuilt and new cases inserted. If only new cases are added to a model and no changes are made to the model's structure, you have the option to refresh the data. In this way, the structure does not have to be re-created. The model is purged of all the existing cases, reloaded with the cases again, and retrained with the new data.

When processing is finished, the status screen appears, as shown in Figure 5-16.

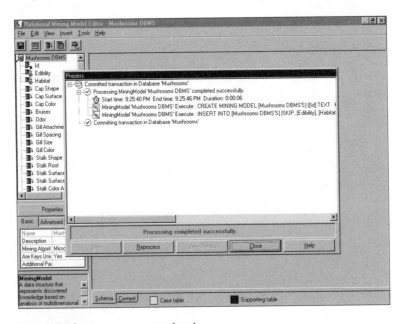

Figure 5-16. *Processing completed.*

Visualizing the Model

One of the most valuable features of a decision tree is the simplicity of the logic behind its construction. The Data Mining Model Editor contains two tabs at the bottom of the screen, the Schema tab, which we have been using thus far to alter the structure of the model, and the Content tab, which shows how the data has been classified and organized within the tree. The Content tab is shown in Figure 5-17.

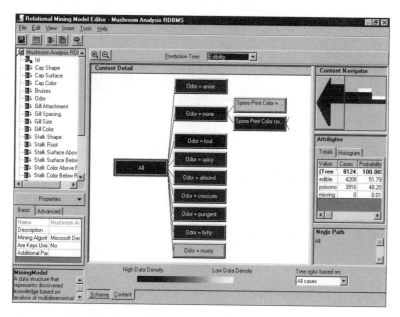

Figure 5-17. *The Content tab.*

The Content tab is a quick and convenient way to look at the model, but the Structure and Properties panes on the sides take up a good portion of the screen real estate. Another way to arrive at a screen that permits easy visualization is to go to the Analysis Manager tree, right-click on the data-mining model that you wish to visualize, and choose Browse to bring up a similar view with more dedicated space for the decision tree. (See Figure 5-18.)

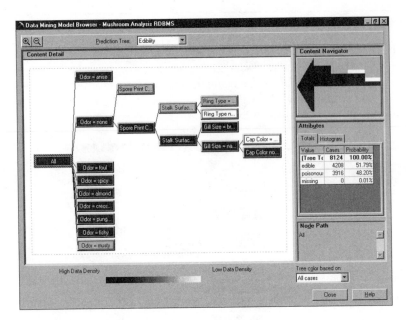

Figure 5-18. *View of the Edibility tree.*

Two magnifying glass icons in the upper-left corner of this window allow you to zoom in on the diagram to get a better view of the tree outline. In the upper middle of the window, there's a drop-down list box that contains a list of all the tree structures in the model. A data-mining model can contain multiple trees—one for each Predictive column. In this model, you made Habitat and Edibility Predictive columns. As a result, you can view Habitat as the current tree by choosing it from the list. The tree will no longer predict whether a mushroom is edible, but it will predict a mushroom's habitat.

As you can see, the diagram of the model looks like a fallen tree with the root to the left and the branches to the right. This hierarchical structure is created by the IF->THEN rules used to classify information. Describing nodes with intuitive rules is one of the advantages of the decision tree technique.

An added bonus of the visualization pane is that the colors give you a feel for the density of the cases in the nodes. The darker the color, the higher percentage of cases corresponding to that value in the attribute is in that node. In the lower-right portion of the window, there is a drop-down list box that contains all the possible values for the Predictive column of that tree. By default, it's set to All Cases so that the color of the nodes will reflect the overall quantity of cases in a node. But if you want to highlight those nodes that contain higher percentages of edible mushrooms, you would only need to select that attribute from that list box and look for the darkest nodes. A view of the edible mushrooms in the tree is shown in Figure 5-19.

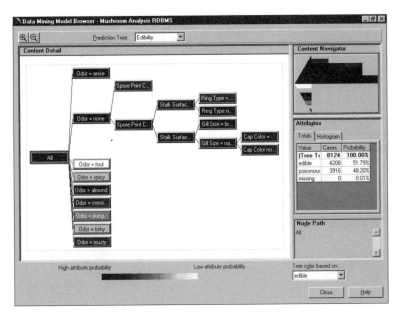

Figure 5-19. *Edible mushrooms.*

Figure 5-20 shows the same tree, but the colors highlight the poisonous mushrooms.

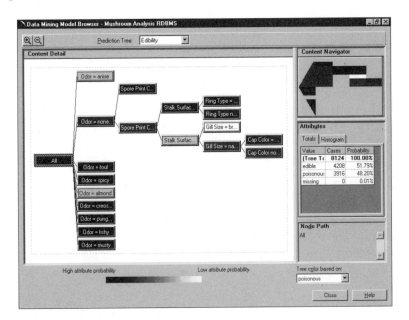

Figure 5-20. *Poisonous mushrooms.*

The nodes and branches of the tree respond to click events from the user, revealing more information. If you click on any of the nodes in the tree, the Attributes pane in the middle-right portion of the window will reflect the data of that node. In addition, the Node Path pane on the lower-right corner will display the description of the rules that govern the inclusion of the cases within the node. On the upper-right panel, the Content Navigator provides a very general overview of the shape of the tree and also allows you to select a visible portion of the tree by clicking on that part of the miniature tree in that panel. For example, if I wanted to see the leaf nodes of a tree, I could either click on the individual branches of the tree in the Visualization pane, or I could click on that portion of the tree in the Content Navigator that I wish to see and the Visualization pane will reflect my choice.

Prediction Columns

Decision trees allow only one variable to be the target of a prediction at one time. That's why when you analyze the data-mining models generated by decision trees, there can be more than one target variable, but for every target variable a new model is created. By choosing different (if any) target variables from the drop-down menu on the top of the visualization pane of the Analysis Manager, you can view each of the different models.

As you can see from the tree, the data has been separated into groups that can be used to make predictions because each node contains data that follows the rules that describe the data based on the attributes Analysis Manager has gathered. You can use this model to determine whether a particular mushroom is edible. To see how the tree works, let's imagine that you found a mushroom in the forest with the characteristics listed in Table 5-6 and you'd like to know whether you can use it for a new cream of mushroom soup recipe you saw on TV.

Table 5-6. Mushroom Characteristics

Field Name	Value
cap_shape	Convex
cap_surface	Smooth
cap_color	Gray
bruises	No Bruises
odor	None
gill_attachment	Free
gill_spacing	Crowded
gill_size	Narrow
gill_color	Black
stalk_shape	Tapering
stalk_root	Equal
stalk_surface_above_ring	Smooth
stalk_surface_below_ring	Scaly

Table 5-6. *(continued)*

Field Name	Value
stalk_color_above_ring	White
stalk_color_below_ring	White
veil_type	Partial
veil_color	White
ring_number	One
ring_type	Evanescent
spore_print_color	Brown
population	Abundant
habitat	Grasses

A decision tree separates data into sets of rules that can be used to describe data or make predictions. In this model, you see that the algorithm created multiple branches based on the odor alone. When the tree color is based on whether a mushroom is poisonous (as in Figure 5-20), the tree seems to indicate that if a mushroom has an odor it's probably poisonous. But if there is no odor, as is the case with this mushroom, then further analysis is needed to determine whether it is poisonous. When you click on the Odor = None node, as shown in Figure 5-21, the Attributes pane tells you that of the more than 8000 total cases, 3528 fall into the odorless category and of those, 120 are poisonous.

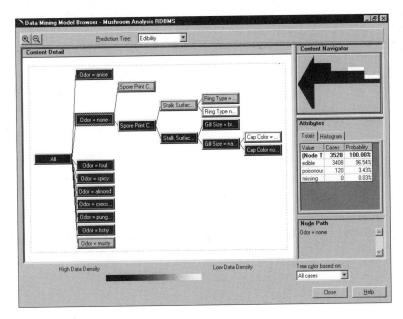

Figure 5-21. *Mushroom odor analysis.*

The Spore Print Color nodes describe the print color of the spores. If you click on the Spore Print Color = Green node, the Attributes pane reveals that if the spores are green, they are poisonous. Your mushroom has brown spores, however, and when you click on the Spore Print Color not = Green Node, as shown in Figure 5-22, the Attributes pane indicates that of 3456 cases of brown-spored odorless mushrooms, only 48 are poisonous.

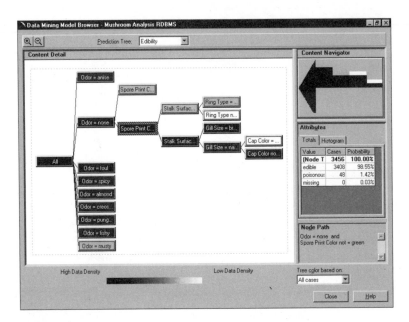

Figure 5-22. *Mushroom color analysis.*

The stalk surface below the ring of your mushroom is scaly, so you're not out of the woods just yet. As the information in the Attributes pane shown in Figure 5-23 indicates, there are only 56 cases of mushrooms like yours and of those 40 are poisonous.

Perhaps it's time to put some gloves on before handling your mushroom any further, but for the definitive conclusion that your mushroom is poisonous, you need to investigate a bit more. The final verdict is determined by the mushroom ring type. Your mushroom is evanescent and according to the information in the Attributes panel shown in Figure 5-24, your mushroom is definitely poisonous!

One of the first tasks undertaken by the decision tree for the mushroom database is to find the combinations of characteristic variables that best set the poisonous mushrooms apart from the edible ones. This process is called *segmentation*.

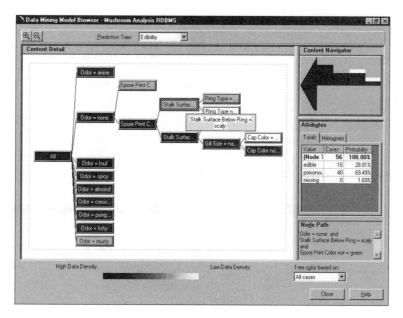

Figure 5-23. *Mushroom stalk surface analysis.*

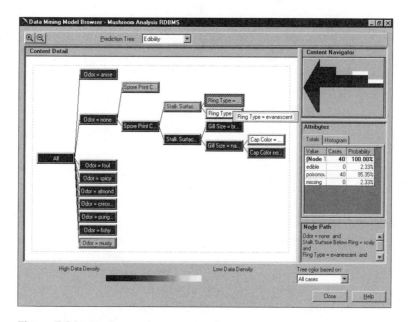

Figure 5-24. *Mushroom ring type analysis.*

This example shows how a predictive task uses the model to make a prediction. Of course, we will be able to make these kinds of predictions automatically and in much greater numbers using predictive queries, which will be covered in more detail in Chapter 12, "Data-Mining Queries."

Dependency Network Browser

Dependency Network Browser, shown in Figure 5-25, is a tool used to view the dependencies and relationships among objects in a data-mining model. To display it from the Analysis Manager Tree pane, right-click a data-mining model and then choose Browse Dependency Network.

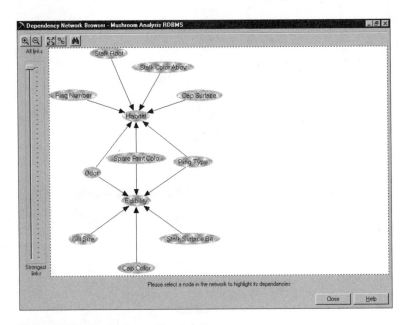

Figure 5-25. *Dependency Network Browser.*

In Dependency Network Browser, a data-mining model is expressed as a network of attributes. Within the model, you can identify data dependencies and predictability among the related attributes. Dependency is indicated by arrows. The direction of predictability is indicated by arrowheads and by the color-coding of the nodes.

Dependency Network Browser Helps Understand Models

Dependency Network Browser presents data-mining content for decision tree mining models from a different point of view than that of Data Mining Model Browser. Data Mining Model Browser allows you to view relationship and distribution information from the Predictive attribute that governs the structure of the tree. Dependency Network Browser allows you to view the entire data-mining model from all the attributes using relationship information alone.

Dependency Network Browser displays all the attributes in the data-mining model as nodes. Arrows between nodes predict links. For example, an arrow from the Odor node to the Edibility node indicates that the Odor attribute predicts the Edibility attribute.

The nodes are color-coded to represent the selected node and the predictability direction of related nodes; click on a node to view its dependency relationships. To improve the view of the relationships, you can drag the nodes or use the Improve Layout button, which automatically distributes and resizes nodes.

The mushroom tree presented by Dependency Network Browser clearly shows which input attributes contribute most to deriving the predictive value. As you move the slider to the left of the window down, Dependency Network Browser removes the weakest dependencies one at a time. Figure 5-26 reveals that the strongest predictor of edibility is odor because the last arrow on the screen is the odor attribute.

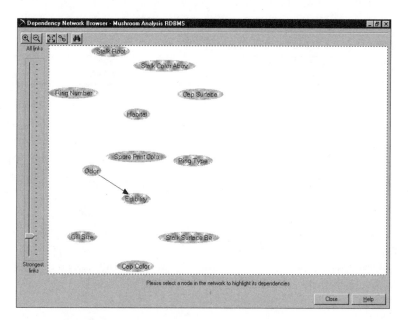

Figure 5-26. *The Links pointer.*

After an attribute is isolated, Data Mining Model Browser allows you to view the details and distribution information for the relationships of the selected attribute.

Dealing with Numerical Data

To function, decision trees algorithms must continuously place data in categorical groups or *bins*. Quantitative values such as salaries or miles are *continuous data*. Although some algorithms are able to make use of the individual values suggested by continuous data, Microsoft decision trees will actually bin the data for you to create a semblance of discrete variables.

The following example shows the advantages of binning data to obtain predictions from your data. Let's say you created a data-mining model using decision trees with cases of car information. To get the best possible price prediction for a used car, you use all the attributes of the car (such as the mileage, year, make, model, body type, and color) as the input types and an optimal selling price as the target variable. Although this seems like a straight-forward problem, you'll be surprised to find that the algorithm creates discrete groups of attributes based on the price or target variable. Although the prices for each make and model range from $500 to $80,000, the predictions usually are a set of four or five values that will look something like $1,030, $8,540, $15,900, and $27,520. Each node will have a division for each value, making it very difficult to decide on a ticket price. One way to make these predictions more accurate is to bin the price attributes before submitting them to the data-mining algorithm. To bin the attributes, create a new field in the case table that contains a price range, much like the one shown in Table 5-7.

Table 5.7 Case Table for Car Fields

...	Year	Make	Price	Price Range
...	...	...	$1,525	$1,000 - $1,999
...	...	...	$8,600	$8,000 - $8,999
...	...	...	$8,250	$8,000 - $8,999
...	...	...	$11,500	$11,000 - $11,999

Although this method won't provide one sale price, it will come up with a price accurate within $999.00. If you're willing to sacrifice accuracy, this method is great, but a car dealership really can't afford to be off by that much money.

Depending on how accurate the prediction must be, binning might or might not be the best data-mining method. The example of used-car pricing showed that binning does not work well when there is a large range of numbers and the predictions must be precise. On the other hand, if you're pricing collectable postage stamps (especially for very rare stamps valued in the hundreds of thousands of dollars), the price range might be small enough to create smaller and more precise bins.

Consider these options before binning:

- Create small bins.
- Avoid creating too many bins. When there are too many bins, the engine, unable to deal with the complexity, doesn't split and classify the data correctly. How many is too many? Well, there's no right answer since much depends on how you intend on using the data-mining model and the nature of the source data used to populate the model. You may want to experiment with this until you find the number of bins that works best for you.
- Create multiple decision trees instead of bins. For example, you could create one decision tree for each car price category. In other words, divide the car population into those that sell for less than $5000, those that sell for less than $10,000, and so on. Next create a separate data-mining model for each population. Because the price range is smaller, the bins created for each model are more precise

Inside the Decision Tree Algorithm

As its name suggests, a decision tree algorithm is a tree-shaped model. There's no limit to the levels, and the more inputs and variables assigned to the algorithm, the bigger—wider and deeper—the tree grows.

CART, CHAID, and C4.5

When a decision tree algorithm is applied to a data-mining problem, the result—or decision—looks like a tree. Although Microsoft uses its own algorithm to generate a decision tree, this algorithm is inspired by other tried-and-proven methods. Let's take a minute to discuss these popular decision tree algorithms used in the world of data mining.

Classification and Regression Trees (CART)

CART is by far the most widely used algorithm because of its efficient classification system that uses various automatic tree-pruning techniques, including cross-validation using a test set.

CART attributes that have strong predictive values are picked once it's determined that they introduce order to the data set. They are used if they split the existing pool of data into two separate nodes, and further branches or leaves are subsequently created.

One of the most useful features of CART is its ability to handle missing data when building the tree. Either it will know not to use a certain record to determine whether a split should be made, or it will use surrogate data. For example, if income information is missing from a record, the effective tax rate can be used in its place because it is a correlative value, even if it's not an exact predictor of income.

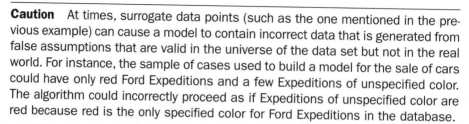

Caution   At times, surrogate data points (such as the one mentioned in the previous example) can cause a model to contain incorrect data that is generated from false assumptions that are valid in the universe of the data set but not in the real world. For instance, the sample of cases used to build a model for the sale of cars could have only red Ford Expeditions and a few Expeditions of unspecified color. The algorithm could incorrectly proceed as if Expeditions of unspecified color are red because red is the only specified color for Ford Expeditions in the database.

One unique feature of the CART algorithm is the binary split restriction that causes the tree nodes to sprout only two branches at a time, which produces a tree that is deeper than algorithm trees that can sprout multiple branches from a single node. A deep tree is considerably more economical with data and as a result is able to detect more structures before too little data is left for analysis. Remember that every node in a hierarchy divides its records among the nodes below it. So a node with 1000 records will create 2 nodes with a certain number of records in each. If a node has a very low record count, it ceases to split, while the other node continues. If there are multiple nodes emanating from a higher level node, each one of them needs to have a split of smaller numbers of records than a purely binary split would have and thus cause the existence of more leaf nodes. Other decision tree algorithms fragment the data rapidly with multiple splits, making it difficult to detect rules that might need a larger number of attributes in a group to make more accurate splits.

Chi-Squared Automatic Interaction Detector (CHAID)

The CHAID algorithm uses Chi-Squared analysis tests to validate the tree. Because Chi-Squared analysis (see Chapter 4) relies on group tables or contingency grids to determine what the distribution of a given value is, the attributes of the data sets must be forced into groups that can be tested. For example, income ranges would have to be placed into discrete attributes such as $10,000 to $19,999 and $20,000 to $29,999.

C4.5

This algorithm is an enhancement to another basic decision tree algorithm known as Iterative Dichotomizer version 3 (ID3), which was developed well over 20 years ago. At the time, it used a logical decision tree to come up with chess moves that would beat a human opponent. Because ID3 was not standardized at the time, many variations and enhancements were made to ID3 before C4.5 was introduced. C4.5 also shares many of its features with CART, and now there is very little difference between them.

To better understand the structure and function of a tree, let's look at a generic diagram of a decision tree structure. To do so, we'll look at a database of credit card holders from the sample FoodMart 2000 database, as shown in Figure 5-27.

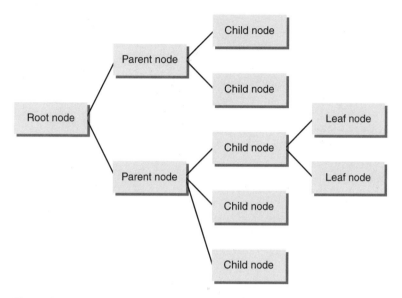

Figure 5-27. *Generic decision tree structure.*

Each element in the tree is actually a node. Every tree starts with one node at the very top that is known as the *root node*. (Although the root node is on the left of Figure 5-27, it is the logical top of the tree.) Many more nodes, all connected by branches, make up the remainder of the tree. Just like a real tree, all subsequent nodes and branches stem from the root node. The *leaf nodes*, located on the end of the branches, are the last nodes on the tree, and they're the ones that contain the values that are ultimately used to make predictions.

What does the presence of pure leaf nodes say about your data?

A tree that has only pure leaf nodes is known as a *pure tree*. Each *pure leaf node* contains 100 percent of a given type of case. This structure defeats the purpose of using a decision tree and most data-analysis professionals actually considered pure trees suspect because in most cases, some very severe overfitting needs to be done to create a tree of this kind. Some data-mining models are built with training sets that contain many different attributes that could be applied. However, unbeknownst to the model builder, only one of these attributes actually determines the probability of reaching a target objective. Consider the fictitious database of surf conditions for various locations shown in Table 5.8.

This data is derived by observing surfers and finding all the factors that contribute to a surfer's decision to frequent a particular beach. Although this is not an exhaustive listing of table elements, it gives an idea of the amount and kind of data that is used and the factor combinations that are possible, such as wave size and quality and water and air temperatures. The last column, the verdict, is the database's recommendation to the surfer. If you processed this data through a Microsoft decision tree algorithm, you'd find that the model contains only one, four-way split that results in four pure nodes. Why? The reason is simple, but not immediately obvious from the data. Surfers (in this fictitious world) only take wave size into consideration when deciding where to surf. The algorithm detects this and thus creates one node for each wave type that contains 100 percent of that kind of wave. The algorithm doesn't recognize other possible splits in the rest of the data that was used to build the model. Although the nodes are 100 percent pure, they still describe something important about the data, namely that only wave size matters to surfers.

Table 5.8. Surf Conditions

Waves	Temperature	Coolness	Break Quality	Verdict
BIG	WARM	VERY	GOOD	RUN
SMALL	WARM	VERY	GOOD	STAY HOME
MEDIUM	WARM	VERY	GOOD	WALK
HUGE	WARM	VERY	GOOD	RUN
BIG	COLD	VERY	GOOD	RUN
SMALL	COLD	VERY	GOOD	STAY HOME
MEDIUM	COLD	VERY	GOOD	WALK
HUGE	COLD	VERY	GOOD	RUN
BIG	FREEZING	VERY	GOOD	RUN
SMALL	FREEZING	VERY	GOOD	STAY HOME
MEDIUM	FREEZING	VERY	GOOD	WALK
HUGE	FREEZING	VERY	GOOD	RUN
BIG	WARM	NOT	GOOD	RUN
SMALL	WARM	NOT	GOOD	STAY HOME
MEDIUM	WARM	NOT	GOOD	WALK
HUGE	WARM	NOT	GOOD	RUN
BIG	COLD	NOT	GOOD	RUN
SMALL	COLD	NOT	GOOD	STAY HOME
MEDIUM	COLD	NOT	GOOD	WALK
HUGE	COLD	NOT	GOOD	RUN
BIG	FREEZING	NOT	GOOD	RUN
SMALL	FREEZING	NOT	GOOD	STAY HOME
BIG	COLD	VERY	BAD	RUN
SMALL	COLD	VERY	BAD	STAY HOME

Table 5.8. *(continued)*

Waves	Temperature	Coolness	Break Quality	Verdict
MEDIUM	COLD	VERY	BAD	WALK
HUGE	COLD	VERY	BAD	RUN
BIG	FREEZING	VERY	BAD	RUN
SMALL	FREEZING	VERY	BAD	STAY HOME
MEDIUM	FREEZING	VERY	BAD	WALK
HUGE	FREEZING	VERY	BAD	RUN
BIG	WARM	NOT	BAD	RUN
SMALL	WARM	NOT	BAD	STAY HOME
MEDIUM	WARM	NOT	BAD	WALK
HUGE	WARM	NOT	BAD	RUN
BIG	COLD	NOT	BAD	RUN
SMALL	COLD	NOT	BAD	STAY HOME
MEDIUM	COLD	NOT	BAD	WALK
HUGE	COLD	NOT	BAD	RUN
BIG	FREEZING	NOT	BAD	RUN
SMALL	FREEZING	NOT	BAD	STAY HOME
MEDIUM	FREEZING	NOT	BAD	WALK
HUGE	FREEZING	NOT	BAD	RUN
BIG	WARM	NEUTRAL	BAD	RUN
SMALL	WARM	NEUTRAL	BAD	STAY HOME
MEDIUM	WARM	NEUTRAL	BAD	WALK
HUGE	WARM	NEUTRAL	BAD	RUN
BIG	COLD	NEUTRAL	BAD	RUN
SMALL	COLD	NEUTRAL	BAD	STAY HOME
MEDIUM	COLD	NEUTRAL	BAD	WALK
HUGE	COLD	NEUTRAL	BAD	RUN
BIG	FREEZING	NEUTRAL	BAD	RUN
SMALL	FREEZING	NEUTRAL	BAD	STAY HOME
MEDIUM	FREEZING	NEUTRAL	BAD	WALK
HUGE	FREEZING	NEUTRAL	BAD	RUN
BIG	WARM	VERY	FAIR	RUN
SMALL	WARM	VERY	FAIR	STAY HOME
MEDIUM	WARM	VERY	FAIR	WALK
HUGE	WARM	VERY	FAIR	RUN

Note The Member Card RDBMS data-mining model used in the following sections is one of the sample data-mining models on the SQL Server 2000 CD-ROM. To install the samples on your computer, select them when you run the SQL Server 2000 Setup program.

As you can see in Figure 5-28, each node of the Member Card RDBMS data-mining model contains information about the characteristics that define each group. You can view the number of instances attached to that node and learn about the distribution of dependent variable values that are being predicted.

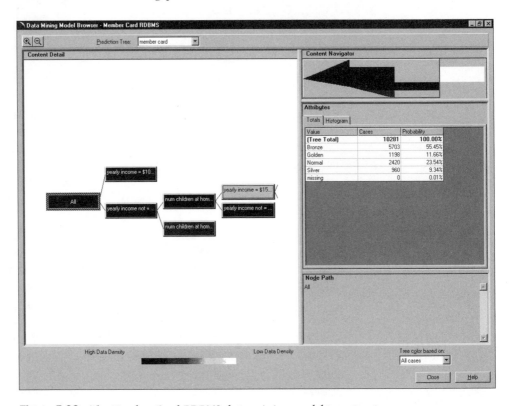

Figure 5-28. *The Member Card RDBMS data-mining model tree structure.*

To view the node contents, click on the node you want to examine. The Attributes panel shows the contents for that node. This panel also contains the quantity of cases for each target variable as well as the percentage of the population it represents.

The Node Path panel describes the grouping criteria of the selected node. The Content Navigator panel provides a rough visual description of the tree shape. The darker the node, the more samples it contains.

The attributes in the root node are all the instances in the training set. In this model, the root node contains five separate instances totaling 10,281 cases, of which 55.45 percent have Bronze cards, 11.66 percent have Gold cards, 23.54 percent have Normal cards, and 9.34 percent have Silver cards.

The first binary split stems from either the root or a parent node. The data is split into two new child nodes. In this model, the data from card holders with incomes between $10,000 to $30,000 go in one child node and the rest of the data goes in the other child node. Presumably, those who fall in the $10,000 to $30,000 group are low-income earners and as you can see from the contents of the node shown in Figure 5-29, two conclusions can already be drawn about this income group:

- These card holders represent a minority of the card holding population (2222 members out of 10,281).
- The vast majority of these card holders have Normal cards.

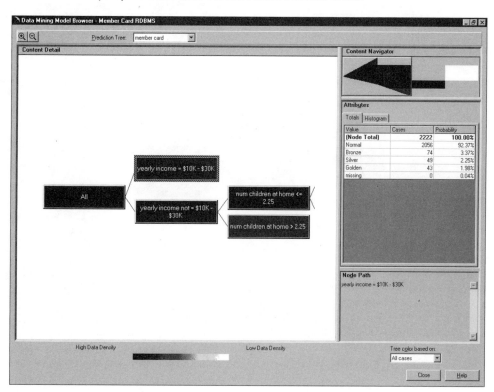

Figure 5-29. *The $10,000 to $30,000 node.*

Because this split has over 92 percent of cases with the same target value, or card type, another split would not be warranted. In data-mining terminology, a node with such a high concentration is considered pure, even though in this case it's really more accurate to say it's "pure enough" because only about eight percent of the cases are other card member types.

The second node in the first split (see Figure 5-30) contains all of those members who do not fall within the $10,000 to $30,000 income bracket, presumably those belonging to a higher income bracket. As you can see, this node contains 8059 of the 10,281 members and a better distribution of card types than the low-income node. What we find here is that the majority of these members have Bronze cards (69.82 percent), and the lowest incidence of card type is the Normal card (4.53 percent).

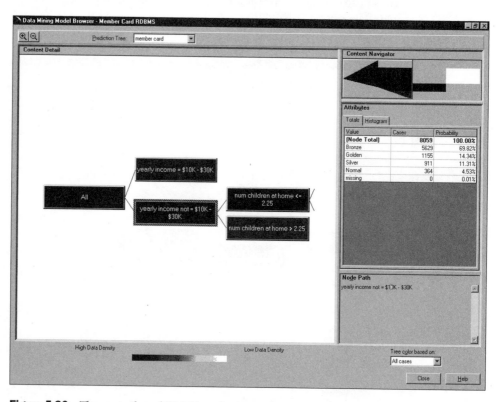

Figure 5-30. *The more than $30,000 node.*

From this model, we learn that the higher number of Gold and Silver cards (14.34 and 11.31 percent, respectively) triggers the algorithm to create yet another split that categorizes all the card members according to how many children they have living at home. Those with one or two children at home seem to be the majority judging by the dark color of the node and the contents displayed in Figure 5-31 that shows 7007 individual cases.

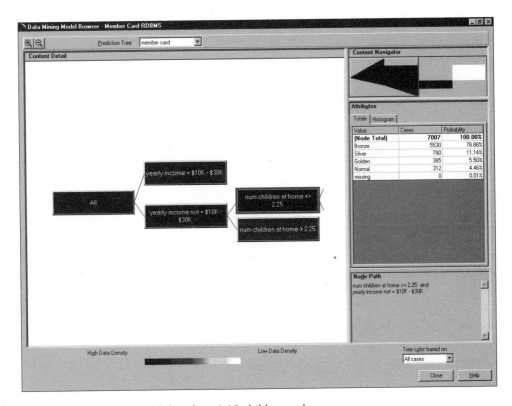

Figure 5-31. *The node with less than 2.25 children at home.*

Note   The algorithm in this example split at 2.25 children. We can only hope that we don't find any .25 individuals in the real world! Numerical attributes will sometimes end up with decimal values even though the original data set contained only whole integers. This is because to determine at which number they can be split, the numerical values are analyzed in order. This sample data set contains cases with more than two children and cases with less than two children. The algorithm determined that 2.25 would be the demarcation between the two nodes. You can avoid this problem by having the numerical values be character types, but this might cause the attribute to be treated as though each value were a separate, discrete entity instead of one having a continuous value.

By examining the contents of the node shown in Figure 5-31, you can see that the majority of card holders with less than 2.25 children living at home (over 77 percent) have Bronze cards.

The node shown in Figure 5-32 shows the members with more than two children living at home. The numbers show that fewer of these folks become card members to begin with. Interestingly, of these members, almost 73 percent have Gold cards and more than

12 percent have Silver cards. As was the case with the $10,000 to $30,000 income bracket node, the case population is too low and concentrated to justify any more splits.

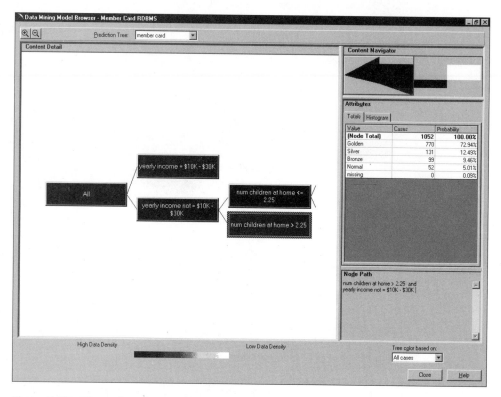

Figure 5-32. *The node with more than 2 children at home.*

Traveling across the nodes brings us to some interesting conclusions:

- If you want to promote Bronze cards, target high-income members with one or two children.

- If you want to promote Gold cards, target high-income members with more than two children.

- Don't bother targeting low-income nonmembers unless you want to subscribe more Normal card members.

The fact is, there is a high enough number of cases in the one or two children node, as compared to the total case set, for the node to benefit from further splits. As you can see in Figure 5-33, another split is created for those who make more than $150,000 per year and those who make less than $150,000 per year.

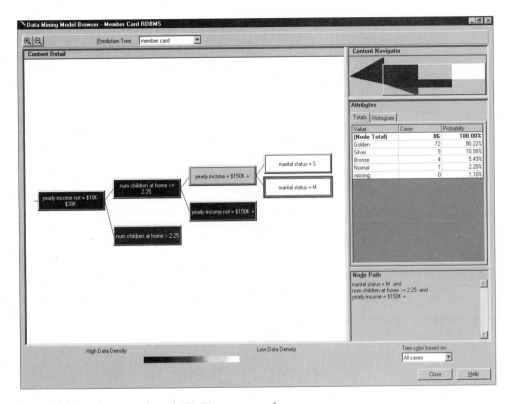

Figure 5-33. *The more than $150,00 income node.*

How Splits Are Determined

Decision trees use an induction algorithm to decide the order in which the splits occur. The inductive algorithm draws conclusions (known as *rules*) based on repeated instances of an event rather than the logical correlation between events. For example, a purely logical algorithm would be able to determine that if John and D.J. are brothers, and D.J. and Bill are brothers, then John and Bill must also be brothers.

Inductive reasoning, on the other hand, will determine that if Box A is a wooden box and is empty, and Box B is also a wooden box and is empty, and Box C is a wooden box and is empty, and Box D is a wooden box and is empty, and Box F is a metal box and is full, and Box G is a metal box and is full, then a wooden Box H, which has never been examined, is probably empty. (This example illustrates why a higher number of cases ensures better accuracy of the data-mining model.)

In the credit card model, the over $150,000 income split was decided based on the algorithm's determination that the income attribute causes much of the data to belong predominately to one of two groups—those who make more than $150,000 per year and those who don't. To find the best split, the algorithm runs through a series of complex calculations on each attribute to find the one that will cause two groups to be created with a predominance of a single class or attribute value. This is essentially an exercise in calculating diversity.

Calculating Diversity

When it comes to deciding which attribute to use to split a node, diversity is the key factor. To calculate the diversity of an attribute, say in the $10,00 to $30,000 income bracket, the algorithm counts all the cases that would fit into that group and all the cases that won't. Then a calculation is made to determine the diversity level of the attribute. But what is diversity exactly? Let's say for instance that you happened to be living in a town with all the members of the "Member RDBMS" sample and only those members. Every person you meet on the street or in the store would fall into one of the above-mentioned categories. The odds of meeting a person who falls in the $10,000 to $30,000 income bracket category as opposed to the odds of meeting someone in a higher income bracket category is a measure of *diversity*. If there is low diversity in one income level attribute, you will meet people in one category far more often the other. If there is high diversity, you will meet an equal number of people from both income groups. In this case, for the algorithm to decide which attribute to use to split, it seeks the least amount of diversity possible in each group. As we can see from the previous examples, there are 2222 of the 10,281 members in the low-income category and 8059 in the other, so when you go outside, you should have 2222 chances out of 10,281 to find a low-income earner, or a 21.6 percent chance. Conversely, you have a 78.3 percent chance of finding someone in the higher income bracket category. To get a diversity index, the algorithm needs to determine the odds of first running into a low-wage earner and then encountering a high-wage earner. The best way to do that is to get the odds of running into the same kind of wage earner twice in a row for each type and add them together. Whatever remains after subtracting that figure from one is the odds of running into two different types, one after the other:

```
1 - ( (21.6% * 21.6%) + (78.3% * 78.3%) ) = 34%
```

The lower the resulting index, the higher the diversity index and the higher chance that the category will get picked for a split. To come up with the lowest index, this formula is applied to all the attributes. The worst result is to wind up with a diversity index of 50 percent.

Upon examining the leaf nodes, we don't find any hard-and-fast rules about the members of the node. For instance, the one or two children and yearly income between $30,000 and $150,000 node indicates that nearly 81 percent of the members have Bronze cards and of the population that fits that classification, about 20 percent use other cards. Presumably, the algorithm could have easily split the rest of the population even further according to all the available attributes, such as by gender and car ownership, until the pure leaf nodes contained 100% of one type of card or another. At some point, the nodes would have so few members that their predictive value would be suspect. The algorithm has built-in checks and balances to make sure that such a thing doesn't happen.

How Predictions Are Derived

Once the tree is built, it can be used for one of its most important purposes—predicting the missing values for new cases. There are two ways to approach making predictions. You can pick a case and follow its pathways, which are determined by its attributes, to see what leaf node it winds up in, or you can use each leaf node to derive a new rule.

Navigating the Tree

Once a tree is filled out, you can use it to predict new cases by starting at the root node of the tree and traversing the route down the branches, which are based on the attributes of the new case, until it gets to the leaf node. The path that the new case follows is based on the very values that caused the split in the first place and not on the independent variables in the new instance.

Let's say that you were to examine a row in the training set for a person with the following characteristics:

Name	Adam Barn
Income	$167,000
Marital Status	Married
Children	1

Because Adam's income does not fall into the $10,000 to $30,000 node, his data will be located on a bottom branch. Since Adam has one child at home, follow the tree upwards to the One Or Two Children At Home node. Now we know that Adam makes more than the $150,000 income required to go up to the Yearly Income Is Above $150,000 node. Adam is married, so we get to classify him in the Marital Status = M node. Now we've reached one of the leaf nodes, and the predicted value is the predominate value in that node, which happens to be Golden, referring to the Gold card. If you took all the values in the set that were used to build the data-mining model, you'd find that this particular tree is 100 percent accurate.

The uncanny accuracy of training sets

Why is it that a case from a training set always seems to come up accurate 100 percent of the time? Let us suppose that Microsoft develops a new kind of certification test that allows the test taker to grade himself. He would take the exam and then give himself the maximum score each time he took the test. The only problem, of course, is that he has no real way of knowing which questions were incorrect without an answer key. In the same way, acquiring data for predictions from the same source as the data used to train the model will cause the predictions to always be 100 percent accurate.

However, if the test taker met with another person who just took the test and allowed this person to grade the exam, the test taker would discover errors by comparing the answers, and the grading accuracy, though not perfect, would still be more accurate. In the same way, for a model to be effective the test cases presented to it must come from a source other than the one used to build the model. Obviously, if you could use more than one test taker to grade the exam, the accuracy of the results would increase, as would the effectiveness of the model if you used a larger sample of data to build it with.

Problem Trees

If by chance you happen to generate a pure tree, then the predictions based on the cases used to build the model will always show 100 percent accurate results. If Adam Barn's case was used as part of the training set, it's 100 percent certain that any predictions using Adam's case as a test set will be perfectly accurate. That's because the attributes used to build the tree will always match the cases. However, once you start making predictions based on cases that are independent of the training set, the 100 percent pure tree will be downright lousy at making predictions not only because the rules supported by the tree are simply too strict to reflect the real world but also because often times, to reach such high levels of purity in a tree, the model has to resort to techniques that cause overfitting. Both of these problems might cause a case to fall into a category that it matches only by chance. For instance, if Bill, a holder of a Normal card, happened to be self-employed, and others in his category were not, you can envision an eager algorithm generating another split that might further divide the 86 cases in that category into 6 self-employed cases and 80 salaried cases. Of those six, another split might be created based on the card holder's educational level. If Adam and Mary, another Normal card holder, were the only Ph.D.'s in the group, they might find themselves in pure leaf nodes because all the other card types for that node would be zero in quantity. However, their reasons for holding a Normal card may be completely unrelated to their educational level or employment status. Maybe Adam is a Normal card member because he has a Gold card from another company, and maybe Mary, a data-mining consultant, is too busy traveling all over the world to upgrade her card; therefore, their membership in the same group is completely coincidental.

Let's suppose for a moment that Lifetime Credit Company wants to review all of its credit card applications and propose the more expensive Gold card to those applicants determined most likely to accept it. Imagine that a new application is presented to the model for D.J. Cornfield, who has the following characteristics:

Name	D.J. Cornfield
Income	$280,000
Marital Status	Married
Children	1
Education	Ph.D.
Employment Status	Self-employed

If you follow D.J.'s attributes along the decision tree, at first he seems like an ideal candidate for the Gold card, until you get to splits concerning his employment status. He's a Microsoft SQL Server consultant, and his Ph.D. is from Harvard University. Now anyone who knows D.J. knows that he's a big spender who will invariably spend a few extra dollars to get the extra service or the extra trimmings on whatever he's buying. If given the choice between the Gold card and the Normal card, you can be sure that he'll go for the Gold. However, the model knows best and will immediately decide that D.J. is actually a bad candidate for the Gold card because apparently he's an incorrigible Normal card member and therefore there is no point in wasting money on that penny-pincher.

As you can see, Lifetime Credit Company would be better off if the algorithm tempered its enthusiasm for splits. Microsoft decision trees usually does a pretty good job of not overgrowing tree branches. That said, you might need to examine the tree to make sure that the nodes contain enough cases to make sense of the rule that determined their membership. If you find that the tree is overgrown, you may need to eliminate some of the splits, a process commonly know as *pruning the tree*. Pruning involves tampering with the underlying structures, a technique we will explore in more detail in Chapter 10, "Understanding Data-Mining Structures."

The other side of the coin is the node that doesn't appear to have a predominate value. In other words, all the possibilities present in a given node have approximately the same chance of occurring. How a prediction for a test case that arrives at such a node is treated depends on the way the prediction is implemented. The best method is usually to allow the operator to decide what to do in such a case. In reality, there are a few options an application may want to take in such a case:

- Remove the node, and use the one above it.
- Allow for a failed, or unknown, prediction.
- Accept the predominate value, even if it's not much more present than the other values.
- Use a default value.

By removing the ambivalent node, you offer the prediction task the possibility of using a node that might have a more informative distribution of target values from which to base a decision. The disadvantage of that tactic is that your prediction will be a little less meaningful. In other words, your prediction will be less precise because as you work your way back up the tree toward the root, you'll have a population that is much larger, is based on fewer attributes to describe them, and as a result is more generalized.

If your application allows for the identification predictions based on perfectly even odds of reaching a target, you could chalk up the prediction as failed. This depends largely on the constructs of the application depending on this prediction. Clearly, you should be prepared for the fact that certain attributes will simply have little or no effect on the outcome of an event. For instance, you could easily try to find out whether car purchases are affected by astrological and numerological charts using a decision tree algorithm only to find that the stars don't seem to have much of an effect on car sales. This should be obvious by the fact that car sales of all models are represented by a relatively even distribution in all the nodes. Rather than considering a failed prediction to be failure, you can take the nonevent as a sign that the attributes used to arrive at a target might not accurately reflect the outcome.

Assigning default values or taking a value as the true outcome because it's represented a few percentage points more than another can be very dangerous in circumstances where the training set does not contain the exhaustive list of all the cases. Consider that even large samples of data will have some built-in imbalances because of the difficulty in obtaining a truly random sampling of data from a larger source. It's perfectly acceptable in the larger scheme of things to accept a few percentage points of difference in the weighting of some attributes in the sample as compared to the totality of the data set, but this difference cannot accurately be used as a predictor. Default values, although dangerous if misused, are actually preferable because they offer at least a certain measure of control by the designer of the data-mining model. Clearly the default values chosen would have to be incorporated into the overall strategy of the data-mining effort in such a way as to continue to provide useful predictions without having to report failure.

Navigation vs. Rules

Although navigating a tree to produce predicted values offers the best way to follow the logic of the data-mining model, it can actually become extremely cumbersome, especially when the tree becomes large in size and deep in branch complexity. As was pointed out earlier, each node in the data-mining model, when visualized in Analysis Manager, shows the description of the characteristics that define the membership in that node.

This description reads very much like a rule, which shows that it's possible to derive a set of rules for a tree by establishing one rule for each leaf node. To create the rule, follow the path between the root and that leaf node. The rules for the leaf nodes in Figure 5-33, read left to right, are as follows:

```
if marital status is married and
    the yearly income is greater than $150,000 and
    the number of children at home is zero, one or two
then the probability of a Gold card is high and
    the probability of other cards is low
```

If you're just looking to establish a prediction for one type of card, such as the Gold card, then reduce the rules to just two outcomes, one for the Gold card and one for the other cards, through the judicious use of the OR connector and the AND joiner. This way of expressing the path of the tree makes it easy to describe how a decision is arrived at. In other words, if someone were to come to you and ask who uses the Gold card, you can simply reply "Married people who make more than $150,000 a year and have zero, one, or two children." In spite of having to go through five nodes to get it, the answer is very clear and succinct.

When comparing rules to trees, we can make the following general statements:

- There are generally as many rules using the AND joiner as there are nodes in the path needed to get from the root node to a leaf node.
- OR can be used to combine some rules, which then reduces the total number of rules to one rule per dependent variable.

Even when not used for prediction, the rules provide interesting descriptive information about the data. There are often additional interesting and potentially useful observations about the data that can be made after a tree has been induced. In the case of the Member Card RDBMS mining model, the following observations can be made:

- Gender and education have no effect on card types.
- People who earn between $10,000 and $30,000 per year almost always have Normal cards.
- Income is the most significant factor in determining card type.

By comparing these conclusions to the tree and the data set used to build the tree, the following further observations can be made about the process:

- The observations above are based on a decision tree algorithm that tried to prioritize its splits by choosing the most significant split first. A different first split might make all the difference in subsequent nodes.
- These observations were made from a sampling of a population of credit card holders. The generalizations made about the sample might not apply to the whole population, particularly if the extraction criterion of the sample itself introduces bias.
- Data mining frequently analyzes information about groups of people. This type of analysis raises important ethical, legal, moral, and political issues when rules regarding gender, race, and national origin are applied to the larger population.

When to Use Decision Trees

I recommend using decision trees under the following circumstances:

- When you want to reliably apply the segmentation scheme to a set of data that reflects a group of potential customers
- When you want to identify possible interactive relationships between variables in a way that would lead you to understand how changing one variable can affect another
- When you want to provide a visual representation of the relationship between variables in the form of a tree, which is a relatively easy way to understand the nature of the data residing in your databases
- When you want to simplify the mix of attributes and categories to stay with the essential ones needed to make predictions.
- When you want to explore data to identify important variables in a data set that can eventually be used as a target.

Summary

Microsoft decision trees is one of the methods, or algorithms, used to build a data-mining model. This method, although one of the most popular, is used for specific types of predictions involving the classification of cases into specific groups.

The decision tree model is used primarily for predictive purposes, but it can also help explain how the underlying data attributes are distributed. In other words, by examining a decision tree, it's easy to draw general conclusions about the population of your data.

The statistical techniques employed to build the decision trees include:

- CART
- CHAID
- C4.5

Splits are determined by applying sophisticated statistical analysis about the data attributes that make up the cases. The general objective is to build trees that are as unbalanced as possible, in terms of the distribution of those attributes. In other words, the algorithm seeks to put as many of one type of attribute as possible in a given node. When possible, the algorithm will try to have all pure nodes, which means that the node contains only cases with 100 percent of a given type of variable.

While building trees, it's a good idea to identify problems with trees that can hamper accurate predictions. These can be caused by overfitting or underfitting data because of a lack of predominate values.

Decision trees also create rules. Every node can be expressed as a set of rules that provides a description of the function of that particular node in the tree as well as the nodes that led up to it.

Another commonly used algorithm to create models is Microsoft Clustering. This algorithm is designed to create a model that cannot be used to make predictions but is very effective in finding records that have attributes in common with each other. In the next chapter, we'll learn how to create a clustered data-mining model and what underlying mechanisms come into play when the algorithm trains the model.

Chapter 6
Creating Decision Trees with OLAP

OLAP is a well-structured format designed primarily to optimize the storage of aggregated data. With OLAP, you can create persistent aggregations along hierarchical dimensions and quickly access values summed according to time dimensions, product dimensions, and geographical locations—much like the GROUP BY statement in SQL. The dimensions offer a means by which to express relationships among data fields in a way that's not easily done with relational data. For example, to store in flat relational tables the hierarchical relationships that exist between employees and their managers in a corporation's human resources database requires relatively complex logic.

OLAP's dimensions are hierarchical by design. It's easy to tell Analysis Manager that there's an employee dimension with 5000 employees at the bottom level, 500 at the middle manager level, 100 at the upper manager level, 20 at the vice president level, and one CEO at the pyramid pinnacle. Of course, this hierarchy can be used to organize just about any grouping of people, species, or product.

Although these levels are really designed to facilitate the aggregation of data by level, it just so happens that this organization is also a convenient way to provide cases for data mining. In a relational data-mining model, you can't store that data-mining model anywhere other than in the Microsoft Analysis Services structures. However, when using data organized with OLAP, you can store a model as a dimension of a cube, as a cube itself, or even as a virtual cube.

Creating the Model

We'll begin by creating our model with the Mining Model Wizard. For a detailed discussion of how to get to and use this wizard, please refer to Chapter 5, "Microsoft Decision Trees," on creating data-mining models using relational data.

Note The example in this section uses the FoodMart 2000 database that ships with Microsoft SQL Server 2000 and the decision tree algorithm to create the data-mining model. The clustering algorithm goes through the exact process to create a model with a few exceptions. I'll point out those exceptions as we go along. The clustered model created through OLAP is essentially the same as the model created with the relational source, which is why you may want to refer back to Chapter 5 from time to time.

Follow these steps to create the model using the Mining Model Wizard:

1. Select source type.
2. Select the source cube for your mining model.
3. Select the data-mining technique.
4. Select the dimension and level the mining model will analyze.
5. Select training data.
6. Create a dimension, a virtual cube, or both. This is an optional step.
7. Finish.

Note You can't use either dimensions that have their Visible property set to False or Virtual dimensions to create data-mining models. Also, you can't use virtual cubes and cubes that contain calculated cells and custom members to create data-mining models.

Select Source Type

The Introduction screen requires no input, but the Select Source Type dialog box, shown in Figure 6-1, requires that you specify the data source, which in this case is OLAP.

Selecting OLAP causes the subsequent screens to be specific to cubes and dimensions as opposed to tables and fields, as was the case with relational data.

Select Source Cube and Data-Mining Technique

In the Select Source Cube dialog box, shown in Figure 6-2, you select the cube that contains the cases that you'll be using to train the model.

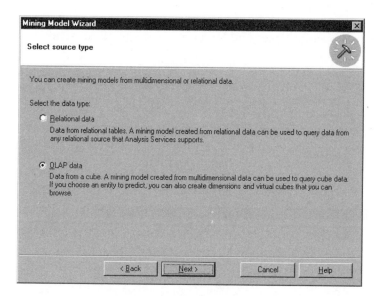

Figure 6-1. *Select source type.*

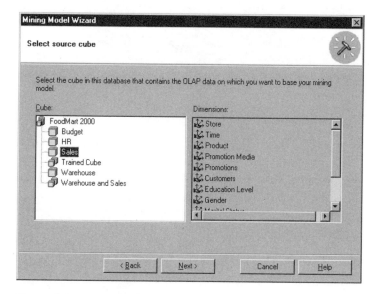

Figure 6-2. *Select source cube.*

Next you select the data-mining technique, as shown in Figure 6-3. You can choose between Microsoft Decision Trees and Microsoft Clustering. If there are any third-party algorithms, these will appear as well.

> **Note** Because you can only create data-mining models from real cubes, as opposed to virtual cubes, you cannot select the virtual cubes even though they might be displayed in the Cube pane. A virtual cube does not contain any data; instead, it serves as a logical representation of either a single cube or a join of two or more cubes. The virtual cube is similar to SQL VIEW in that regard. You also are not allowed to choose cubes that contain virtual members in the form of calculated fields.

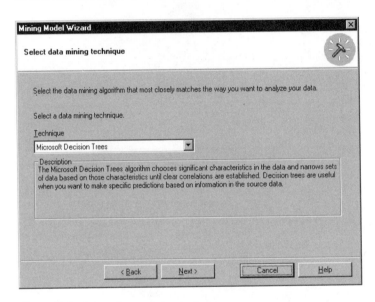

Figure 6-3. *Select data-mining technique.*

Select Case

In the Select Case screen, select the dimension that contains the cases that are to be used to train the data-mining model. (See Figure 6-4.) Also, optionally choose the level that you're interested in using. If you don't choose a level, the wizard assumes the lowest level in the dimension. The dimension level constitutes the input fields.

Note Dimension levels are similar to fields in a relational database, except that dimensions can be composed of multiple hierarchical levels. In a relational table, you would have a date field, but in a cube, you could have a date dimension which contains the year as the highest level. For each year, you would have twelve months in a month level, and for each month, you would have that month's allocated number of days in a day level, and so on.

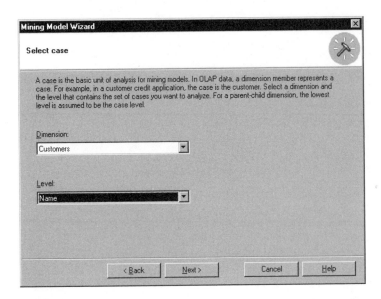

Figure 6-4. *Select case.*

Note Because OLAP deals mainly in aggregates, there is no notion of a case key, such as an ID, because unique row identifiers are normally lost during aggregation.

Select Predicted Entity

In the Select Predicted Entity screen, shown in Figure 6-5, you have three options for the source of your predictions.

- Measure of the source cube
- Member property of the case level
- Members of another dimension

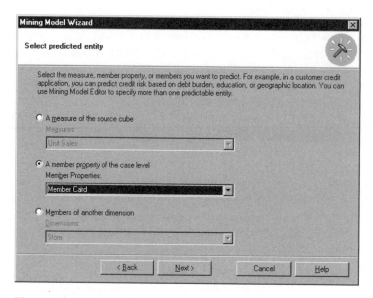

Figure 6-5. *Select predicted entity.*

Note The Select Predicted Entity screen is available only if you choose OLAP with the decision tree algorithm. Unlike the decision tree algorithm, clustering does not provide any real predictive abilities.

A Measure of the Source Cube

If you want to make predictions based on the measures—the numerical values—in the cube, you would choose the A Measure Of The Source Cube option. Bear in mind that because Microsoft Decision Trees is designed primarily for discrete values, it doesn't deal with numerical values in the way you might normally expect because of the tendency of the Microsoft Decision Trees algorithm to use the numbers to make small numbers of discrete groups known as *bins*.

As was mentioned in Chapter 5, Microsoft Decision Trees will have a tendency to bin a wide range of numbers into a much smaller set of discrete values that it can place in a decision tree node. That's fine unless you want the decision tree to predict a very specific value.

Member Property of the Case Level

All dimension levels in OLAP can contain member properties to aid in describing that level. For example, employee levels will likely be expressed as employee numbers so that OLAP can create aggregations based on those numbers. However, when it comes time to generate a report or to display the data from the cube, you're going to want to display employee names, which are more descriptive, even if the names aren't suitable for aggregation. Each level can have multiple properties associated with it, and each of those properties can serve as predictive attributes for the data-mining model. One of those properties is chosen in Figure 6-5.

Members of Another Dimension

If there is relationship between the dimension containing the cases and another dimension, you can use that related dimension as the source of your prediction attributes. If the dimension you choose does not have any relation to the cases, then you'll most likely generate an error at processing time because there will be no entries in the model.

Select Training Data

In the next step, you select data for training your model. The dimension that you selected in the Select Case screen is selected by default, but you must also choose at least one other dimension as a case. (See Figure 6-6.) Failure to do so will not cause an error, but will result in a rather flat tree.

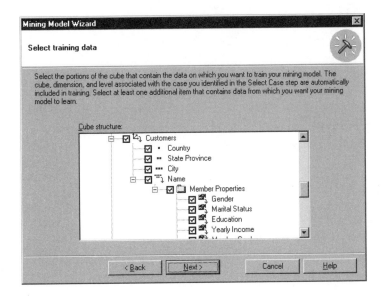

Figure 6-6. *Selecting training data.*

Select Dimension and Virtual Cube

The next step is optional but offers some very powerful features available only when using OLAP as a data source and Microsoft Decision Trees as your data-mining algorithm. Regardless of the options you choose, a data-mining model will be created in the Analysis Services structures. However, the Create A Dimension And Virtual Cube screen, shown in Figure 6-7, asks if you also want to create a data-mining dimension and a virtual cube as output from the data-mining algorithm. If you choose to create the dimension, you'll also be able to create the virtual cube. You can only create the virtual cube if the dimension is first chosen as an output option.

Note If the source cube happens to contain a measure that is a distinct count, the option will be unavailable to you. Select Dimension And Virtual Cube.

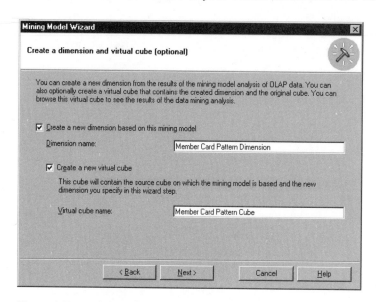

Figure 6-7. *Virtual dimension and cube.*

The Dimension

The *dimension* is the result of the output of the data-mining model. If you look at any OLAP dimension, you'll notice that it forms a hierarchical tree in which branches may have sub-branches, each of which may have sub-branches of its own.

Analysis Services capitalizes on the tree-like structure of the dimension by replicating the tree structure of the Microsoft Decision Trees data-mining model into an OLAP dimension tree.

After completing this data model, we'll discuss the contents of that dimension and how it can be used to analyze data.

The Virtual Cube

The *virtual cube* is almost identical to the cube from which the cases came except that it also contains the dimension that was created in the current session. Even if you choose not to build a new dimension or a new virtual cube, you'll still create a data-mining model. Go ahead and create the virtual dimension. Later in this chapter, you'll get a chance to use this cube to better analyze your source cube.

Completing the Data-Mining Model

The last step, shown in Figure 6-8, is to name the data-mining model.

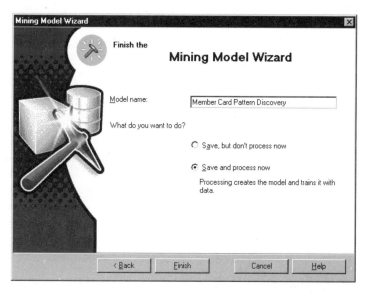

Figure 6-8. *Naming the data-mining model.*

One click on the Finish button and the process of creating dimensions and cubes and building the data-mining model begins. A processed cube is shown in Figure 6-9.

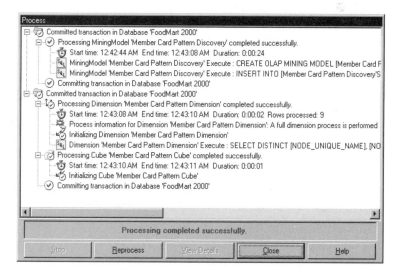

Figure 6-9. *A successfully processed cube.*

A Word About Transactions

There are multiple tasks that need to be completed in succession when processing a cube or a data-mining model. These include:

1. Creating structures
2. Querying source data
3. Inserting data into the structures
4. Creating calculated fields

Before Analysis Services declares that the cube or data-mining model is complete, it checks that all the steps have been completed. If any of the steps fail, all the previous steps must be undone lest they get partially processed and used for the model. This could produce a cube or a data-mining model that looks usable but is actually incomplete. The following figure shows a tree-like structure of all the processes that took place while trying to create a cube for which one of the steps was not completed. The lower tasks need to be complete before the upper tasks of the tree can be completed. If any of the tasks fail, as happened in the model shown here, all the dependent tasks also fail.

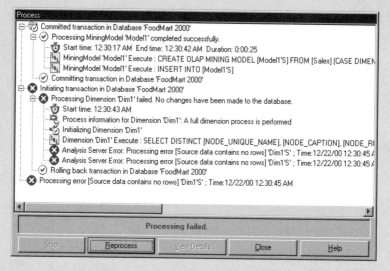

To insure the integrity of an OLAP or data-mining structure, Analysis Services uses a mechanism known as *transactions*. Transactions allow you to bunch multiple steps into a single task that must either succeed or fail as one unit. If the individual steps succeed, the engine issues a *commit;* if any step fails, the engine issues a *rollback,* which restores the data structures to their original state.

Transactions are used to insure the integrity of these operations by wrapping the multiple steps involved. RDBMS engines are best able to accomplish this because the same engine that's responsible for the manipulation of the data is also responsible for its storage. This makes it easy for the engine to have full visibility of the transaction completion stage and gives it the ability to physically undo any writes to the data structures. Analysis Services has a great deal of control over all the events except for the data storage because the data is actually stored in files that are the responsibility of the operating system. To get around this, Analysis Services makes all the changes in temporary files, and once the tasks are complete, it overwrites the original files with the temporary ones.

When you look at a data-mining processing screen in action, you'll notice that the first statement is an Initiate Transaction statement followed by a Committing Transaction statement. Once the transaction is complete, the Initiate Transaction statement becomes the Transaction Complete statement.

OLAP Mining Model Editor

When the processing is done, click the Close button and wait for the OLAP Mining Model Editor to appear. (See Figure 6-10.)

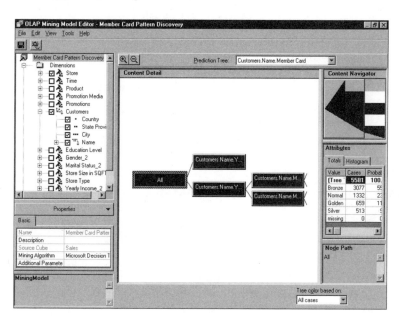

Figure 6-10. *OLAP Mining Model Editor.*

This editor functions in basically the same way as the Relational Mining Model Editor. The few differences are because OLAP is the source of the model and not a relational database.

Content Detail Pane

The first thing you'll notice is that the nodes in the trees don't have regular field names as they do with relational data, although they still function the same as with relational data. They have the name, level, and property of the OLAP dimension used to derive the rules for inclusion in that node.

Structure Panel

Figure 6-10 shows that the structure is represented not by fields as in the relational data-mining model, but as a hierarchy of levels representing the structure of the dimensions within the cube. You can make changes to the structure of the model by adding, changing, or removing dimensions, levels, and properties for the Input or the Predictable columns.

Prediction Tree List

The Prediction Tree list contains the various decision tree structures that are in the model. Each decision tree is represented by the prediction field that will be derived through its use. In this example, when the choices in the drop-down menu are presented to us, we see a fully qualified property from a level in a dimension as the option value.

If you followed the steps on pages 115–123, you've created a virtual cube and a virtual dimension in addition to a data-mining model. These structures are excellent tools for the power of OLAP to provide leverage to better understand the data-mining models. Now that you know how to create a virtual cube and a data-mining model from the cube, it's time to discuss the ways and methods used to analyze data. Before we get to this, let's look at how an OLAP-based data-mining model differs from the one we created in Chapter 5 using relational data. Gaining an understanding of this part will make the subsequent sections involving the use of the virtual cubes and dimensions much clearer.

Analyzing Data with the OLAP Data-Mining Model

Creating a data-mining model from OLAP is similar in many ways to creating it from a relational database source.

The undirected data-mining tasks that we're seeking to accomplish would seem to be ultimately the same regardless of the source, except for the fact that OLAP, unlike the relational model, offers us the unique possibility of relating the data-mining model itself to the OLAP cube that was used as the source.

Note   The data-mining model, regardless of the source, requires a flattened source, even if you're using OLAP as the source. To flatten the source, the engine creates an intermediary structure to allow the dimension levels to be allocated to individual fields. This will cause the OLAP structure to appear as a regular two-dimensional table with one column per dimension level for the time it takes to populate the model.

Remember that even if relational databases are sometimes used for decision support, they are best used as support for transaction processing, such as order entry, accounting, and billing. A valuable by-product of these transaction processing tasks is the table data that can later be mined. But because these relational databases are not generally designed for ease of reporting, mining this data requires putting it into a separate data-mining model, which tends to disconnect the source from the model. Once the model is created, it's often somewhat difficult to go back and find out how that model applies to the data in those tables.

In contrast to the relational databases, OLAP is designed for reporting and decision support to the practical exclusion of transaction processing. In fact, it's hard to imagine how OLAP could ever be adapted to transaction processing at all. However, whatever shortcomings exist in OLAP's transaction processing ability are more than compensated for by its ability to provide structure to existing data. As with data mining, OLAP uses relational data as a source and puts the data in its own structure, often disconnecting itself from the original source of data. Unlike data mining, OLAP provides primarily numerical data in the form of sums, counts, or averages. The dimensions simply provide a context to those numbers in such a way that the summed numbers can be viewed according to specific dimensional characteristics. OLAP cubes allow a user to browse this data and see how sales figures relate to time, geography, and store front locations. Data-mining models are not really capable of indicating anything about sales figures as they relate to time and geography, but they can do something that OLAP cannot. They can function beyond their predictive capabilities and tell you, for example, that of your 1000 stores located nationwide, 50 of these share common characteristics which account for 25 percent of your sales.

Wouldn't it be nice to know what the sales figures are for those stores that seem to have something in common? If it happened that their sales were unusually low or unusually high, then it could be cause for further investigation and perhaps even a call to action.

If the source of that data was a relational model, it would be possible to issue a query that takes into account the characteristics of the decision tree nodes and then sum those sales figures to get an answer. With a few more queries, it would then be possible to compare these figures to other figures and see whether that value is low or high.

If the source is OLAP, Analysis Services has a set of tools that allow you to analyze those sales figures using the generated model. In other words, you could instantly see the customer sales figures described by one of the nodes without having to issue any queries.

Using the Generated Virtual Cube

If you created a data-mining model as outlined earlier in this chapter, you have a virtual cube as well as a data-mining model. To browse the contents of the cube, right-click on your cube and choose Browse Data, as shown in Figure 6-11.

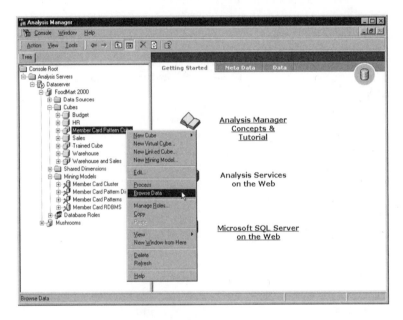

Figure 6-11. *Browsing the cube data.*

The cube browser window uses a flex-grid control to display the data. The lower part of the screen contains the numerical data, or measures, which is aggregated according to the dimensions chosen in the drop-down lists at the top of the window.

In a virtual cube, all the measures actually originate from the cube that was used when processing the data-mining model. All the dimensions also come from that cube, so in essence, this virtual cube is an exact representation of the original cube to which it's linked. In other words, this virtual cube contains all the data that was used to train the data-mining model. There is one extra element, and that is the dimension that was created along with this cube. (See Figure 6-12.)

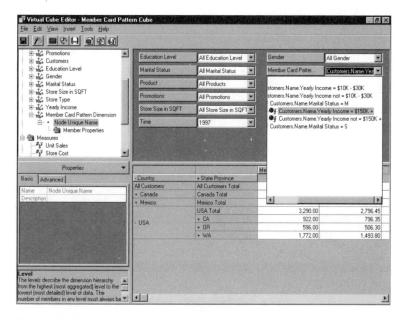

Figure 6-12. *Virtual dimension levels.*

You'll notice that this dimension contains levels that are placed in a similar structure as the nodes of the decision tree present in the data-mining model. In fact, every node in the decision tree has an equivalent level in the virtual dimension. This comes in handy when analyzing data from the cube. Before analyzing the cube, let's look at what makes up a dimension.

Using the Generated Dimension

Dimensions originate in hierarchies derived from data in tables. For example, an employee database can have various of levels of management. These levels are identified by the operator who defines the cube and are then picked up by the OLAP dimension processor, which creates a structure that represents the management hierarchy in the database.

Another way to create a dimension is to use Multidimensional Expressions (MDX) to create calculated member levels containing very specific records. This allows the member levels to include only those records that meet the criteria for the nodes in the decision tree.

What Is MDX?

Wherever large quantities of formatted, structured data is stored, a query language is nearby waiting to retrieve it. Microsoft SQL Server, DB2, and Oracle use SQL as the standard query language, and Microsoft OLAP uses MDX, a query language tailored specifically to access cubes. MDX is also used to create calculated members and custom member formulas that specify rules for inclusion in a data set.

At first glance, MDX looks like SQL because they share some key words, but it's actually a very different language. An in-depth discussion of MDX is beyond the scope of this book, but the Analysis Services portion of the SQL Server Books Online, and other books, such as *Microsoft OLAP Unleashed*, by Timothy Peterson (SAMS, 1999), offer longer discussions on this technology.

Besides having the same structural look, dimensions are also similar to decision trees in that they both use rules of inclusion in a member set. In the same way that a decision tree node applies rules to determine which case records are included, cube dimensions use MDX.

To get a better idea of how this process works, go to the Shared Dimensions folder of the cube, right-click your dimension, and choose Browse Dimension Data. (See Figure 6-13.)

Note Dimensions derived from a data-mining model are easily recognized by the miner's pickaxe icon.

Figure 6-13. *Browse the dimension data.*

The dimension structure and the MDX expression used to make that level are shown in Figure 6-14.

Notice that the expression that describes the Yearly Income Over $150,000 is identical to the one in the node of the tree that has the same rules. (See Figure 6-15.)

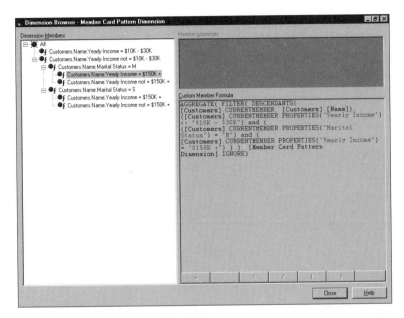

Figure 6-14. *The virtual dimension comprised of MDX statements.*

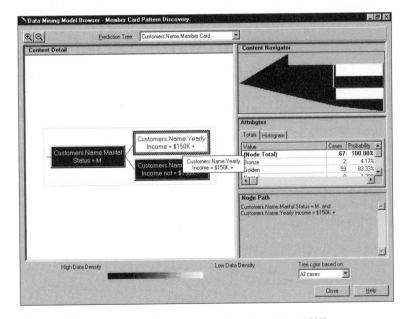

Figure 6-15. *The virtual dimension level with income 150K+.*

The virtual dimension level feature is significant because it allows you to browse the data in the cube according to the nodes that are present in the data-mining model. Browsing in this manner allows you to view the measures in the cube according to the rules present in the mining model. (See Figure 6-16.)

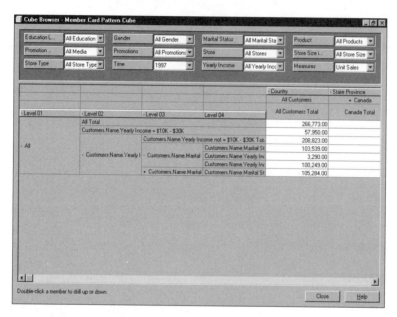

Figure 6-16. *The actual sales figures by dimension level.*

As you can see in this example, the unit sales can be measured according to their membership in a given data-mining model node. Notice that the people who earn lower incomes are responsible for far lower sales than people in higher income groups. This might or might not be a surprise depending on the kinds of products the company sells.

As compared to the relational data-mining model, the OLAP-based model offers unprecedented analytical power to the user. With the power afforded by MDX and calculated members, it's possible to find what percentage of the overall population each member group represents, or the standard deviation, to get a better understanding of the data.

Note Whenever OLAP uses calculated fields or calculated members as is the case with the generated dimensions, there is a real possibility that queries and browsing done with these dimensions will be far slower than with ordinary dimensions, mostly because the cube is making the calculations on the fly, which precludes OLAP from taking advantage of the speed gains that come with using stored aggregates.

Summary

As far as the data-mining portion of Analysis Services is concerned, all data-mining models created with decision trees are treated exactly the same regardless of the structure of the source data because the data-mining processor formats the information in the same way before training the model. All the information is converted to single-table structures with columns and rows so that all the information is temporarily placed in a flat structure that the data-mining processor can deal with. As a result, a data-mining model created with OLAP is fundamentally the same as one created using a relational data source.

By using OLAP as the data source, Analysis Services is able to provide unique options during the creation of the data-mining model that is not be available if using a relational database as the source for the case data. You can choose to create additional OLAP structures, such as a virtual cube and a virtual dimension. These are extremely valuable in that they offer an operator who wants to browse the data the ability to do so with the help of the patterns that were discovered and organized in the data-mining model.

Chapter 7
Microsoft Clustering

System administrators spend a good portion of their time keeping tabs on network and machine performance, which they monitor with tools that track numerous performance counters. These tools usually use windows that display graphs that track the changes in these counters over time. When the system is complex enough, a tool's display area seems cluttered with a multitude of overlapping graphs, each displaying a mass of multicolored, crisscrossing lines that are constantly moving as the values for the counters change over time. (See Figure 7-1.) If you ever observe a system administrator as she's monitoring the machine and network performance, you'll probably notice that she only needs to glance at the screen once to know whether anything is wrong. This may surprise you at first—after all, there must be hundreds of these counters moving and changing all the time, so how does she know that something isn't amiss? If you ask, she'll most likely reply that everything "looks okay." The reason that she can quickly determine there are no problems is because the graphs and the charts display a repeating visual pattern that doesn't change much while things are functioning within normal parameters. The system administrator would, of course, be unable to just glance at the counters and provide you with definite values for any of the performance counters, but she's not interested in the real numbers. For her periodic checks, she's only interested in the big picture—the overall health and load of the system, which she can see with one glance at the screen.

This scenario demonstrates how you can quickly analyze complex, rapidly-changing data by looking at the big picture. Sometimes the data that you're mining contains so many variables that it's virtually impossible to really "see" the pattern in the data. If the system administrator was asked to monitor the system by watching numbers stream down a character-based screen instead of with graphs, the sheer quantity of data in the many counters would quickly overwhelm the operator and make it impossible to identify a problem. She would surely be forced to resort to some tool that could use the computing power of a machine to read and interpret the information for her. There are simply too many data points to comprehend. This is true for any kind of data with many variables. Depending on the type of data available for analysis, data miners are also interested in the big picture. Microsoft Clustering is the algorithm that offers this window into the data.

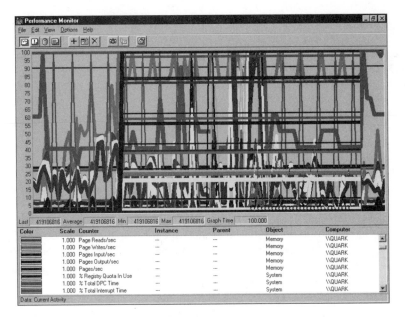

Figure 7-1. *Performance monitor graphs.*

The Search for Order

Humans have a natural tendency to classify and group objects with similar characteristics. When we see a strange looking animal, our brains immediately try to identify it as a mammal or a reptile, a carnivore or an herbivore. We do this in order to draw a conclusion about that particular animal and decide our course of action. If it's a small furry herbivore, we'll probably want to pet it, but if it's a large carnivorous reptile, we'll surely run!

Looking for Ways to Understand Data

Our brains deal with a complex problem by dividing it into a number of smaller bite-sized problems that are easier to solve. For instance, if you were asked to measure employee efficiency for a multinational corporation with 10,000 employees, to make the task manageable, you would measure the efficiency of various groups of employees and not the efficiency of each individual. To accomplish this task, you would find significant similarities between employees that allow you to make global statements about them, such as the following fictitious statements:

- Sales works the most hours but is the least productive.
- Finance works the least hours but is the most productive.
- Upper managers work more hours than CEOs.
- Junior managers work more hours than upper managers.

This example uses groups found in most companies, but to discover meaningful groups that are specific to this company, I would have to evaluate all the employee characteristics and classify them into groups based on similarities, such as profession, job description, geographical location, and so on, as the example in Figure 7-2 shows. Identifying the groups and their members is the primary task of the clustering algorithm.

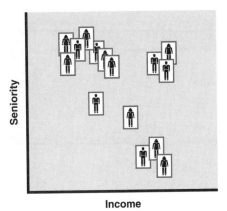

Figure 7-2. *Clusters of employees.*

Clustering as an Undirected Data-Mining Technique

Clustering works in a way that facilitates undirected data mining; by undirected, I mean there are no dependent variables used to find a specific outcome. In other words, when preparing the data-mining model, you don't really know what you're looking for or what you'll find. The application of clustering as a technique amounts to dumping your whole basket of data into the system and letting it "magically" arrange the data into neat piles. All the algorithm does is find records and assign those records to the groups that it defines. Generally speaking, clustering is rarely used to derive information that can be used directly for any sort of specific decision-making; more often it's used to identify groups of records that can be studied further with another method, such as decision trees. Figure 7-3 is an example of a cluster chart.

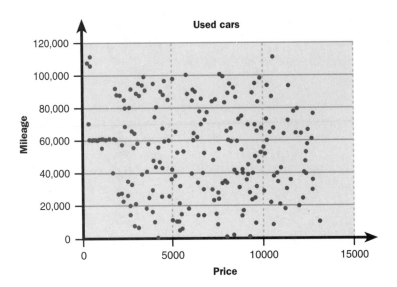

Figure 7-3. *A cluster chart.*

How Clustering Works

The clustering algorithm is an iterative process that seeks to identify groups and group members. In order to best appreciate the results you'll get from this process, let's look at the inner workings of the algorithms as they turn the raw cases into models.

Overview of the Algorithm

As you will see, clustering creates values that represent points in space. These points permit the process to measure the records in terms of their proximity to one another. Like countries on a map, clusters have boundaries that surround the records that reside within the cluster. To know the membership of a given record, it's enough to know in which cluster it resides. The model generated by the clustering algorithm also contains references to coordinates that locate the record in a point in space. These coordinates point to other records that belong to the same cluster.

The K-Means Method Clustering Algorithm

The *K-Means* clustering algorithm is one of the most common methods for arriving at a set of clusters. Almost any commercial data-mining application incorporates some variation of this clustering algorithm. The main feature of K-Means clustering is the predetermined *K variable*, which you set to the number of clusters you want. For example, if you decide you want ten clusters, you set K equal to 10.

Clustering can produce two extreme results depending on the value you choose for K. You could choose to set K equal to one, in which case you'll have a relatively meaningless result because all the data is grouped in one node. The other extreme is to make K equal to the number of records in the case set, which will provide an equally meaningless result because grouping has occurred. Any other number of clusters is possible depending on the value you assign to K. There is really no hard and fast rule on choosing the value for K and it's often a good idea to try several variations.

Note   When creating clusters with the Microsoft Clustering algorithm, the default number of clusters is always 10. As discussed, this number can be modified to fine tune the results.

Finding the Clusters

When presented with the data, the algorithm first has to decide upon the possible clusters that are likely to exist. (See Figure 7-4.) The algorithm does this a number of ways. One method is to identify every distinct value for a given attribute, select every fourth or fifth record, and offer those up as possible cluster values. An alternative method retrieves a sample of records and tries to determine the clusters based on the number of values that are farthest apart. A third method is to select records randomly.

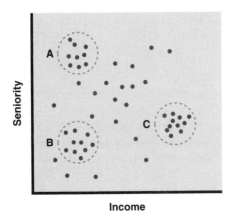

Figure 7-4. *Finding the clusters.*

Known vs. Unknown Clusters

Sometimes you'll know the number of clusters in advance, and other times you won't. For instance, a French department store teamed up with a marketing firm and a clothing designer house to try once again to revolutionize, not the fashion industry, but the clothing retail industry. They decided that rather than cut clothes to standard sizes, such as small, medium, or large, they would actually make them to fit predetermined body shapes and types. They figured that somehow this would allow them to produce clothing that fit better and would serve a (pardon the pun) wider range of customers while at the same time dramatically reduce manufacturing costs. They applied a clustering algorithm to the database of customer body measurements and came up with 120 body types that had common physical attributes. Now all they had to do was make clothes according to the body types and not the measurements. In this case, they had already decided upon the clusters that would exist in order to classify the population of customers into each one. This is a very simplified version of the actual process, but it serves to illustrate the use of predetermined groups.

A commercial real estate firm used clustering to learn the characteristics of good tenants who paid rent on time. The French department store had the advantage of knowing the specific clusters they were looking for and establishing the value of each. This advantage clearly left no room for fuzzy, useless groupings. The real estate firm didn't have this advantage because their tenants were too varied. In the end, of the 19 clusters they got, only one proved to be useful. It seemed that the best tenants were small business owners who were also homeowners for more than ten years. The research showed that many small business owners used their homes as collateral for their business loans. To avoid losing their homes, these business owners were highly motivated and had solid, well-thought out business plans.

Finding the Center of the Cluster

The initial cluster values are randomly determined samples that provide a start point. So if you chose a K value equal to 10, then ten points will be randomly chosen and temporarily assigned the status of the center of a cluster. Once the initial cluster values are determined, then the algorithm cycles through the records and places each record in one of the clusters. As it does this, it continually seeks the records that most closely match the center points of all the other records and reassigns them. This is done by calculating a simple average of the values in that cluster and grabbing those points that fall closest to that average. This exercise, illustrated in Figure 7-5, is repeated for each record until all the records are placed in a cluster.

Note Because the initial centers of the clusters are determined randomly, it's very possible to find that the same data generates different clusters when reprocessed.

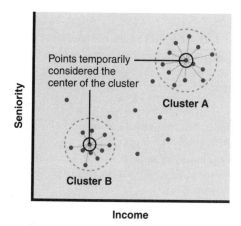

Figure 7-5. *Finding the cluster centers.*

The Boundaries

While the centers of the clusters are continually being adjusted, the boundaries between clusters are also moving. The boundaries between clusters are defined as the halfway point between the center values of each of the clusters. (See Figure 7-6.) Over the course of World War II, Eastern Europeans living near the Soviet border found themselves living in different countries without ever leaving home as a result of battles over border territory. Cluster boundaries also move; records that once belonged to one cluster can suddenly find themselves in another cluster.

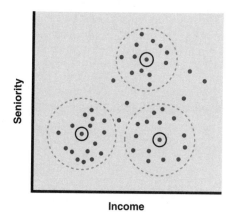

Figure 7-6. *Cluster boundaries.*

What Is Being Measured Exactly?

The preceding explanation might make clustering seem inordinately simple because the values we are dealing with are easily quantifiable and can be averaged and calculated to determine their placement in a given cluster. If all the cases involved only numerical attributes the clustering algorithm would be extremely easy to understand indeed.

The reality is quite different, of course. In our everyday world, we have many ways of recognizing similarities without resorting to mathematical calculations. For example, most of us would consider a bicycle to be more similar to a motorcycle than to a car. In a data-mining operation, these subjective comparisons must be converted to numbers that prove the similarity. We usually find ourselves working with databases that contain characteristics that don't necessarily map to a number, such as:

- Colors
- Geographical locations
- Automobile makes
- Languages
- Animal species

We could attach a numerical value to these attributes and assign them some point in space. Although this sounds very feasible, it creates some new problems.

Conceptual Attributes

The algorithm cannot measure the differences between conceptual values. In other words, if our records contain mammals, fish, reptiles, birds, and insects, the computer would not know that a chimpanzee is far closer to a human than to a bat is or that frozen yogurt is closer to ice cream than carrot cake is. These differences should be far greater than say, the difference in eye color between species, but the algorithm can never be entirely accurate because it doesn't understand what we mean by "closer" in this context.

Clustering Factors

Listed below are the four factors that affect the clustering process.

- Rankings
- Interval values
- Measures
- Categorical values

Rankings

Ranking orders the values from higher to lower or lower to higher. Ranking says nothing about the values or their relative distance from each other. For example, you may be the fastest sprinter in the country and I may be the second fastest, but this ranking does not tell us how much faster you are.

Interval Values

Unlike ranking, *interval values* do measure the difference between one measure and another. If you weighed 150 pounds and I weighed 200 pounds, the interval value tells us that the difference in our weight values is 50 pounds.

Measures

While ranks and intervals express relative values, *measures* express an absolute value relative only to zero. It's important not to confuse measures with intervals by following what seems to be logical but is ultimately flawed reasoning. For example, you might draw the following incorrect conclusions:

- 10 degrees is twice as cold as 20 degrees.
- At 300 pounds, Fred is twice as fat as Joe, who weighs 150 pounds.
- 80 decibels is twice as loud as 40 decibels.

Categorical Values

Categorical values sort similar things and place them into groups. For instance, a stack of books could be grouped into fiction and nonfiction and then again by subject and genre. The key is to remember that a category only groups similar things; the differences between categories are not measured or given a value. In other words, you could never say that a reference book is greater than or less than a novel, but you can say that they are not equal to each other.

Measuring "Closeness"

As you can see, there are many ways to measure "closeness," or how similar things are to one another. There are three main methods used to measure closeness.

- Distance between points in space
- Record overlap
- Vector angle similarity

Distance Between Points In Space

This is the most straightforward method of measuring similarity. The record attributes are assigned a numerical value that represents a coordinate position along one or more axes. To get your distance value, measure the distances between X and Y values on each axis, square them, add them, and take the square root of the sum, as shown in Figure 7-7.

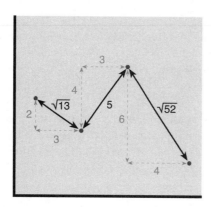

Figure 7-7. *Distance between points.*

Vector Angle Similarity

Vector angle similarity seeks to find values that have the similar angles from the X or the Y axis of a chart and indication of "sameness" that might not otherwise be so obvious when the distance of individual points are being measured on their own. There are times when the relationship between the values of the attributes within the records is used as a value for the entire record. In other words, we are looking for a relationship between records and their attributes. When this relationship is needed, it's better to find the difference between the vector angle—the angle formed by a line through the origin and a point representing a record's attributes—than the distance between points in space.

For instance, in a cluster chart of vehicles that includes automobiles, ships, and trains, we know that a Volkswagen Beetle is more similar to a truck than to a small speed boat. But because cars and trucks are similar in scale, but not in real size, we need to find another way besides size to identify them as the same type of vehicle. They are similar because they both have four wheels, a steering wheel, a muffler, and two axles. In fact, the truck is really very similar to a Beetle except for size. The same method can be used to identify the similarities between a kayak and the Titanic. Because other attributes have values that are easy to measure, we run the risk in this type of data sample of finding similarities based on more obvious, but irrelevant values, such as size, weight, and manufacturer.

If we measure the angle between vectors to find similarity, instead of the distance between points in space, we are protected from values that are influenced by difference in the relative size of the numbers instead of their proportional value. Vector angle measurements can be taken by creating a point for every value of the record and drawing a line between the point values as shown in Figure 7-8.

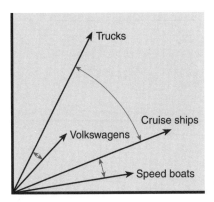

Figure 7-8. *Vector angle measurements.*

The Record Overlap Problem

When dealing with records that are made up mostly of categorical variables, the best option always looks for similarity within records and then groups them by the number of common attributes, as shown in Figure 7-9. Of course, the process is a bit more complicated if there are many similar fields that cause the differences between fields to be less remarkable. This becomes more difficult when the differences are few. To better account for the differences, they are weighted double or triple their value. For example, you may have an attribute for height in your cases which is defined as "Short", "Average", "Tall", and "Gigantic". It may happen that the persons in your cases all have different heights, but because of the broad classifications allowed for height, a very high number of them appear to fall within the "Average" height node. This renders the height attribute meaningless unless you choose to force the values into broader classifications by multiplying everyone's height measurements by 10 in an attempt to make their height differences more apparent. That way, a difference of 3 inches in real life appears as a difference of more than two and a half feet to the algorithm.

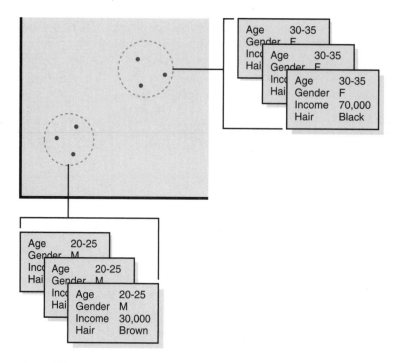

Figure 7-9. *Record overlap.*

When to Use Clustering

Clustering is the best choice of algorithms when you have a very large quantity of data that has a high degree of logical structure and many variables, such as point-of-sale transactions data or call-center records data. Clustering results can allow you to

- Visualize relationships
- Highlight anomalies
- Create samples for other data-mining efforts

Visualize Relationships

One very important advantage of clustering is the ease with which a point chart or graph can be generated to display the model. A visual display allows a user or operator to see the similarities among records at a glance.

Highlight Anomalies

The graphs also make it easy to see the records that just don't fit. For instance, if a school district were to analyze performance of all fifth grade students, a point graph like the one in Figure 7-10 could be made.

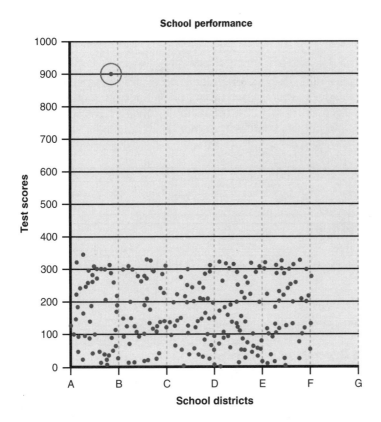

Figure 7-10. *School performance chart.*

As you can see, there is one school that performs extremely well compared to all the others. The cluster does not explain why one school out performed all the others, but it does unequivocally show its difference from the rest.

Election Results

In the 2000 U.S. presidential election, the vote count in the state of Florida was so close, a recount was mandated. In Palm Beach county, a higher number of ballots than expected went to Patrick Buchanan, of the fringe Reform Party. Using clustering, a local statistician published a report that showed the probability of this candidate receiving such a high vote count.

The statistician began his report by showing a cluster point chart of the number of Buchanan votes by county. The chart showed points fairly evenly spread out along a horizontal axis, which represented the counties. However, the Palm Beach county point was higher than all the other points. In fact, it was at the very top of the chart. By itself, this chart said nothing about the validity of the ballots, or Buchanan's popularity in that county. It did, however, bring home the point that this level of electoral support for Buchanan was unusual enough to warrant close attention.

Create Samples for Other Data-Mining Efforts

Many data-mining algorithms such as decision trees require a significant population sample to analyze. Clearly, when a population is very large, the decision tree might become so large that it becomes difficult to traverse all the necessary rules needed to arrive at a leaf node. When you embark upon a data-mining project, it's often more useful to preselect a portion of the population first. For instance, you might have access to a nationwide customer database with millions of records, but you would like to target a general population of online shoppers in an effort to find out who shops online and how they are different from "brick and mortar" shoppers. To target this group, instead of choosing known categories, you could apply a clustering algorithm and then choose the cases present in the more meaningful nodes from which to begin the decision tree process.

Weaknesses of Clustering

Unlike decision trees, clustering data isn't easily interpreted and you frequently need to experiment to get some meaningful clusters. The main weaknesses of the clustering algorithm are

- Results are difficult to understand.
- Data types are difficult to compare.

Results Are Difficult to Understand

Unlike decision trees, there are no nodes to traverse and no rules to follow; in fact, there are no real predictions to be made. As a result, the clusters you end up with are somewhat difficult to understand. In Analysis Services, you'll find what looks like a set of rules in a node, but in fact these are simple descriptions of the records that fell into that cluster.

In some cases, you might end up with many clusters, some that are of no use and others that are very useful. Because the clusters do not offer any logical explanation for their existence, it's very easy to overlook interesting groups. As a result, it's necessary to analyze the meaning and value of each cluster.

Data Types Are Difficult to Compare

Because clustering relies on numerical data to plot points in space, comparing numbers that measure different types of things becomes a significant challenge. For example, we know that 30 degrees is much colder than 80 degrees, and we also know that an automobile that costs fifty dollars more than another comparable model is an insignificant difference. The difference in both cases is 50, but their relative difference (comparing degrees to dollars) is not easy to express in the model. To deal with this, a proportional equalizer of sorts is applied to the values to minimize their differences. For example, the car prices might be divided by 1000 so that the variations in auto prices occur in the same proportion as the temperatures.

Creating a Data-Mining Model Using Clustering

The process to create a data-mining model using the clustering algorithm starts in a similar manner as the process used to create a decision tree algorithm. In this section, we'll create the model using the Data Mining Model Wizard. Since the wizard forces you to use default values, we'll also look at modifying the model using the Data Mining Model Editor.

Using the wizard, the steps are as follows:

1. Select the source type.
2. Select the table or tables for your mining model.
3. Select the data-mining technique to be used by your mining model.
4. Edit the joins.
5. Select the Case Key column for your mining model.
6. Select the Input and Predictable columns.
7. Finish.

The database used for the example is based on a sample of census data used to determine the characteristics of people earning more than $50,000 per year.

> **Note**   This data comes from one of the many "data-mining ready" databases in the University of California, Irvine, Machine Learning Repository, which graciously offers their data for free on the Web. More information can be obtained at *http://www.ics.uci.edu/~mlearn/MLRepository.html*.

The attributes are shown in Table 7-1.

Table 7-1. Attributes for the Over $50,000 Income Group

Field Name	Source
ID	Primary key ID generated by Microsoft SQL Server
Age	Input
capital-gain	Input
capital-loss	Input
Class	Input
education	Input
education-num	Not Used
Fnlwgt	Not used
hours-per-week	Input
Marital-status	Input
native-country	Input

Select Source Type

As with decision trees, clustering can use either a relational database or an OLAP cube as a data source. In this example, we'll be choosing the relational database as a source as shown in Figure 7-11.

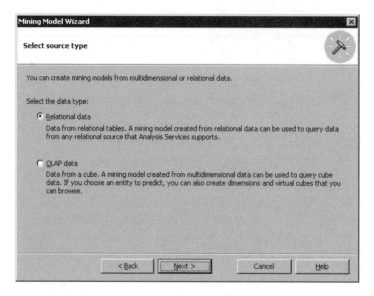

Figure 7-11. *Selecting the type of data source.*

Select the Table or Tables for Your Mining Model

The available tables in the given database are listed in the panel shown in Figure 7-12. We'll choose the census table, which contains a sample of about 32,500 records from a fictional census database. Although this data set was originally designed to predict which persons are most likely to make over $50,000 per year, the number of characteristics present in this table makes it a suitable candidate for clustering.

The available fields of the table are listed in the right panel, and if you needed to you could view the first 1000 records of this table by clicking on the Browse Data button. If we didn't already have an adequate data source defined, we could use the New Data Source button to create another.

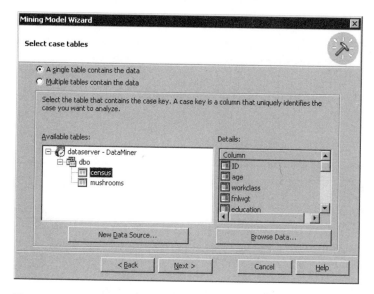

Figure 7-12. *Selecting the case table.*

Select the Data-Mining Technique

As Figure 7-13 shows, the only data-mining techniques available are decision trees or clustering, at least until you add a third-party algorithm or your own algorithm. For the purposes of this exercise, we'll choose clustering.

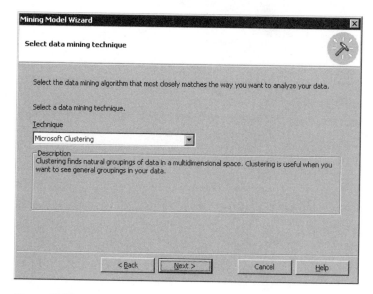

Figure 7-13. *Selecting clustering technique.*

Edit Joins

The Edit Joins dialog box is displayed only if you are creating a mining model from multiple tables. Since we chose only one table, this option will not appear.

Select the Case Key Column for Your Mining Model

Every table should have a unique ID field. If the data you retrieved does not have one, add one that can be used at this step, as shown in Figure 7-14.

> **Tip** To create a unique ID on a SQL Server 2000 table, add a new field of UNIQUEIDENTIFIER type and make *newid()* the default value. By making the field a NOT NULL type, the SQL Server engine automatically updates the field with a unique GUID value.

Picking a field that contains a potential input value as the key field excludes it from being used as an input value. This is why it's important to have a dedicated, nonsignificant field as the ID in this step.

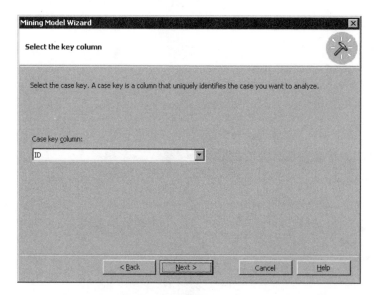

Figure 7-14. *Selecting key column.*

Select the Input and Predictable Columns

Unlike decision trees, which is a predictive model generator, clustering makes no distinction between input and predictable fields. As far as the clustering algorithm is concerned, all chosen fields are inputs. That's why the dialog box only has one panel for the chosen fields. Double clicking on a field in the left panel causes that field to be used as an attribute for clustering. Once the fields have been chosen, as in Figure 7-15, click Next.

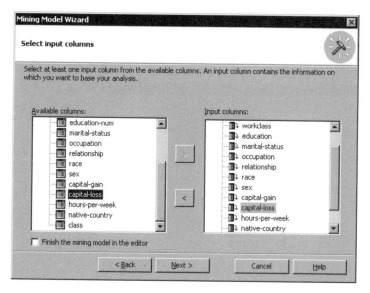

Figure 7-15. *Selecting Input columns.*

Finish

The Finish dialog box prompts you for the name of the data-mining model and offers you the option to process it right then. If you have no further parameters to change through the Data Mining Model Editor, processing it is a good choice.

Determining the Best Value for K

The clustering algorithm used by Microsoft strongly resembles the K-Means method for clustering. This method requires that the algorithm be told in advance how many clusters, or values for K, will exist. When you first build a clustering model, you are given 10 as the value for K by default, which may be the ideal number or it may not. Either way, the results can be drastically different based on the number chosen. The records might not contain data that lends itself to the number chosen. For example, you might have a database containing sales data involving eleven different product types. If you chose 10 as the value for K, then you run the risk of missing a possible clear division of the data into 11 clusters—one for each product. As we'll see later in this section, the Data Mining Model Editor gives you a chance to adjust the value for K and reprocess the model in an attempt to find that ideal number.

154 | PART II Data-Mining Methods

Processing the Model

Creating the model is an iterative process that continually seeks the center of the cluster as each new case is added to the model. For this reason, it usually takes longer to create a clustering model than a decision tree model. As the model is being processed, or trained, you'll notice that the bottom portion of the processing screen often makes reference to the candidate model with an iteration number, as shown in Figure 7-16.

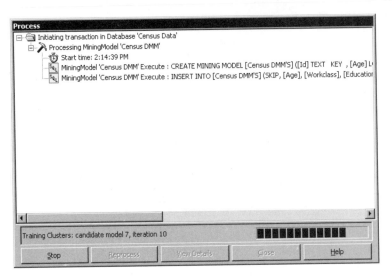

Figure 7-16. *Training clusters.*

This process was outlined in the "Finding the Clusters" section earlier in this chapter. Once the model is processed, click the Close button to go to the Data Mining Model Editor.

Viewing the Model

As shown in Figure 7-17, all the fields are considered input fields. Changing their status from "input" to "input" and "predictable" will not generate a different type of cluster model. To see the contents of the model, click the Content tab.

Organization of the Cluster Nodes

The clusters are represented graphically in much the same way as the decision trees are, except that the "tree" (as shown in Figure 7-18) always has only one level. What appears to be the root node is actually a cluster that contains all the records used to train the model. This node is valuable because it can tell you at a glance how many records there are and even how many records contain given attributes. To get a count of a given attribute, you only need to choose the attribute you're seeking to measure from the Node Attribute Set menu. This makes the Attributes pane show the totals for each of the attributes for that given node.

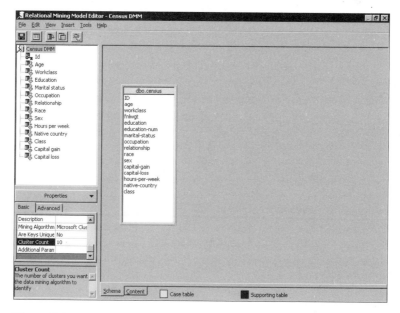

Figure 7-17. *Data Mining Model Editor.*

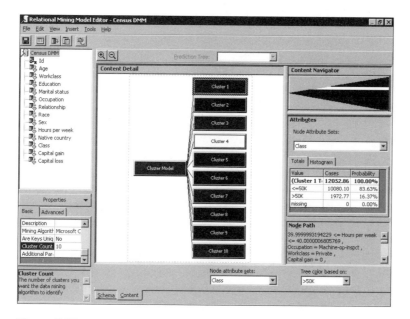

Figure 7-18. *Viewing the contents of the model.*

The nodes' names are nondescript (named Cluster 1, Cluster 2, Cluster 3, and so on); but each cluster does have a set of rules that describes the records contained within the cluster. You can see the list of rules that determine what data is included in a given group by clicking on the node and looking at the contents of the node path.

Why are some records part of a cluster when they don't seem to belong?

You might occasionally notice some records in the cluster that are not accounted for in the rules of the cluster. For example, you might find that the node's rules make no mention of records with a class of greater than $50,000 (>50K), yet the Node Attributes pane shows that 12 percent of the records do indeed have this attribute. This apparent anomaly occurs because the record's other characteristics are enough to place it in a given cluster even if that attribute is not included in the node definition. To understand this better, remember that as far as the clustering algorithm is concerned, a record is simply a point in space. A node is nothing more than a logical circle drawn around those points. While some of the points will be dead-center in that circle, others will be on the fringes of the same circle. Those fringe points might have some attributes that fall outside the strict node definition.

Order of the Cluster Nodes

The numbered order of the clusters is another significant feature that indicates the quantity of records in the cluster. The clusters are numbered and arranged in descending order. In other words, Cluster 1 contains more records than Cluster 2, and Cluster 2 contains more records than Cluster 3, and so on. This is very significant in the clustering models because the more records in a cluster, the more confidence we can have in the significance of the commonality of the records within that cluster. Conversely, the bottom clusters can be very significant in identifying anomalies in the data, as was shown in the school performance results example discussed earlier in this chapter.

Analyzing the Data

As I mentioned earlier, at first glance the most meaningful nodes are likely to be the ones with the most records and the least meaningful nodes are likely to be the ones with the fewest records. A deeper analysis of the middle nodes can certainly lead to some interesting insights. That said, it's expected that a certain number of nodes, if not all, will be meaningless because the commonality of the records is coincidental or based on a commonality that doesn't allow us to make any global statements. For example, some nodes might contain records about persons who are involved in a wide array of different professions. If the professions don't have anything in common, there is very little we can generalize about them.

The cluster we just generated seems to be somewhat devoid of meaning. Perhaps it's because there are relatively few cluster nodes and many attributes. This forces the engine to find common ground using many different attributes and even many variations of the values of those attributes. If you were to look at the first node of the cluster and the last node, you'd see that nothing about them allows us to draw any conclusions. Maybe if we increased the number of clusters, we would find more significant results.

To illustrate this, let's change the number of clusters from 10 to 20. To do this, change the Cluster Count property value in the Basic tab. When you click the Process Mining Model button, you'll get a warning that you must save the model before processing. Just click OK, and continue. If the structure of the model had not been changed, as is the case when a new set of training data is introduced, then you'd have the option to simply refresh the data—a process that amounts to emptying the model and retraining it with the new data. However, we did change the structure by demanding more clusters, so the dialog box only offers the choice of fully reprocessing the model. This is equivalent to building the model from scratch.

Once the option to reprocess is chosen, the twenty-cluster model is reprocessed as shown in Figure 7-19.

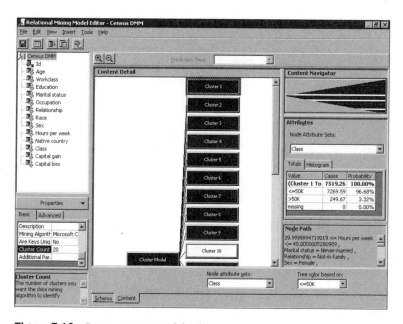

Figure 7-19. *Data Mining Model Editor.*

Now let's take a look at the nodes again. The first node contains about 20 percent of the whole sample and shows more than 96 percent of the persons making less than $50,000 per year. The group described in this node is made up of African American females who are unmarried, separated, or divorced. Another interesting node is the very last one, which includes one unmarried, part-time fisherman who made more than $40,000 in capital gains in one year.

These nodes are a bit more descriptive and do contain some data that could be significant. Unlike decision trees, which groups records according to precise rules, the clustering algorithm tries to place "similar" records in groups. Each record might precisely match a cluster's criteria and therefore be placed in the center of the cluster, or it might match only several criteria and hover on the border between two or more other clusters. The K value often defines how inclusive or exclusive each cluster is.

Summary

Clustering is an undirected data-mining method designed to discover basic classification inherent in databases. Clustering does not attempt to predict unknown data values as decision tree algorithms do, but it does offer a way to discover records that are similar enough to each other to be considered part of given groups that the algorithm itself identifies.

The aim of this kind of data mining is to gain an understanding of the natural similarities among groups of records. This knowledge can lead to further study of the behavior of these groups to see whether any generalizations can be made.

Part III
Creating Data-Mining Applications with Code

With systems such as SQL Server 2000 and Analysis Services, the complexity of the engine is often hidden behind intuitive, interactive user interfaces. Analysis Services provides the Analysis manager as the GUI interface for the user, but the convenience of the user interface does often come at the expense of flexibility and power. A programmer can take better advantage of all the data-mining engine features to perform many administrative as well as application development tasks by using the programming interfaces. This section will deal with the tools needed to accomplish these tasks with code. We'll look at the tools available to us, the object interfaces provided by the Analysis Server engine, and many examples of programs written using code—both to manage data-mining models and make predictive queries.

Chapter 8
Using Microsoft Data Transformation Services (DTS)

As we saw in Chapters 1 and 2, one of the most important prerequisites for a successful data-mining effort is the preparation of the case data, which you need to do before you can begin mining any data. In many, if not most, cases the source of the training for your data-mining models is going to come from disparate sources and nonrelational data formats, such as flat files or Microsoft Excel spreadsheets. As part of any enterprise-wide data-mining effort, organizations need to centralize and normalize their data into a data warehouse. In Chapters 1 and 2, I discussed the need for these steps, the preferred methodology, and the pitfalls to avoid. So now that we know what is needed to create data-mining models, it makes sense to incorporate more Microsoft SQL Server tools to help us in the entire data-mining effort. *Microsoft Data Transformation Services* (DTS), although not specifically an Analysis Services tool, is a very important tool that gathers data from many different sources so that it can be cleansed and warehoused before it is used in OLAP and data mining.

Sometimes the data increases over time, as is the case with supermarket sales data, weather data, and stock market price data. When this is the case, the data-mining models are continuously updated with new data that enriches the model and allows for more timely predictions. In addition to all the transformational capabilities of DTS, it can also create a unit (which acts much like an application) that can be automated with SQL Server Agent.

In this chapter, I'll explain how DTS works and how to program it, and I'll show you, step-by-step, how to automatically download the mushroom data used in Chapter 5 from the mushrooms database's FTP site, run the DTS transformation steps needed to format and store the data, and train the data-mining model. We'll create a unit to do all this with the click of a button or through an automated task.

What Is DTS?

DTS is many things, including a

- Collection of COM objects, each geared toward a specific task
- Hub of OLE DB data connections
- Workflow development platform
- Application development environment

Unlike other programming environments, DTS is strictly batch-oriented. This means that it will run steps in a sequential order without waiting for user input or any other user "events." It's expected to provide an easy way to define those steps and establish the flow of execution to allow you to go from beginning to end in a perfectly predictable manner (barring errors and other exceptions).

The basic DTS unit is a *package*, which is the named collection of a given collection of tasks. Just as Microsoft Visual Basic programs are contained within a project and just as SQL Server tables are contained within a database, DTS objects are contained in a package. A package can contain any one of the following four types of objects:

- Connections
- DTS Tasks
- Transformations
- Workflows

As a unit, packages can be edited, stored in databases or files, password protected, scheduled for execution through the SQL Server Agent, and retrieved by version. Each package contains one or more steps that are executed sequentially or in parallel when the package is run. When executed, the package connects to the correct data sources, copies data and database objects, transforms data, notifies users of the processes of events, and optionally creates written logs of the events that transpired.

DTS Tasks

A *DTS task* is an object that has a specific function that is executed as a step. The type of task depends on the functionality required. By default, DTS performs a whole slew of tasks as described in the following sections.

Transform

The *Transform Data task* is used to copy data between any OLE DB–compliant source and the destination data. When the source and destination objects are defined, the individual columns are exposed and given a default mapping, which is usually ordered sequentially so that the first column of the source maps to the first column of the destination and so on. This lets you customize the transformation task by defining different column mappings or by eliminating certain columns from the transformation procedure altogether. Many times the simple column mappings are not enough; for example, many data sources will store the date in one field and the time in another, but SQL Server 2000 contains a single date field that incorporates both the date and the time. When transforming the data from the source, you have the option of specifying, through the use of scripting, that the destination's date/time field is the concatenation of the source's date and time field. We'll take a closer look at scripting in DTS later in this chapter. Other times, the source data contains only obscure code that can be converted to meaningful descriptions by look-ing up the values in a third data source. The transformation task has facilities to handle this as well. The flexibility of this task makes it a cornerstone of almost every DTS package.

> **Note**   The Transform Data task is often referred to as the *DataPump task*, espe-cially in the object properties of a package.

Bulk Insert

The *Bulk Insert task* is the T-SQL BULK INSERT command encapsulated in an object. For it to work, the following conditions must be met:

- The data destination is a single SQL Server table.
- The data source is a flat text file.
- The columns of the source and the destination have a 1-to-1 mapping.
- The source and the destination have the same number of columns.
- There are no transformation steps taken or implicit conversions made between the source and the destination.

Bulk Insert is the fastest way to import text data into a SQL Server 2000 table as long as the following restrictions are met:

- The database option Select Into/Bulkcopy is set to true.
- The target table has no indexes, or if the table has indexes, it is empty when the bulk copy starts.
- The target table is not being replicated.

Bulk Insert is typically used when the number of rows to be imported is in the millions, when time is of the essence, and when logging is not necessary. When these conditions exist, the records are usually inserted into a staging table, preferably in a special staging database, and then processed from this staging table.

Data Driven Query

A *Data Driven Query task* allows you to loop through the source data as you would with an ADO record set or a SQL Server cursor. This is especially useful when the contents of each individual record contain values that are used to determine what action to take on one or multiple tables. In other words, as you navigate through each row, you could issue almost any SQL statement including INSERT, UPDATE, DELETE, and stored procedure calls. The creation of a Data Driven Query task is a bit more involved than the other packages because of all the options available to you, but it does offer the ultimate in flexibility even if it's at a high cost to the performance of the task. Just remember that these aren't batches, but record-by-record transactions, so if you can find a way to do this with one of the tasks mentioned earlier, you're better off.

Execute Package

In a data-mining environment, the executable processes can be divided and run separately. Programmers are familiar with the notion of breaking applications into parts and having each part perform specific tasks for purposes of readability and code re-use. The *Execute Package task* allows you to only train the model, or to only use the model several times to make predictions, or to do both processes consecutively. It allows you to create packages that perform specific tasks. These packages can be called from other packages, which allows you to break a task into smaller pieces. This flexibility makes it easy to choose to do one or the other, or both, without creating the same package three times. Just as in a programming language, the Execute Package task has mechanisms that allow parameters to pass from one package to another, just as one would do with a stored procedure or a function.

I'll cover the next five tasks briefly because they're not especially relevant to data mining. If you would like more information about some of these tasks, consult SQL Server Books Online, or pick up a copy of *Professional SQL Server 2000 DTS (Data Transformation Services)* by Mark Chaffin, Brian Knight and Todd Robinson (Wrox Press), a book completely dedicated to DTS.

Transfer Error Messages

With sp_addmessage, a SQL Server system stored procedure, a user can add user-defined error messages that are application specific. If your application is going to run on other servers, you would use this task to transfer those messages.

Transfer Master Stored Procedures

The *Transfer Master Stored Procedures task* copies the stored procedures from a master database on one SQL Server 2000 server to another.

Transfer Databases

The *Transfer Databases task* copies the contents of a database in a SQL Server 7 server to a SQL Server 2000 server.

Transfer Jobs

The *Transfer Jobs task* copies the contents of the jobs stored in the msdb database in a SQL Server 2000 server to another SQL Server 2000 server.

Transfer Logins

The *Transfer Logins task* copies the logins defined in the master database from one SQL Server 2000 server to another SQL Server 2000 server.

Copy SQL Server Objects

The *Copy SQL Server Objects task* transfers objects from one SQL server to another. Any number and combination of objects can be transferred, but remember that this is not a disaster recovery mechanism for SQL Server. It's useful for creating occasional test environments or moving specific objects such as lookup tables from one server to another.

Dynamic Properties

The *Dynamic Properties task* works by retrieving values from sources outside a DTS package at package run time and using them to assign values to objects that require run-time variables specific to a given server or other dynamic element. In this way, a package can act like a reusable application and retrieve values from an outside source, leaving the rest of the package as is. This is particularly useful for cases in which

- The raw data-mining source files have dynamic names or sequential numbers in the name.
- You need to connect to an available server or FTP site, where the name of the server or site is not known until package run time.
- The target of the prediction or the location of the test data used to make predictions changes periodically or is unknown until run time.

The source of the dynamic data used by the package can come from any one of these sources:

- A data file containing a property value that can be read and assigned. Unlike the initialization file selection, the data file selection supports property values greater than one line in length.
- A .ini file, such as myprogram.ini, or any .ini file that you create. This is good for single-line value pairs as opposed to registry-style hierarchies of definitions.
- A SQL Server query, as long as it returns just one row. Just make sure that you use the TOP 1 or GROUP BY in such a way that you're guaranteed to get just one row back from the query.
- A DTS package global variable. These can be set and initialized in the package designer.
- An operating system environment variable set within Microsoft Windows 2000 or Microsoft Windows NT.
- A constant used as the default value for a variable in case the conditions for assigning that variable never occur.

Message Queue

Message Queue is a task the interacts with *Microsoft Message Queue* (MSMQ), a transaction monitoring and COM+ packaging system.

ActiveX Scripting

ActiveX Scripting is a task that executes a program written entirely in a scripting language, such as Microsoft VBScript or JScript. The scripting task is a way not only to manipulate the variable and the other objects in the same package, but also to accomplish any number of tasks including instantiating Microsoft ActiveX objects and servers such as Microsoft Word and Excel. The task designer provides a rich environment to create the scripts by providing syntax checkers, keyword and function lists, and an object browser.

> **Note**   By default, all the ActiveX scripting tasks provide VBScript and JScript as language options. You aren't limited to those languages if you install other Windows Scripting Host (WSH)–compliant languages, such as PerlScript or even ActivePython. My personal favorite is Practical Extraction and Reporting (Perl) language, which can be retrieved free from *http://www.activestate.com*. By installing Perl on the server with SQL Server 2000, the Perl keywords and syntax checker automatically become available in the development environments involving the ActiveX scripting languages.

Execute SQL

Execute SQL is a task that is designed, as the name strongly suggests, to execute any T-SQL statement that you could run from SQL Query Analyzer. This task could be used for any number of processes, including creating tables, updating information, and deleting records.

Execute Process

The *Execute Process task* can run an executable program, such as a batch file or a .exe file. It runs in its own process, so the rest of the SQL Server environment is reasonably safe from the program's effects on memory and other resources. Typically, this might run a batch or a program that opens connections to other network resources or retrieves files, or it might run a program that generates a text file to be imported by SQL Server in a subsequent step.

Send Mail

Send Mail is a very handy task that programmatically sends mail to a recipient. This can be used to notify managers that a report is available or, in a more likely scenario, to notify a system administrator that a task failed.

FTP

The *FTP task* automates the retrieval of a file or a collection of files to a local directory from an FTP site. It handles the logging-in process as well as the actual file transfers. In addition, you can perform data transfers from any UNC path without it being an FTP site.

Analysis Services Processing Task

The *Analysis Services Processing task* processes Analysis Services objects. Originally designed for processing cubes only, it still uses the Cube icon even though it's capable of processing cubes, dimensions, and of course, data-mining models.

Data-Mining Prediction Query Task

When you install Analysis Services, the *Data-Mining Prediction Query task* package becomes available. This package is designed to help create and run prediction queries based on a data-mining model and output the results to another source such as a SQL Server table or any other OLE DB–compliant data store such as Excel.

Custom and Third-Party Tasks

If the tasks described so far don't meet the requirements of your batch process, you can take advantage of the extensibility offered by DTS that lets you create custom tasks using Microsoft Visual C++, Visual Basic, Delphi, or any language that can create COM-compliant applications. You can then integrate these custom tasks into the DTS Designer user interface and save them as part of the DTS object model. The tasks then become available for use within the DTS Designer whenever a new package is created.

Connections

Connections are the basis for all activity in the DTS package. To successfully execute DTS tasks that copy and transform data, a DTS package must establish valid connections to its source and destination data and to any additional data sources, such as lookup tables.

OLE DB is the main provider type of DTS connections and allows a wide variety of data sources to be used. These can range from traditional relational database sources such as SQL Server or Microsoft Access to more loosely structured data, such as from Excel spreadsheets and text files.

Sources

DTS contains built-in features that let you graphically add and configure a data source that contains either the raw data that will be manipulated or a final data structure that will store the output of a DTS task. You can use a data source, file, or data link as a source.

A Data Source Connection

Data Source Connections give you access to:

- Standard databases such as SQL Server 2000
- Access 2000
- Oracle
- DBASE
- Paradox
- OLE DB for ODBC
- Excel 2000 spreadsheets
- HTML files
- OLE DB providers

A File Connection

DTS provides additional support for text files. When specifying a text file connection, specify the format of the file. For example, you would specify

- Whether a text file is delimited by a character or in a fixed field format
- Whether the text file is in a Unicode or an ANSI format
- The row delimiter and column delimiter if the text file is in fixed field format
- Whether there is a special character qualifier to separate text columns from numeric or data columns
- Whether the first row contains column names

A Data Link Connection

The connection string used by the data source is stored in a separate text file and accessed at connection time.

Configuring a Connection

When creating a DTS package, you configure connections by selecting a connection type from a list of available OLE DB providers. The properties you configure for each connection vary depending on the individual provider for the data source. A DTS package can have multiple connections defined for the same data source, or the same connection can be reused for various tasks. A few factors to take into account before creating connections in a DTS package include the order of the execution of the tasks, whether your packages will be moved to other servers, and the security of your accounts.

Single Thread per Connection

If the package is designed so that the tasks execute in a perfectly linear order without any parallel tasks, then a single connection is fine. Packages can be designed to have multiple tasks execute simultaneously. In this situation, a single connection becomes a bottleneck and performance can be greatly enhanced by using a separate connection for each task.

Dynamic Connection Properties

If your package can be moved or copied to different servers, you may need to edit the direct connections made in a package. To make it easy to modify the connection parameters for a connection or connections, use a data link file, which saves the connection string in a separate text file. Alternatively, consider using the Dynamic Properties task to change the connection information at run time.

Security Account Information

When creating a connection for a SQL Server data source, you have the option of specifying a given username and password or of using integrated security. Although using integrated security simplifies package creation because no specific credentials need to be supplied, keep in mind that the account used to access the server will be the currently logged on user's account or the service account of the SQL Server Agent if you have scheduled the package to run as a job. Using integrated security can cause numerous bugs because access is denied to SQL Server objects that are needed by certain tasks. If possible, consider creating a specific account with appropriate rights to the tasks in the package and use that account when creating connections. This ensures a consistent user environment regardless of the means by which the package was launched.

DTS Package Workflow

DTS steps and precedence constraints determine the order that the tasks in the package are executed and under what logical conditions they are allowed to run. The simplest, most straightforward way to accomplish this is to use the DTS Designer because all the graphical workflow elements can be dragged, dropped, and interconnected using the mouse. That said, Visual Basic, Visual C++, or even Perl code provides the same functionality without DTS Designer.

DTS Package Steps

Steps are used to control the order in which tasks are executed in a DTS package. *DTS package steps* represent the execution units in the DTS object model, and they define which tasks execute in what sequence when the package is run and which ones run parallel to each other.

There are no step objects to manipulate per se; instead, they are implicitly created whenever precedence constraints are created between tasks. To give you some perspective on that, consider that without any precedence constraints, all the tasks in a package would execute simultaneously, unless they all rely on the same connection (but then the order of execution would be different every time).

When creating a package using code, you can control the relationship between a step and a task more precisely. You can create multiple steps for different package operations and associate the execution of those steps with a single task. For example, suppose you write a package in Visual Basic and specify in several parts of the package that errors can be generated. By linking the steps associated with those errors, you can make the different types of errors execute the same Send Mail task. That Send Mail task can send an e-mail notifying the system administrator that the package failed.

> **Note**   DTS Designer allows you to execute an individual package step. This action is useful for testing and troubleshooting individual steps without having to run the entire package. To execute a single package step in DTS Designer, right-click the task you want to execute and choose Execute Step from the menu.

Precedence Constraints

Precedence constraints sequentially link tasks in a package. In DTS, you can use three types of precedence constraints, which can be accessed either through DTS Designer or programmatically.

Unconditional

If you want Task 2 to wait until Task 1 completes, regardless of the outcome, link Task 1 to Task 2 with an Unconditional precedence constraint.

On Success

If you want Task 2 to wait until Task 1 has successfully completed, link Task 1 to Task 2 with an On Success precedence constraint.

On Failure

If you want Task 2 to begin execution only if Task 1 fails to execute successfully, link Task 1 to Task 2 with an On Failure precedence constraint. If you want to run an alternative branch of the workflow when an error is encountered, use this constraint.

Using Multiple Precedence Constraints

You can issue multiple precedence constraints on a task. For example, you can have a given task execute only when two other previous tasks succeed, or only if one of the tasks succeeds and the other fails.

DTS Designer

The *DTS Designer* is a combination of integrated development environment, workflow engine, and application platform.

It has the graphical user interface similar to any classical workflow designer that calls for objects of different types to be arranged on a virtual whiteboard and have sequences and dependencies attached to them. The DTS Designer graphical user interface allows you to build and configure packages by using drag-and-drop methods and by completing property sheets on the various DTS objects included in the package. Unlike a normal workflow designer, the objects themselves contain functionality that can be defined with parameters or complete programs. Once these objects have been defined and the rules set for their execution order, the package can be launched and the graphical elements come alive to provide visual cues that mark the progress of the tasks.

You can use DTS Designer to do the following:

- Create a simple database object transfer task.
- Create a package that includes complex workflows with multiple steps and dependencies.
- Edit an existing package that was stored in one of the four storage repository types.

Opening the DTS Designer

You can access DTS Designer through SQL Server Enterprise Manager, through the Data Transformation Services node of the console tree. Under the tree, you'll find three storage repositories for the package. I'll discuss these later in this section. If you right-click on this node, you can choose to open a package that happens to be stored in a .dts file.

DTS Designer Work Area

The user interface for the virtual whiteboard includes the DTS Designer main panel, which consists of the following parts:

- A design sheet to create workflows with graphical objects that represent DTS tasks, DTS transformations, and precedence constraints
- A menu bar containing menus for package operations, edit operations, data sources, tasks, and workflow items
- A toolbar containing buttons for: creating, saving, and executing a package; printing a workflow; cutting, copying, and pasting graphical objects in a workflow; annotating a workflow; and changing both the workflow layout and the size of a workflow on the design sheet
- A Connection toolbar containing connections for data sources

- A Task toolbar containing DTS tasks
- You can dock the Connection and Task toolbars by right-clicking on them and choosing Undock from the menu (You can redock a toolbar by right-clicking its title bar and choosing Dock from the menu.)
- Context menus to configure and edit package components and workflow (for example, connections, tasks, and workflow objects)

Saving a DTS Package

When you save a DTS package, you save all DTS connections, DTS tasks, DTS transformations, and workflow steps and preserve the graphical layout of these objects on the DTS Designer design sheet. The options described in the following sections are available for saving packages.

Package Name

Specify a unique name for the package with *package name*. The msdb tables use this name as a primary key.

Owner Password

Specify a password for the package to protect sensitive user name and server password information in the package from unauthorized users with *owner password*. If the package has an owner password, the data is encrypted with the standard encryption API. This option is available only for packages saved to SQL Server or as a structured storage file.

User Password

Set a password for a package user with *user password*. This password allows a user to execute a package. However, this option does not allow a user to view the package definition. If you set the user password, you must also set the owner password. This option is available only for packages saved to SQL Server or as a structured storage file.

Location

Specify the format and location of the saved package with the *location* option. You can save to a SQL server, which then stores it in the msdb database, and then to either Meta Data Services, a structured storage file, or a Visual Basic file. When you save the package to a SQL server or to Meta Data Services, you have the following options:

- **Server name** Specifies the name of the SQL Server installation storing the package.
- **Use Windows Authentication** Specifies the security mode used to connect to SQL Server. The Windows Authentication used will be the Microsoft Windows login of the user creating the package.

- **Use SQL Server Authentication** Specifies the security mode used to connect to an instance of SQL Server.

- **User Name** Specifies a user name for the connection to an instance of SQL Server.

- **Password** Specifies a password for the connection to an instance of SQL Server.

When you save the package to Meta Data Services, you can also scan by displaying the Scanning Options dialog box and specifying how objects referenced by the package should be scanned into Meta Data Services. This capability allows you to relate source and destination objects in a package to database meta data (for example, primary and foreign keys in a table, in an index, and in column information, such as data type) stored in Meta Data Services.

When you save the package as a COM-structured storage file or a Visual Basic file, you have the following options:

- **Filename** Specifies the package filename and path. If the package is a structured storage file, it should be stored with the extension .dts. If the package is a Visual Basic file, it should be stored with the extension .bas.

- **Browse** Displays the Save As dialog box, where you can specify the filename, extension, and storage location.

You can save a package to:

- **Microsoft SQL Server** With this default save option, you can store a package in the SQL Server msdb database, which contains tables especially for storing packages. This offers the robustness and security of SQL Server but does constrain the access to the package to times when that particular SQL Server is available and running. You can take advantage of the backup features of SQL Server to insure the safety of the packages from loss as well as take advantage of the DTS object transfer utility to move the package from one server to another.

- **Meta Data Services** With this save option, you can maintain historical information about the data manipulated by the package. However, Meta Data Services and the repository database must be installed and operational on your server. You can track the columns and tables that are used by the package as a source or destination. You also can use the data lineage feature to track which version of a package created a particular row. You can use these types of information for decision-support applications.

- **A structured storage file** With this save option, you can copy, move, and send a package across the network without having to store the file in a SQL Server database. The structured storage format allows you to maintain multiple packages and multiple package versions in a single file.

- **A Visual Basic file** If you were so inclined, you could create an entire DTS package represented entirely in code without resorting to the DTS Designer at all. Alternatively, you can also decide to do the opposite and take an already designed DTS package and convert it to Visual Basic code.

  With this option, the whole package saves as Visual Basic code, and you can later open the Visual Basic file and modify the package definition in your development environment.

> **Note** When you save a package to the SQL Server repository or to a structured storage file, you can secure the package with one or more passwords. When you save a package to Meta Data Services or as a Visual Basic file, the DTS package security options are not available. However, you can keep packages saved to Visual Basic files secure through a source code control system such as Microsoft Visual SourceSafe, and create a compiled version which hides the details of the code.

dtsrun Utility

The *dtsrun utility* executes a package created using DTS. The DTS package can be stored in the Microsoft SQL Server msdb database, a COM-structured storage file, or SQL Server Meta Data Services. The syntax is as follows:

```
dtsrun
[/?] |
Package retrieval:


        /~S
        /~U
        /~P
        /~E
        /~N
        /~M
        /~G
        /~V
        /~F
        /~R


    Package operation (overrides stored Package settings):


        /~A Global Variable Name:typeid=Value
        /~L Log file name
        /~W Write Completion Status to Windows Event Log <True or False>


    DTSRun action (default is to execute Package):
```

The following do not execute the package; instead they perform an administrative operation on it.

```
/!X
/!D
/!Y
/!C
```

The following is a list of arguments:

- **/?**   Displays the command prompt options.
- **~**   The tilde specifies that the parameter to follow is an encrypted value stored as a hexadecimal string. This is done to protect a batch file that would otherwise contain clear text values for the username, passwords, and servers. It can be used with the **/S**, **/U**, **/P**, **/N**, **/G**, **/V**, **/M**, **/F**, and **/R** options.
- **/S** *server[\sql server instancename]*   Specifies the name or the instance of SQL Server to connect to.
- **/U** *username*   The SQL login used to connect to an instance of SQL Server.
- **/P** *password*   A user-specified password used with a login ID.
- **/E**   Specifies that a Windows NT or Windows 2000 trusted connection will be used as opposed to the SQL Server login and password
- **/N** *packagename*   The name the DTS package was saved as.
- **/G** *guid_string*   The package ID assigned to the DTS package when it was created. The package ID is stored as a GUID data type.
- **/V** *guid_string*   The version ID assigned to the DTS package when it was first saved or executed. A new version ID is assigned to the DTS package each time it is modified. The version ID is a GUID. This is used by the storage engine to keep track of version and execution history. This history is known as the lineage of the package.
- **/M** *password*   An optional password assigned to the DTS package when it was created. To launch the package you must have the password. If no password was specified, then this switch is not necessary.
- **/F** *filename*   The name of a COM structured storage file containing DTS packages. This is the result of saving the package as a .dts file. If *server_name* is also specified, the DTS package retrieved from SQL Server is executed and that package is added to the structured storage engine.
- **/R** *repository_database_name*   The name of the repository database containing DTS packages.

- **/A** *variable_name:typeid=value* Specifies a package global variable, where *typeid* = type identifier for the data type of the global variable as described in Table 8-1. The entire argument string can be quoted, and the argument can be repeated to specify multiple global variables.

Table 8-1. Global Variable Types and their ID Values

Data type	Type ID
Integer (small)	2
Integer	3
Real (4-byte)	4
Real (8-byte)	5
Currency	6
Date	7
String	8
Boolean	11
Decimal	14
Integer (1-byte)	16
Unsigned int (1-byte)	17
Unsigned int (2-byte)	18
Unsigned int (4-byte)	19
Integer (8-byte)	20
Unsigned int (8-byte)	21
Int	22
Unsigned int	23
HRESULT	25
Pointer	26
LPSTR	30
LPWSTR	31

To set global variables with this command switch, you must have either Owner permission for the package or the package must have been saved without DTS password protection enabled.

- **/L** *filename* Specifies the name of the package log file where the events of package execution will be stored including times, steps, and any errors.
- **/W** *Event_Log* Specifies whether to write the completion status of the package execution to the Windows Application Log. Specify True or False.

- **/Z**   Indicates that the command line for dtsrun is encrypted using SQL Server 2000 encryption.

The next four commands perform administrative functions without executing the package.

- **/!X**   Blocks execution of the selected DTS package. Use this command parameter when you want to create an encrypted command line without executing the DTS package to use that command line in your batch files.

- **/!D**   Deletes the DTS package from an instance of SQL Server. It is not possible to delete a specific DTS package from a structured storage file. The entire file needs to be overwritten using the **/F** and **/S** options.

- **/!Y**   Displays the encrypted command used to execute the DTS package which was encrypted with the **/!X** command.

- **/!C**   Copies the command used to execute the DTS package to the clipboard. This option can also be used in conjunction with **/!X** and **/!Y** to make it easy to paste the generated command on to a batch file.

To execute a DTS package saved as a COM-structured storage file, use

```
dtsrun /Ffilename /Npackage_name /Mpackage_password
```

To execute a DTS package saved in the SQL Server msdb database, use

```
dtsrun /Sserver_name /UusernName /Ppassword
   /Npackage_name /Mpackage_password
```

To execute a DTS package saved in Meta Data Services, use

```
dtsrun /Sserver_name /Uusernrame /Ppassword
   /Npackage_name /Mpackage_password /Rrepository_name
```

Using DTS to Create a Data-Mining Model

Having covered the essentials of DTS, I'll now walk you through the creation of a DTS package. Upon request, DTS will build our Mushrooms data-mining model. This case is especially interesting because the source file resides in a remote FTP site that you can access from your Internet connection. This file is a comma-delimited text file that contains well formatted rows but with cryptic codes in the columns that need to be translated to create a legible data-mining model. The file needs to be placed in a SQL Server 2000 table, and then the data-mining model needs to be created. This is the first part of our DTS package. Later, in Chapter 12, we'll expand the package to include tasks for automatically issuing predictions against test data presented to it for analysis.

The steps to create the DTS package are as follows:

1. Download the Mushrooms file from the FTP site.

2. Delete the contents of the SQL Server staging table that will be used to import the mushroom data.

3. Import the file into a SQL Server table—while converting the cryptic codes used to describe the characteristics of the mushrooms into meaningful labels.

4. Train the data-mining model from the data in the SQL Server table.

Preparing the SQL Server Environment

Before we can do steps 1 through 4, we need to prepare the SQL Server database for the data-mining operation.

- Build the mushrooms table.

- Create a lookup table that contains the code to label translations for the mushroom characteristics.

Let's start with the mushrooms table. Run the code shown below in the Query Analyzer of your SQL Server database.

```
if not exists (select * from dbo.sysobjects
    where id = object_id(N'[dbo].[mushrooms]')
    and OBJECTPROPERTY(id, N'IsUserTable') = 1)
BEGIN
CREATE TABLE [mushrooms] (
    [ID] [varchar] (50) NULL ,
    [edibility] [varchar] (50) NULL ,
    [cap_shape] [varchar] (50) NULL ,
    [cap_surface] [varchar] (50) NULL ,
    [cap_color] [varchar] (50) NULL ,
    [bruises] [varchar] (50) NULL ,
    [odor] [varchar] (50) NULL ,
    [gill_attachment] [varchar] (50) NULL ,
    [gill_spacing] [varchar] (50) NULL ,
    [gill_size] [varchar] (50) NULL ,
    [gill_color] [varchar] (50) NULL ,
    [stalk_shape] [varchar] (50) NULL ,
    [stalk_root] [varchar] (50) NULL ,
    [stalk_surface_above_ring] [varchar] (50) NULL ,
    [stalk_surface_below_ring] [varchar] (50) NULL ,
    [stalk_color_above_ring] [varchar] (50) NULL ,
    [stalk_color_below_ring] [varchar] (50) NULL ,
    [veil_type] [varchar] (50) NULL ,
    [veil_color] [varchar] (50) NULL ,
```

```
    [ring_number] [varchar] (50) NULL ,
    [ring_type] [varchar] (50) NULL ,
    [spore_print_color] [varchar] (50) NULL ,
    [population] [varchar] (50) NULL ,
    [habitat] [varchar] (50) NULL
)
END
```

This table should be empty until we actually import the test file. We do need to create the lookup table and populate it with proper values as shown here.

```
create table lookups
(
    lookup_id uniqueidentifier not null
        default newid() primary key clustered,
    type varchar(50),
    code char(1),
    value varchar(50)
)
go
create index ix_type_code on lookups(type,code)
    with fillfactor= 100
go

insert into lookups (type,code,value)
    values ('cap_shape','b','bell')
insert into lookups (type,code,value)
    values ('cap_shape','c','conical')
⋮
```

and so on, until you have a table that contains the values shown in Table 8-2.

Table 8-2. Mushrooms Lookup Table

Type	Code	Value
bruises	t	bruises
Cap_color	b	buff
Cap_color	c	cinnamon
Cap_color	e	red
cap_color	g	gray
cap_color	n	brown
cap_color	p	pink
cap_color	r	green
cap_color	u	purple

(continued)

Table 8-2. *(continued)*

Type	Code	Value
cap_color	w	white
cap_shape	b	bell
cap_shape	c	conical
cap_shape	f	flat
cap_shape	k	knobbed
cap_shape	x	convex
cap_surface	f	fibrous
cap_surface	g	grooves
cap_surface	y	scaly
edibility	e	edible
edibility	p	poisonous
gill_attachment	a	attached
gill_attachment	d	descending
gill_attachment	f	free
gill_color	b	buff
gill_color	e	red
gill_color	g	gray
gill_color	h	chocolate
gill_color	k	black
gill_color	n	brown
gill_color	o	orange
gill_color	p	pink
gill_color	r	green
gill_color	u	purple
gill_color	w	white
gill_size	b	broad
gill_spacing	c	close
gill_spacing	w	crowded
habitat	g	grasses
habitat	l	leaves
habitat	m	meadows
habitat	p	paths
habitat	u	urban
habitat	w	waste
odor	a	almond

Table 8-2. *(continued)*

Type	Code	Value
odor	c	creosote
odor	f	foul
odor	l	anise
odor	m	musty
odor	n	none
odor	p	pungent
odor	y	fishy
population	a	abundant
population	c	clustered
population	n	numerous
population	s	scattered
population	v	several
ring_number	n	none
ring_number	o	one
ring_type	c	cobwebby
ring_type	e	evanescent
ring_type	f	flaring
ring_type	l	large
ring_type	n	none
ring_type	p	pendant
ring_type	s	sheathing
spore_print_color	b	buff
spore_print_color	h	chocolate
spore_print_color	k	black
spore_print_color	n	brown
spore_print_color	o	orange
spore_print_color	r	green
spore_print_color	u	purple
spore_print_color	w	white
stalk_color_above_ring	b	buff
stalk_color_above_ring	c	cinnamon
stalk_color_above_ring	e	red
stalk_color_above_ring	g	gray
stalk_color_above_ring	n	brown

(continued)

Table 8-2. *(continued)*

Type	Code	Value
stalk_color_above_ring	o	orange
stalk_color_above_ring	p	pink
stalk_color_above_ring	w	white
stalk_color_below_ring	b	buff
stalk_color_below_ring	c	cinnamon
stalk_color_below_ring	e	red
stalk_color_below_ring	g	gray
stalk_color_below_ring	n	brown
stalk_color_below_ring	o	orange
stalk_color_below_ring	p	pink
stalk_color_below_ring	w	white
stalk_root	b	bulbous
stalk_root	c	club
stalk_root	e	equal
stalk_root	r	rooted
stalk_root	u	cup
stalk_root	z	rhizomorphs
stalk_shape	e	enlarging
stalk_surface_above_ring	f	fibrous
stalk_surface_above_ring	k	silky
stalk_surface_above_ring	y	scaly
stalk_surface_below_ring	f	fibrous
stalk_surface_below_ring	k	silky
stalk_surface_below_ring	y	scaly
veil_color	n	brown
veil_color	o	orange
veil_color	w	white
veil_type	p	partial

Creating the Package

The first step is to create a new package. Right-click on the Data Transformation Service node in the Enterprise Manager to get the menu shown in Figure 8-1.

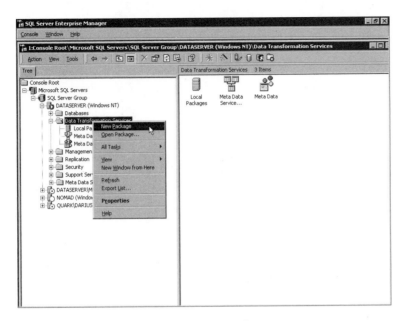

Figure 8-1. *Menu option for a new DTS package.*

Choose New Package from this menu to open a blank "canvas" for us to work with, as shown in Figure 8-2.

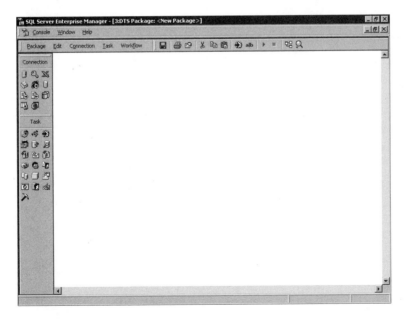

Figure 8-2. *Blank work area.*

Notice the toolbars on the left of the canvas. The Connection toolbar contains all the different connection types including OLE DB, Excel, inbound text files, outbound text files, and others. The Task toolbar contains all the built-in tasks that were described in the first part of this chapter. To bring any of these elements to the canvas, click the connection or task you want to use.

The very first thing we need to create is the FTP task. Do this by clicking the File Transfer Protocol Task button. The File Transfer Protocol Task Properties dialog box appears to permit you to add all the settings you need. (See Figure 8-3.)

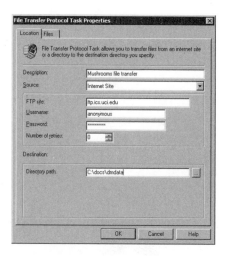

Figure 8-3. *Configuring the FTP task.*

To configure the FTP task, use the same settings as in Figure 8-3. Remember that the FTP site refers to the root directory of the FTP site without the sub directories. In the Files tab of the File Transfer Protocol Task Properties dialog box, we specify where the source files are specifically located. Note that you must specify the local directory where the files will be transferred.

> **Warning** In a DTS package, all references to directories and drives are evaluated in terms of the computer that's launching the DTS package. A DTS package always runs locally to the machine that called it. For this reason, a directory setting that worked fine when you ran the package on your development computer may fail when run as a job on the server because that particular path does not exist there. This problem can be circumvented either by standardizing directory trees in the development vs. production servers, using UNC path names, or using dynamic properties to set these values at run time.

Go to the Files tab in the File Transfer Protocol Task Properties dialog box, and you will see a directory tree panel on the left in the Source section and chosen files on the right in the Destination section, as shown in Figure 8-4. Travel down the directory tree to arrive at the location where the mushroom file resides. The path to take is as follows:

```
.../pub/machine-learning-databases/mushroom
```

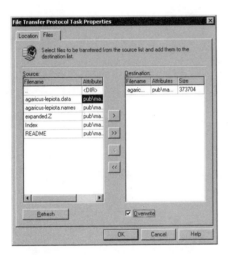

Figure 8-4. *Locating the source files.*

The list of source files will appear. Choose agaricus-lepiota.data, click on the single arrow pointing to the right to copy it to the right panel, and then click OK. To create the text file connection in the next step, we will actually need a sample of that file, so right-click on the FTP task and choose Execute Step to execute only that step, as shown in Figure 8-5. If there were any other steps in the package, this would be a way to ensure that only this one runs without launching the whole package.

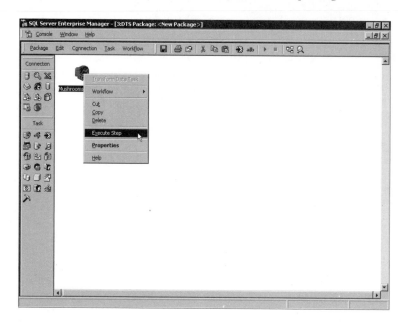

Figure 8-5. *Transferring the file.*

DTS considers text files as connections, so on the upper-left sidebar, click the Text File (Source) button that has an arrow pointing to the right (indicating that it's an incoming file). The Connection Properties dialog box shown in Figure 8-6 will appear. Make sure to specify it's a new connection.

Note Giving these tasks and connections an explicit, meaningful name makes it easier to read the DTS package because these names appear on the canvas of the DTS Designer as well as on any error messages stored in text files.

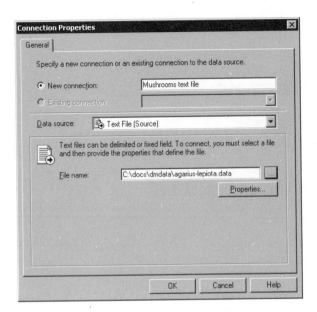

Figure 8-6. *Naming the text file and creating the connection.*

Click OK. The Text File Properties dialog box appears, as shown in Figure 8-7.

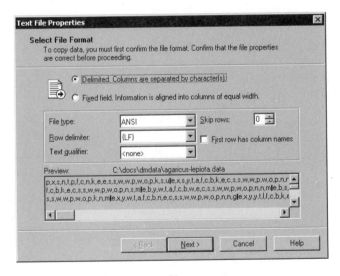

Figure 8-7. *Configuring text file properties.*

In the Text File Properties dialog box, set the properties that determine for DTS the format of the file. In this case, use the settings shown in Figure 8-7 and click the Next button to bring up the Specify Column Delimiter screen shown in Figure 8-8.

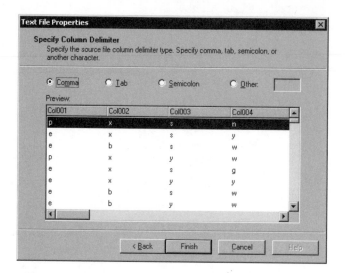

Figure 8-8. *Creating a new DTS package.*

This screen permits you to specify the characters used as delimiters and also gives you a quick sample of how your choice affects how SQL Server interprets the format of the file. If you can see the default column headers and a clear separation between the columns, then chances are good you picked the right delimiter. Click Finish, and then click OK to close the Connection Properties dialog box. Once you're done, the canvas should have a connection to a text file and an FTP task, as shown in Figure 8-9.

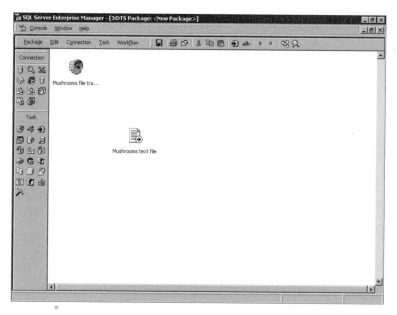

Figure 8-9. *The canvas.*

To work with SQL Server, we need to create our first database connection. To do this, click the Microsoft OLE DB Provider For SQL Server button in the left corner of the Connection toolbar. This brings up the Connection Properties dialog box. Specify the name, the type of OLE DB connection, the SQL Server name, and the user credentials, as shown in Figure 8-10. Click OK when you're finished.

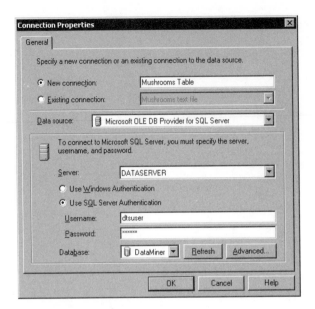

Figure 8-10. *The OLE DB Connection parameters.*

Now that you have set up the connections, select the text file connection first, hold down the Ctrl key, and click on the database connection. The order in which you select the connections determines the direction of the transformation we're going to create next. Now that the two connections are highlighted, click the Transform Data Task button on the toolbar. A black transformation arrow should appear between the connection icons, as shown in Figure 8-11.

Next click on the FTP task, hold down the Ctrl key, and select the text file connection. Choose On Success from the Workflow menu to create a precedence constraint on the transformation, as shown in Figure 8-12. Once done, the transformation commences only if and when the file is successfully transferred through the FTP connection.

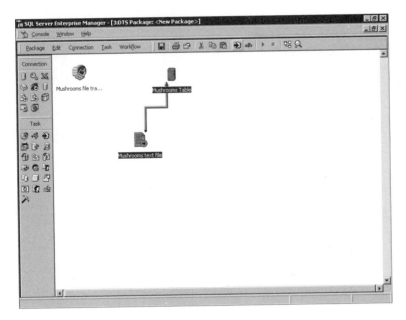

Figure 8-11. *Creating a new transformation.*

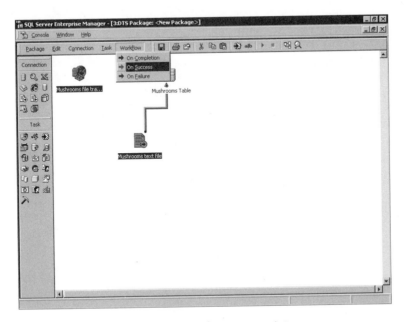

Figure 8-12. *Creating a new precedence constraint.*

A success arrow appears between the two connection icons, as shown in Figure 8-13.

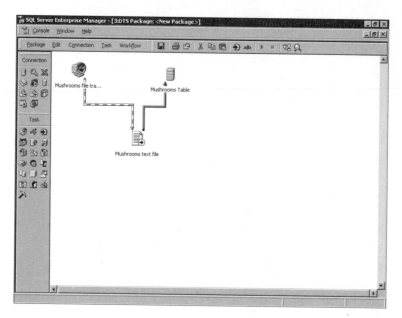

Figure 8-13. *Success constraint.*

But wait! We need to make sure that the table is empty before importing the data files. That's no problem since the order in which the objects are created has no effect on the order of their execution. To check the table, we create an Execute SQL task and issue the TRUNCATE TABLE command as has been done in Figure 8-14.

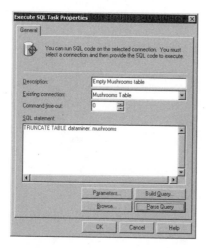

Figure 8-14. *Creating a new Execute SQL task.*

As done previously, we create another success constraint between this new task and the FTP task. (See Figure 8-15.) Now we won't even get the file unless we can successfully empty this table of all residual cases. The Execute SQL task replaces the FTP task as the first step to run in the package.

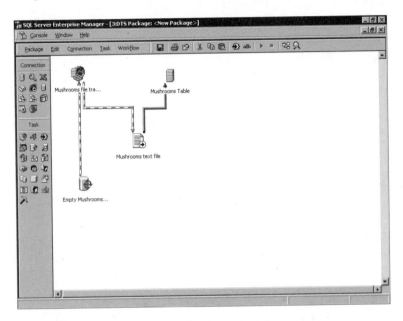

Figure 8-15. *New success precedence constraint.*

Remember the lookup table we created to convert the single character codes in the mushrooms text file to meaningful labels? To avoid the necessity of sharing a connection with the task that fills the table with the cases, we'll click the Microsoft OLE DB Provider For SQL Server button and create a new connection for the lookup table, as shown in Figure 8-16.

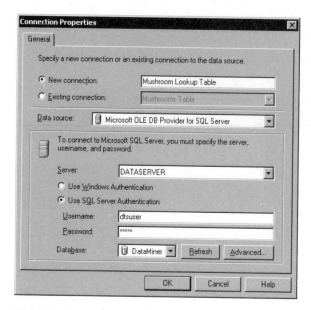

Figure 8-16. *Creating a new database connection.*

The canvas now has two separate connections to the same database. (See Figure 8-17.)

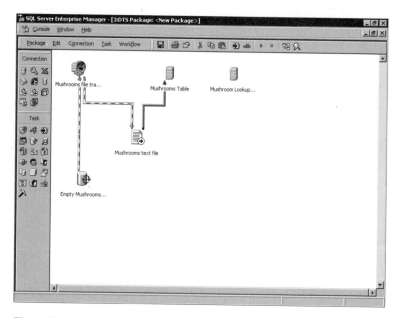

Figure 8-17. *Separate database connections.*

Now we must configure the trickiest part of the package, the transformation itself. To open the Transformation properties, right-click on the black transformation arrow and choose Properties from the menu shown in Figure 8-18.

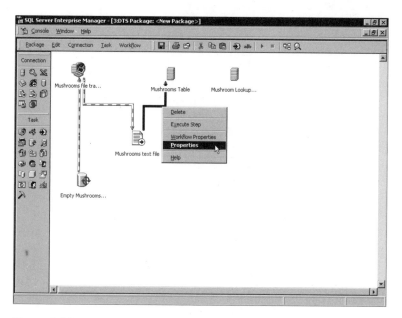

Figure 8-18.   *Opening the Transformation properties.*

This opens the Transform Data Task Properties dialog box shown in Figure 8-19, which is designed to help configure the properties of the transformation. The Source tab on this dialog box is simply a reiteration of the characteristics of the two connections. If we had used a database connection instead of a text file as a source, we could have chosen to use the results of a query as our source.

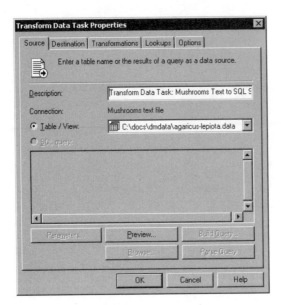

Figure 8-19. *Source tab.*

Click the Destination tab. You may pick the specific destination table or create one on the fly. For this exercise, choose the mushrooms database we created earlier. Note that the structure of the table is listed as a reminder. (See Figure 8-20.)

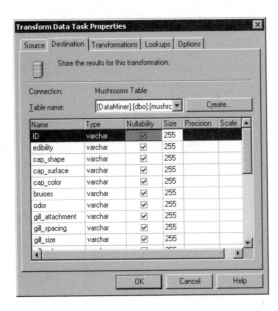

Figure 8-20. *Destination tab.*

Click the Transformation tab, click the Select All button, and then click the New button. You may pick a variety of transformation types, but since we need to intervene with a lookup table to translate codes, pick the ActiveX Script option, as shown in the Create New Transformation dialog box. (See Figure 8-21.)

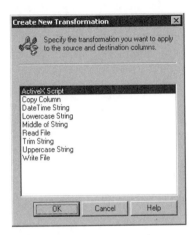

Figure 8-21. *Transformation types.*

Click OK to bring up the Transformation Options dialog box, shown in Figure 8-22.

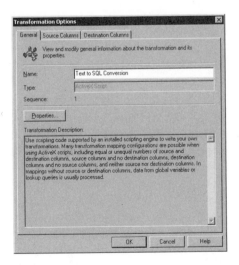

Figure 8-22. *ActiveX Script Transformation Options dialog box.*

Click the Properties button to bring up the ActiveX Script Transformation Properties dialog box shown in Figure 8-23. The ActiveX Script Transformation Properties dialog box lets you choose a scripting language. The transformation script is already generated for you. If you choose a language other than VBScript, such as JScript or PerlScript, click the Auto Gen button to regenerate the script in that language. The problem (shown in Figure 8-23) is that our table has an ID field that is not present in the source text file, so the automatic column mapping is off-center because it tried to match the first field in the text file, the Edibility field, with the ID field in the table. This causes the other fields to be off their mark.

Figure 8-23. *Scripting properties.*

To make sure the column mappings are correct and because we're going to be using code to intervene in the transformation process, it's far more convenient to have one code snippet with all the transformations as opposed to many small code snippets for each column. The first thing you need to do is click Cancel in both the ActiveX Script Transformation Properties dialog box and the Transformation Options dialog box to return to the Transform Data Task Properties dialog box. Now click the Select All button and then the Delete button. These actions eliminate all the column mappings. Now select all the fields in the left side that represent the text file columns, and then select all the fields in the right side, except for the ID field, as shown in Figure 8-24. Finally, click on the New button and create an ActiveX script transformation as you did before. This will create one mapping path that includes all the selected columns. Click OK in both the ActiveX Script Transformation Properties dialog box and the Transformation Options dialog box to return to the Transform Data Task Properties dialog box.

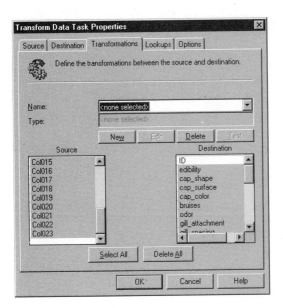

Figure 8-24. *Column remapping.*

Now click the Lookups tab to see a list of lookups, as shown in Figure 8-25. We're going to take advantage of the Lookups tab because we need to be able to use the lookup table we created earlier to convert some of the code values in the text file into meaningful labels. At this point we could create a separate lookup for each field (about 23 of them) and give them each a different name. However, by using parameters, we can get away with creating just one table and using the ActiveX script transformation to pass the proper parameters. Here you must give the lookup a name (which later will be referenced in code) and the connection that will supply the lookup values. Remember the second SQL Server connection we created?

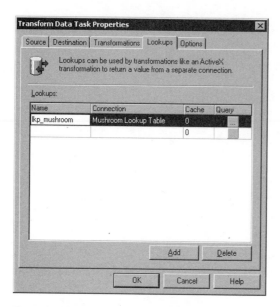

Figure 8-25. *Creating the lookup.*

Click the Query button to invoke the Query Designer shown in Figure 8-26. The query is very simple: We're interested in getting a value returned to us based on the name of the field that contains the value and the code, or the one character value that the field contains. The type and the code are the unknown values, or parameters, that we're going to use to retrieve the correct value. To indicate to the lookup function that we want to be able to pass a parameter, put a "?" in place of the variable. We can have as many of these values as we choose. Click OK to return to the Transform Data Task Properties dialog box.

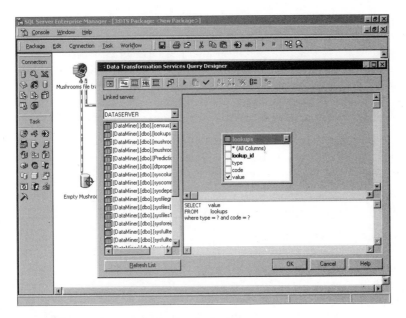

Figure 8-26. *Query Designer for the lookups.*

The Options tab of the Transform Data Task Properties dialog box, shown in Figure 8-27, allows us to configure some additional properties for the transformation.

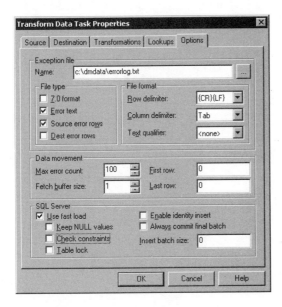

Figure 8-27. *The Options tab.*

The top portion of the Options tab allows you to create a text file that contains any errors and determine what types of error information will be stored in the text file. This file is indispensable for debugging purposes after the fact. When converting data from outside sources, as in this example, you're always subject to errors caused either by file corruption from the supplier of the file or from changes made to the file structure without your knowledge. This debugging function can alert you to those types of errors not only by signaling the errors, but also by listing a certain number of rows that caused the problem.

The middle portion of the Options tab lets you decide how many errors you will allow before interrupting the task. It also lets you decide how many rows you want to import and even what range of rows they belong to.

The bottom portion of the Options tab affects how the data will load. By choosing Fast Load, you are asking SQL Server to attempt to dispense with logging the inserts to the table.

Note By executing a nonlogged operation such as this in a database, you render the logs useless for recovery purposes because as soon as SQL Server detects a nonlogged operation, it disallows any transaction log backups. To restore the recoverability of the database, a full database backup must be performed immediately after the Bulk Insert. This is why it's often best to have all staging tables, such as this one, in a separate staging database where the transaction logs do not need to be used for recovery.

Locking the table and disabling constraint checking speeds up the Bulk Insert task. The batch size is relevant when you have many rows to insert at once. By leaving the default value to 0, you're basically saying that all the records will be inserted into SQL Server in one single transaction. That can hurt performance and tax resources. By setting it to a value of 10,000, for example, you allow SQL Server to write every 10,000 rows that come in.

Now let's go back to Figure 8-23 and change the ActiveX Script so it will account for the lookups we created. Take a look at the code in Figure 8-23.

DTSDestination(<*fieldname*>) refers to the field in the SQL Server table. The DTSSource (<*fieldname*>) refers to the column in the text file. Ordinarily, the transformation would be relatively simple:

```
DTSDestination("Field1") = DTSSource("Col1")
```

Because we are using transformations, we need to make the same change to every one of the fields:

```
DTSDestination("Field1") = DTSLookups("LKP_MUSHROOMS").Execute _
    ("Field1",DTSSource("Col1"))
```

The syntax of the lookup function is simple:

```
DTSLookups("LookupName").Execute(Parameter1, Parameter2, …)
```

The parameters are read in order and replace the "?" characters in the lookup query definition we created earlier. The function then returns a value that we use to update the destination column.

Click the Transformation tab, and click the Edit button to open the Transformation Options dialog box. Click the Properties button to open the ActiveX Script Transformation Properties dialog box, and then modify the function as shown in Figure 8-28. Close all the dialog boxes to return to the DTS Designer canvas.

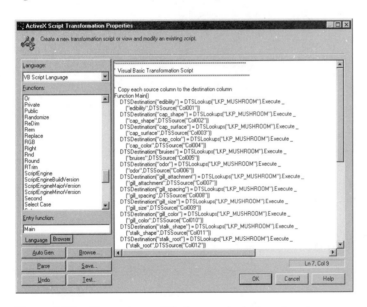

Figure 8-28.   *The script modified to use the lookup function.*

To create the data-mining processing task, click the Analysis Services Processing Task button to open the Analysis Services Processing Task dialog box shown in Figure 8-29. First you'll be shown the Analysis Servers that are available. Choose a server, and drill down to the database that you want to process. Since we're interested in processing the data-mining model, we'll drill all the way down to the "Mushroom Analysis RDBMS" data-mining model that you created in Chapter 5.

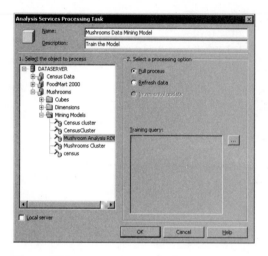

Figure 8-29. *Creating an Analysis Services processing task.*

When you choose a data-mining model, the processing options correspond to the options that you would use for data-mining as opposed to OLAP, for example. In this case, choose Full Process, which takes a little longer but rebuilds the structure of the data-mining model. Notice that you can, if you wish, specifically write a query that will populate the data-mining model. A default query is used if you do not specify one.

Now create a success precedence constraint so that the data-mining model gets processed only after the staging table containing the cases is successfully populated by the transformation task. (See Figure 8-30.)

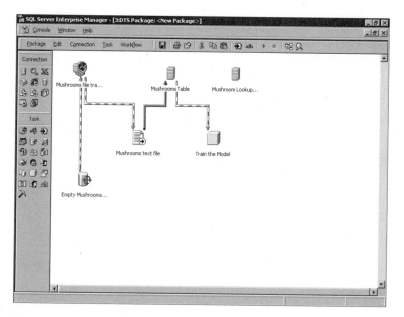

Figure 8-30. *Adding the precedence constraint to include the mining model.*

Now choose Save As from the Package menu to bring up the Save DTS Package dialog box shown in Figure 8-31. As mentioned earlier, there are various locations to store the package. The most flexible is the .dts file which can be transferred, e-mailed, or carried on a disk. But for the purposes of this example, save it in SQL Server, which then stores it in the msdb database.

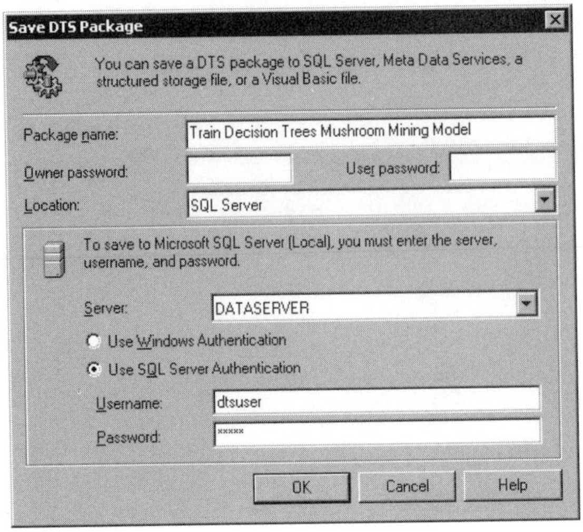

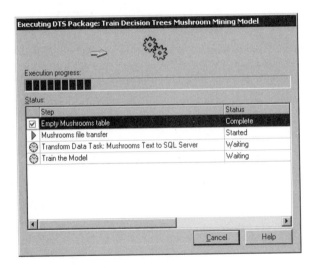

Figure 8-31. *Saving the package.*

The simplest way to execute the package is to click the Execute button located on the toolbar, or choose Execute from the Package menu. A dialog box appears and provides immediate feedback of the progress of each step in the package as it executes. (See Figure 8-32.)

Figure 8-32. *Executing the package.*

If you go back to the Data Transformation node in Enterprise Manager and select the SQL Server node, you'll notice the package is stored there for future use. (See Figure 8-33.)

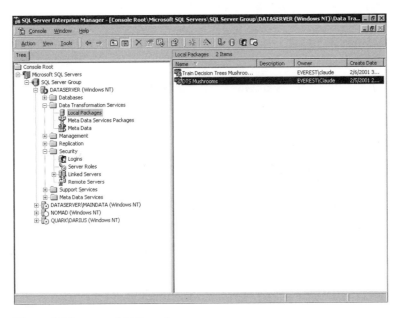

Figure 8-33. *List of DTS packages.*

If you would like to schedule this package to run at preset times, say at 11 P.M. every night, all you need to do is right-click on the package you wish to schedule and choose Schedule Package from the menu. (See Figure 8-34.)

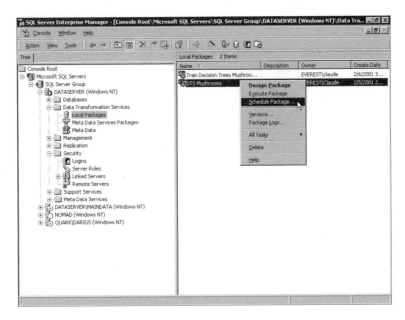

Figure 8-34. *Package options.*

This brings up the Edit Recurring Job Schedule dialog box (shown in Figure 8-35), which allows you to set the dates and times that the package should run unattended. Once the schedule is set, the job is added to the list of jobs in the SQL Server Agent.

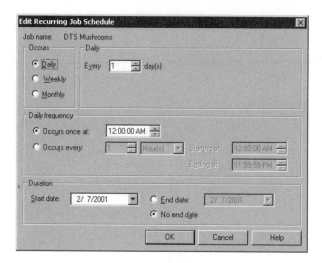

Figure 8-35. *Edit Recurring Job Schedule dialog box.*

Summary

A data-mining strategy must include the data preparation steps, especially because the predictive and analytical qualities of the data-mining model are highly dependent on the successful conversion of raw data into structured cases. This means that the cases not only must prove to be structurally coherent, but also must pass any and all integrity tests that are necessary before declaring them fit to represent data to be analyzed. DTS is a very powerful tool that was designed for that purpose. It also happens to be a tool that offers more than enough flexibility to create batch-oriented programs that aid in bringing the data all the way from its raw form to the final data-mining model, relational database, or OLAP cube. The structure of the DTS facilitates its transportation, execution, and scheduling, which allows it to be integrated with a wide variety of SQL Server tools and programming interfaces.

Chapter 9
Using Decision Support Objects (DSO)

Decision Support Objects (DSO) is a library of Component Object Model (COM) classes and interfaces that provide access to the functionality of the core Analysis Services engine insofar as the administrative tasks are concerned. The internal structure of the objects contained within Analysis Services is reflected in the object model exposed by DSO. This makes it easy to manage Analysis Services programmatically.

Installing DSO

To be able to access DSO from a computer where Analysis server is not installed, you may either install the client components of Analysis Services, which will automatically install the appropriate DLLs, or you may copy the following files to your computer:

- **Msmddo80.dll**   The DSO library, version 8.0
- **Msmdso.rll**   The DSO resource file, version 8.0
- **Msmdnet.dll**   The Analysis Services network interface
- **Msmdlock.dll**   The Analysis Services lock manager

The DLLs are installed in the following location:

    <drive>:\Program Files\Common Files\Microsoft Shared\DSO

The resource file, Msmdso.rll, does not need to be registered and is installed by default in the following location:

    <drive>:\Program Files\Common Files\Microsoft Shared\DSO\Resources\1033

To register the DLL files, you should use Regsvr32.exe or use the *DLLSelfRegister* functions of the DLL files. Additionally, registry entries for each file should be made under the following registry key:

```
HKEY_LOCAL_MACHINE\SOFTWARE\Microsoft\Windows\CurrentVersion
\SharedDLLs
```

As we saw in the Analysis Manager in Chapters 5 and 6, the objects in Analysis Services are organized in a hierarchy. First we have a server that contains connections, cubes, shared dimensions, and data-mining models. The cubes contain partitions and the data-mining model contains columns, data sources, and roles. Figure 9-1 shows this hierarchy.

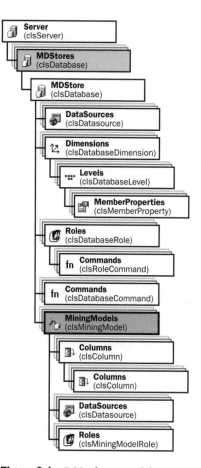

Figure 9-1. *DSO object model.*

Scripting vs. Visual Basic

As I describe the functionality of each object, I'll provide code samples to illustrate their use in real applications. The following examples use Microsoft Visual Basic 6; you could also use Microsoft Visual C++. However, it's very probable that someone might use this technology on the Web or with Microsoft Windows Scripting Host, so the question is, can you use VBScript (or any other scripting language, for that matter) with DSO? The answer is yes—but you shouldn't. The reason for this relates to the way DSO was built. Each object in DSO exposes much of the functionality of the collection of its subobjects in the hierarchy through an interface named *MDStores*. In other words, if you want to scroll through the collection of databases in a *Dso.Server* object, you would find them in the collection, not of databases, but of *MDStores*. Each *MDStore* of the *Server* object happens to be a database object. Each database can contain a certain number of cubes, which are also contained within the *MDStores* interface. Each *MDStore* of the *Database* object is a cube.

Note   The mining models, as we'll soon see, are not represented by an *MDStores* collection because they are at the same level as the cubes in the hierarchy.

To be able to take advantage of these *MDStores* interfaces, the language must be able to create object data types so that you can write the following:

```
Dim dsoServer as Dso.Server
Set dsoServer = new Dso.Server
```

The *dsoServer* object needs to be dimensioned as the object type for there to be a *dsoServer.MDStores*. If you were to use a scripting language, there is an undocumented *Databases* collection in DSO that can also be used as I'll show you here in plain VBScript (using Windows Scripting Host):

```
Dim dsoServer
Dim db

Set dsoServer = wscript.CreateObject("dso.server")
DsoServer.Connect "dataserver"

For each db in dsoServer.Databases()
    Wscript.echo db.name
Next

DsoServer.Close
```

I have run into very few, if any, problems proceeding in this way. However, according to Microsoft, these undocumented collections are not supported and may or may not exist in future versions of DSO. The lack of support should be discouragement enough from using DSO directly from a scripting language.

If you wish to use DSO through script, I recommend that you create your own ActiveX DLL, which serves as a wrapper for the DSO component. This DLL is the one you can safely use in a scripting environment.

The *Server* Object

The *Server* object in the DSO hierarchy represents the root object in the model tree and handles the functionality related to the Analysis server. The *Server* object uses the *Server* interface, with a *ClassType* property of clsServer.

The *Server* object is used to

- Connect to and disconnect from an Analysis server.
- Start, pause, and stop the Analysis server service (*MSSQLServerOLAPService*) provider.
- Provide detailed information, such as the version and edition, of an Analysis server.
- Create other *Service* objects, such as databases, data sources, commands, dimensions, cubes, data-mining models, and roles.
- Manage object locking in Analysis Services, controlling read/write access in a multiple user situation.
- Provide access to DSO *Database* objects using the *MDStores* collection.

To connect to a server, just create an instance of the server like this:

```
Dim dsoServer As New DSO.Server
```

Then call the *Connect* method and supply the name of the Analysis server you wish to connect to:

```
dsoServer.Connect "myServerName"
```

Managing the service status of the Analysis server is only slightly more complex than most other interactions with other components of DSO only because of its need to communicate through the service management component of the Win32 API, which utilizes many cryptic-looking values that are simplified using the following constants:

```
' Constants regarding the current state of the service
Const OLAP_SERVICE_ON = &H4
Const OLAP_SERVICE_PAUSED = &H7
Const OLAP_SERVICE_STOPPED = &H1


' Return error constants
Const SERVICE_CONTINUE_PENDING = &H5
Const SERVICE_PAUSE_PENDING = &H6
Const SERVICE_PAUSED = &H7
Const SERVICE_ON = &H4
Const SERVICE_START_PENDING = &H2
Const SERVICE_STOP_PENDING = &H3
Const SERVICE_STOPPED = &H1
Const SERVICE_ACCEPT_PAUSE_CONTINUE = &H2
Const SERVICE_ACCEPT_SHUTDOWN = &H4
Const SERVICE_ACCEPT_STOP = &H1
Const SERVICE_ACTIVE = &H1
Const SERVICE_CHANGE_CONFIG = &H2
Const SERVICE_CONTROL_CONTINUE = &H3
Const SERVICE_CONTROL_INTERROGATE = &H4
Const SERVICE_CONTROL_PAUSE = &H2
```

```
Const SERVICE_CONTROL_SHUTDOWN = &H5
Const SERVICE_CONTROL_STOP = &H1
Const SERVICE_ENUMERATE_DEPENDENTS = &H8
Const SERVICE_INACTIVE = &H2
Const SERVICE_INTERROGATE = &H80
Const SERVICE_NO_CHANGE = &HFFFF
Const SERVICE_PAUSE_CONTINUE = &H40
Const SERVICE_QUERY_CONFIG = &H1
Const SERVICE_QUERY_STATUS = &H4
Const SERVICE_STATE_ALL = (SERVICE_ACTIVE or SERVICE_INACTIVE)
Const SERVICE_USER_DEFINED_CONTROL = &H100

Const SERVICE_WAIT_MAX_SECONDS As Integer = 45


Friend Function AnalysisServiceManager(oServer As Object, _
    ByVal iCmd As Integer, _
    ByRef lngRunStatus As Long, _
    ByRef lngError As Long) As Boolean

Dim bReturnValue    As Boolean
Dim lngServerStatus As Long
Dim lngControlCmd   As Long

lngRunStatus = oServer.ServiceState
bReturnValue = False
lngControlCmd = icmd
lngError = 0

On Error GoTo ManageError

Select Case icmd

    ' Run this when the request is to start the service.

    Case SERVICE_ON

    ' The status of the service must be checked in case
    ' it's either running already or in the process of
    ' starting.

        Select Case lngRunStatus
            ' If it's already running, then do nothing and
            ' act as though it was started successfully and
            ' return true.

            Case SERVICE_ON
                bReturnValue = True

            ' If the service is not running, then changing
            ' the state of the service control property will change
```

(continued)

```
                        ' the behavior of the service. In this case, changing
                        ' the state to a running state (SERVICE_ON) will
                        ' make the service attempt to start. Failure to do so
                        ' will invoke the error manager automatically.

                        Case SERVICE_PAUSED, SERVICE_STOPPED
                            oServer.ServiceState = lngControlCmd
                            bReturnValue = True
                    End Select

            ' A request is being made to pause the server.

            Case SERVICE_PAUSED

                Select Case lngRunStatus

                        ' Again, if the service is already paused, there's
                        ' no need to make a fuss …

                        Case SERVICE_PAUSED
                            bReturnValue = True

                        ' If the service is running, it gets paused
                        ' by simply changing the value of the state.

                        Case SERVICE_ON

                            oServer.ServiceState = lngControlCmd
                            bReturnValue = True

                        ' Trying to pause a stopped service, on the
                        ' other hand, is a problem. The user needs
                        ' to know that the attempt failed, so the
                        ' return value is false.

                        Case SERVICE_STOPPED
                            bReturnValue = False

                End Select

            ' A request is made to stop a running server.

            Case SERVICE_STOPPED

                Select Case lngRunStatus

                        Case SERVICE_STOPPED
                            bReturnValue = True
```

```
        Case SERVICE_ON
            oServer.ServiceState = lngControlCmd
            bReturnValue = True

        ' Stopping a paused server is a problem
        ' and the caller needs to be notified via
        ' a FALSE return value.

        Case SERVICE_PAUSED
            bReturnValue = False

    End Select
End Select

' lngStatus holds the value of the current state of the
' service. Since this is a variable passed by reference,
' the value will update the variable that was declared
' in the calling program.

lngStatus = oServer.ServiceState

OlapServiceControl = bReturnValue

Exit Function

ManageError:
' Manage any error caught by the server object,
' which generally will be due to making requests
' that are incompatible with the service's ability
' or from some server configuration error such as an
' invalid service login.
' Also can occur if the state change fails to take
' effect within 60 seconds

lngStatus = oServer.ServiceState
lngError = Err.Number
OlapServiceControl = False

End Function
```

The code would get called as follows:

```
Dim dsoServer As New DSO.Server
Dim lSuccess As Boolean ' Contains the return status of the function
Dim lngStatus as Long ' Sent by reference and contains the status of
                        ' the service after the function runs
Dim lngErr as Long      ' Contains any error values that may have
                        ' resulted. If the function returns FALSE,
                        ' this variable may contain the error number
                        ' needed to obtain a more complete description
                        ' of the problem.
```

(continued)

```
dsoServer.Connect "dataserver"

' This is the function call
lSuccess = AnalysisSrvcMgr(dsoServer, SERVICE_ON, lngStatus, lngErr)
```

This code sample shows how to display the properties of a server:

```
Public Sub displayProperties(oServer As DSO.Server)

    ' For illustration sake, we'll show the output going to the
    ' debug window.
    With oServer
        Debug.Print "Name:                " & .Name
        Debug.Print "Description:         " & .Description
        Debug.Print "Connection Timeout: " & .ConnectTimeout
        Debug.Print "LockTimeout:         " & .LockTimeout
        Debug.Print "Edition:             " & .Edition
        Debug.Print "Version:             " & .Version
        Debug.Print "Log File:            " & .ProcessingLogFileName
    End With

End Sub
```

Here is a code sample showing how to create the database:

```
Public Sub CreateDatabase()
    Dim dsoServer As New DSO.Server
    Dim dsoDataBase As DSO.MDStore

    Dim strDataBaseName As String
    Dim strDescription As String

    ' You need to define name of the Analysis server
    ' where this will occur.
    dsoServer.Connect "dataserver"

    ' The name of the database is mandatory ...
    strDataBaseName = Me.txtDbName.Text
    ' ... but the description is optional
    strDescription = "Database Created from DSO Code"

    ' Check whether that database name has already been used.
    ' The server has a collection which contains all the
    ' databases that exist within. By scrolling through
    ' the server's MDStores interface, you can see whether
    ' the proposed name is in use already.
    If dsoServer.MDStores.Find(strDataBaseName) Then
        MsgBox "There is a database called " & strDataBaseName & _
            ". Please try another name."
        Exit Sub
    End If
```

```
' Simply by adding the new database to the collection
' you've caused DSO to create the physical database
' on the server.
Set dsoDataBase = dsoServer.MDStores.AddNew(strDataBaseName)

' This is where the description gets set. If the string
' is empty, it won't do anything.
dsoDataBase.Description = strDescription

' The information you provided gets committed through
' this update command.
dsoDataBase.Update

End Sub
```

Before any other object can be created in a database, a connection to a data source needs to be made as is the case here, when we would like to connect to our mushrooms database:

```
Private Sub AddDataSource()
    Dim dsoServer As New DSO.Server
    Dim dsoDB As DSO.MDStore
    Dim dsoDS As DSO.DataSource

    Dim strDBName As String
    Dim strDSName As String
    Dim strDSConnect As String

    ' Initialize variables for the database name,
    ' data source name, and the ConnectionString property
    ' for the data source.
    strDBName = "Mushrooms"
    strDSName = "dataserver"
    strDSConnect = "Provider=MSDASQL.1;User ID=sa;" & _
        "Data Source=FoodMart;Connect Timeout=15"

    ' Create a connection to the Analysis server.
    dsoServer.Connect "dataserver"

    ' Locate the database first.
    If dsoServer.MDStores.Find(strDBName) Then
        Set dsoDB = dsoServer.MDStores(strDBName)

        ' Check to see whether the data source already exists.
        If dsoDB.DataSources.Find(strDSName) Then
            MsgBox "Data source " & strDSName & _
                " already exists for database " & strDBName
        Else
            ' Create a new data source.
            Set dsoDS = dsoDB.DataSources.AddNew(strDSName)
            ' Add the ConnectionString properties.
```

(continued)

```
                    dsoDS.ConnectionString = strDSConnect
                    ' Update the data source.
                    dsoDS.Update
                    ' Inform the user.
                    MsgBox "Data source " & strDSName & _
                        " has been added to database " & strDBName
                End If

            Else
                MsgBox strDBName & " is missing."
            End If

End Sub
```

While parameters of the server are being changed you may need to ensure that you're able to get a lock on the server to implement the changes:

```
Public Sub LockServer(oServer As DSO.Server, _
    ByVal iLockType As Integer)

' The values for iLockType can be of the following types:

' ---- OlapLockExtendedRead ----
' Serves as a guarantee that the server whose properties
' are being read won't change in either the object itself
' or any dependent objects. Applying this to a server will
' prevent any databases belonging to that server from being processed.
' Note that multiple users can gain this read lock, but that
' no processing can occur until all the locks are released.

' ---- OlapLockProcess ----
' The object's Process method can be started, and other applications
' have read-only capabilities on that object until the lock is
' released. Only one olapLockProcess lock can be applied to an
' object at a time, and other applications can only apply
' olapLockRead locks while the olapLockProcess lock is in place.

' ---- OlapLockRead ----
' Allows read-only access to the properties of that object. Others
' may place this lock concurrently as well, but no user can issue
' a write lock until all the read locks have been released.

' ---- OlapLockWrite ----
' The properties of the object can be modified using the Update
' method. No other lock can be placed on this object until this
' lock is released.

Dim strDescr As String
```

```
' The description is useful for other applications that may need to
' see this description to describe the lock that was placed.

strDescr = "Lock placed for testing purposes"

oServer.LockObject iLockType, strDescr

End Sub
```

To unlock an object or a series of objects, it's enough to call one of these methods:

```
' This unlocks the server lock only

dsoServer.UnlockObject

' Unlocks the server and any objects within
' the same object model. This returns a Boolean value if
' it's successful.

lRetval = dsoServer.UnlockAllObjects
```

The *Database* Object

The *Database object* represents a database in Analysis Services. The database contains cubes and data-mining models, both of which are located at the same level. As mentioned previously, the database objects are accessed through the *MDStores* collection of the DSO *Server* object, but only the cubes can be accessed through this interface. As we'll see soon, you need to explicitly name the data-mining collection to access the data-mining models from the database.

The *Database* object is used to

- Create, edit, and delete commands, data sources, cubes, dimensions, data-mining models, and roles applicable to a database in Analysis Services.
- Manage transactions involving objects that belong to the database, such as cubes, dimensions, and mining models.
- Provide access to events, using the *Database* interface, which is used to supply client applications with progress information on currently executing database tasks.

When reading the code that follows, note that although the data-mining model objects are the same regardless of the algorithm chosen, there are properties that are of use only in the case of a given algorithm as opposed to another. Tables 9-1 and 9-2 detail the uses of each of the properties according to the algorithm.

Table 9-1. Properties of the Data-Mining Model Object

Property	OLAP	Relational
CaseDimension	Defines the case dimension used by the data mining model.	Not used.
CaseLevel	Defines the case level within the case dimension used by the data-mining model. A read-only property, it identifies the lowest level in the dimension whose data-mining model column has its *IsDisabled* property set to False.	Not used.
Description	Contains a user-friendly description of the data-mining model.	
FromClause	Not used.	Defines the case table, in the form of a FROM clause, used by the data-mining model.
JoinClause	Not used.	Defines any supporting tables, in the form of a JOIN clause, used by the data-mining model.
MiningAlgorithm	Defines the data-mining algorithm provider, such as Microsoft_Decision_Trees or Microsoft_Clustering, used by both types of data-mining models.	
SourceCube	Defines the OLAP cube used by the data-mining model for training data.	Not used.
SubClassType	Is set to *sbclsOlap* when the *MiningModel* object is created.	Is set to *sbclsRelational* when the *MiningModel* object is created.
TrainingQuery	Defines the Multidimensional Expressions (MDX) query used to insert training data into the data-mining model. In most instances, this property is left blank; DSO will construct an appropriate training query if this property is not used.	

Table 9-2. Data-Mining Column Properties

Property	OLAP	Relational
DataType	Defines the expected data type of the data-mining column.	
Description	Contains a user-friendly description of the data-mining model column.	
ContentType	Should contain a value from the SUPPORTED_CONTENT_TYPES column of the MINING_SERVICES schema rowset. For example, if the column contained text data that corresponded to income ranges for customers, the *ContentType* property would be set to DISCRETE to reflect the discrete valuations of the data. If, on the other hand, the column contained actual salaries, the property would be set to either CONTINUOUS or DISCRETIZED, depending on the capabilities of the data-mining algorithm provider.	

(continued)

Table 9-2. *(continued)*

Property	OLAP	Relational
IsKey	Not used. This property is read-only and is automatically set to True for the lowest enabled level in the case dimension specified in the *CaseDimension* property of the mining model.	Defines the key columns for the data-mining model. Set to True to specify a key column in the case set.
IsInput	Defines the Input columns for the data-mining model. For a set of related columns, changing the *IsInput* property for one of the columns automatically changes the property for the other related columns.	
IsPredictable	Defines the predictable columns for the data-mining model. A column can have both *IsInput* and *IsPredictable* set to True. For a set of related columns, changing the *IsPredictable* property for one of the columns automatically changes the property for the other related columns.	
IsDisabled	Defines the columns to be used in analysis for the data-mining model.	
Distribution	This property is used to optimize the mining model by giving the mining-model algorithm some indication of the statistical nature of the data in the column. The values for this property should come from the SUPPORTED_DISTRIBUTION_FLAGS of the MINING_SERVICES schema rowset.	
SourceOlapObject	The value of this property is an object within the OLAP cube. For instance, this property might contain a DSO level object or a DSO member property object.	Not used.
SourceColumn	Not used.	The value of this property is the fully qualified name of a field in the case or supporting table for the data-mining model.

DSO lets us create either a Relational data-mining model or an OLAP data-mining model. We'll look at both, starting with the relational model.

Creating the Relational Data-Mining Model Using DSO

This code sample demonstrates the use of Visual Basic to create a relational data-mining model using DSO. Notice how the DSO object model relies on the *MDStores* interface until it begins to access data-mining objects, in which case the *MiningModel* object is used. This code accomplishes exactly the same thing you do when you create a data-mining model using the wizards in Analysis Manager. The data source connections are established, the data-mining model is defined, and the model is finally trained with the data from the relational database.

```
Public Sub newRelationalDMM()
    Dim dsoServer As New DSO.Server
    Dim dsoDataBase As DSO.MDStore
    Dim dsoDataSource As DSO.DataSource
    Dim dsoDMM As DSO.MiningModel
    Dim dsoCol As DSO.Column
    Dim dsoRole As DSO.Role

    Dim strLQ As String, strRQ As String
    Dim strModelname As String
    Dim strFrom As String
    Dim strSrcName As String

    ' Constants used for DataType property
    ' of the DSO.Column object.
    ' Note that these constants are identical to
    ' those used in ADO in the DataTypeEnum enumeration.
    Const adInteger = 3
    Const adWChar = 130

    strSrcName = "dataserver"
    strModelname = "MushroomsRDBMS"

    ' Connect to the server on this computer.
    dsoServer.Connect "dataserver"

    Set dsoDB = dsoServer.MDStores("Mushrooms")

    ' Retrieve the open and close quote characters for
    ' the mushrooms data source.
    strLQuote = dsoDB.DataSources(strSrcName).OpenQuoteChar
    strRQuote = dsoDB.DataSources(strSrcName).CloseQuoteChar

    ' The mushrooms table is the fact table for this
    ' relational data-mining model; this variable will
    ' make it easier to understand the code that
    ' follows.
    strFrom = strLQ & "mushrooms" & strRQ

    ' Check for the existence of the model on this computer.

    If Not dsoDB.MiningModels(strModelname) Is Nothing Then
        ' If this model exists, delete it.
        dsoDB.MiningModels.Remove strModelname
    End If

    ' Create a new relational mining model
    ' called CustSalesModelRel.
    Set dsoDMM = dsoDB.MiningModels.AddNew(strModelname, _
        sbclsRelational)
```

```
' Create a new ALL USERS mining model role.
' In this way, everyone can use and query the model.

Set dsoRole = dsoDMM.Roles.AddNew("All Users")

With dsoDMM
    .DataSources.AddNew strSrcName, sbclsRegular

    .Description = "Analysis of Mushroom edibility"

    ' Set the case table for the model to the
    ' Mushrooms table.

    .FromClause = strFrom

    ' Select the algorithm.

    .MiningAlgorithm = "Microsoft_Decision_Trees"

    ' Let DSO define the training query. This gets
    ' filled automatically by DSO based on the data
    ' source and the definition of the model.

    .TrainingQuery = ""

    ' Save the existing structure to the repository.

    .Update
End With

' Create the Mushroom table's ID column as a key column.

Set dsoCol = dsoDMM.Columns.AddNew("ID", _
    sbclsRegular)

' Set the column properties for the new column.

With dsoCol

    ' Set the source field from the case table for
    ' the column.

    .SourceColumn = strFrom & "." & strLQ & _
        "id" & strRQ
    .DataType = adInteger
    .IsKey = True
    .IsDisabled = False
End With

' The next several columns are the attribute columns
' used by the model to make predictions.
```

(continued)

```
Set dsoCol = dsoDMM.Columns.AddNew("Cap Shape", _
    sbclsRegular)
With dsoCol
    .ContentType = "DISCRETE"
    .SourceColumn = strFrom & "." & strLQ & _
        "cap_shape" & strRQ
    .IsInput = True
    .IsPredictable = False
    .DataType = adWChar
    .IsDisabled = False
End With

Set dsoCol = dsoDMM.Columns.AddNew("Cap Surface", _
    sbclsRegular)
With dsoCol
    .ContentType = "DISCRETE"
    .SourceColumn = strFrom & "." & strLQ & _
        "Cap_Surface" & strRQ
    .DataType = adWChar
    .IsInput = True
    .IsPredictable = False
    .IsDisabled = False
End With

Set dsoCol = dsoDMM.Columns.AddNew("Cap Color", _
    sbclsRegular)
With dsoCol
    .ContentType = "DISCRETE"
    .SourceColumn = strFrom & "." & strLQ & _
        "Cap_Color" & strRQ
    .DataType = adWChar
    .IsInput = True
    .IsPredictable = False
    .IsDisabled = False
End With

Set dsoCol = dsoDMM.Columns.AddNew("Bruises", _
    sbclsRegular)
With dsoCol
    .ContentType = "DISCRETE"
    .SourceColumn = strFrom & "." & strLQ & _
        "Bruises" & strRQ
    .DataType = adWChar
    .IsInput = True
    .IsPredictable = False
    .IsDisabled = False
End With

Set dsoCol = dsoDMM.Columns.AddNew("Odor", _
    sbclsRegular)
With dsoCol
```

```
        .ContentType = "DISCRETE"
        .SourceColumn = strFrom & "." & strLQ & _
            "Odor" & strRQ
        .DataType = adWChar
        .IsInput = True
        .IsPredictable = False
        .IsDisabled = False
End With

Set dsoCol = dsoDMM.Columns.AddNew("Gill Attachment", _
    sbclsRegular)
With dsoCol
        .ContentType = "DISCRETE"
        .SourceColumn = strFrom & "." & strLQ & _
            "Gill_Attachment" & strRQ
        .DataType = adWChar
        .IsInput = True
        .IsPredictable = False
        .IsDisabled = False
End With

Set dsoCol = dsoDMM.Columns.AddNew("Gill Spacing", _
    sbclsRegular)
With dsoCol
        .ContentType = "DISCRETE"
        .SourceColumn = strFrom & "." & strLQ & _
            "Gill_Spacing" & strRQ
        .DataType = adWChar
        .IsInput = True
        .IsPredictable = False
        .IsDisabled = False
End With

Set dsoCol = dsoDMM.Columns.AddNew("Gill Size", _
    sbclsRegular)
With dsoCol
        .ContentType = "DISCRETE"
        .SourceColumn = strFrom & "." & strLQ & _
            "Gill_Size" & strRQ
        .DataType = adWChar
        .IsInput = True
        .IsPredictable = False
        .IsDisabled = False
End With

Set dsoCol = dsoDMM.Columns.AddNew("Gill Color", _
    sbclsRegular)
With dsoCol
        .ContentType = "DISCRETE"
        .SourceColumn = strFrom & "." & strLQ & _
            "Gill_Color" & strRQ
```

(continued)

```
            .DataType = adWChar
            .IsInput = True
            .IsPredictable = False
            .IsDisabled = False
        End With

        Set dsoCol = dsoDMM.Columns.AddNew("Stalk Shape", _
            sbclsRegular)
        With dsoCol
            .ContentType = "DISCRETE"
            .SourceColumn = strFrom & "." & strLQ & _
                "Stalk_Shape" & strRQ
            .DataType = adWChar
            .IsInput = True
            .IsPredictable = False
            .IsDisabled = False
        End With

        Set dsoCol = dsoDMM.Columns.AddNew("Stalk Root", _
            sbclsRegular)
        With dsoCol
            .ContentType = "DISCRETE"
            .SourceColumn = strFrom & "." & strLQ & _
                "Stalk_Root" & strRQ
            .DataType = adWChar
            .IsInput = True
            .IsPredictable = False
            .IsDisabled = False
        End With

        Set dsoCol = dsoDMM.Columns.AddNew("Stalk Surface Above Ring", _
            sbclsRegular)
        With dsoCol
            .ContentType = "DISCRETE"
            .SourceColumn = strFrom & "." & strLQ & _
                "Stalk_Surface_Above_Ring" & strRQ
            .DataType = adWChar
            .IsInput = True
            .IsPredictable = False
            .IsDisabled = False
        End With

        Set dsoCol = dsoDMM.Columns.AddNew("Stalk Surface Below Ring", _
            sbclsRegular)
        With dsoCol
            .ContentType = "DISCRETE"
            .SourceColumn = strFrom & "." & strLQ & _
                "Stalk_Surface_Below_Ring" & strRQ
            .DataType = adWChar
            .IsInput = True
            .IsPredictable = False
            .IsDisabled = False
        End With
```

```
Set dsoCol = dsoDMM.Columns.AddNew("Stalk Color Above Ring", _
    sbclsRegular)
With dsoCol
    .ContentType = "DISCRETE"
    .SourceColumn = strFrom & "." & strLQ & _
        "Stalk_Color_Above_Ring" & strRQ
    .DataType = adWChar
    .IsInput = True
    .IsPredictable = False
    .IsDisabled = False
End With

Set dsoCol = dsoDMM.Columns.AddNew("Stalk Color Below Ring", _
    sbclsRegular)
With dsoCol
    .ContentType = "DISCRETE"
    .SourceColumn = strFrom & "." & strLQ & _
        "Stalk_Color_Below_Ring" & strRQ
    .DataType = adWChar
    .IsInput = True
    .IsPredictable = False
    .IsDisabled = False
End With

Set dsoCol = dsoDMM.Columns.AddNew("Veil Type", _
    sbclsRegular)
With dsoCol
    .ContentType = "DISCRETE"
    .SourceColumn = strFrom & "." & strLQ & _
        "Veil_Type" & strRQ
    .DataType = adWChar
    .IsInput = True
    .IsPredictable = False
    .IsDisabled = False
End With

Set dsoCol = dsoDMM.Columns.AddNew("Veil Color", _
    sbclsRegular)
With dsoCol
    .ContentType = "DISCRETE"
    .SourceColumn = strFrom & "." & strLQ & _
        "Veil_Color" & strRQ
    .DataType = adWChar
    .IsInput = True
    .IsPredictable = False
    .IsDisabled = False
End With

Set dsoCol = dsoDMM.Columns.AddNew("Ring Number", _
    sbclsRegular)
With dsoCol
    .ContentType = "DISCRETE"
```

(continued)

```
            .SourceColumn = strFrom & "." & strLQ & _
                "Ring_Number" & strRQ
            .DataType = adWChar
            .IsInput = True
            .IsPredictable = False
            .IsDisabled = False
        End With

        Set dsoCol = dsoDMM.Columns.AddNew("Ring Type", _
            sbclsRegular)
        With dsoCol
            .ContentType = "DISCRETE"
            .SourceColumn = strFrom & "." & strLQ & _
                "Ring_Type" & strRQ
            .DataType = adWChar
            .IsInput = True
            .IsPredictable = False
            .IsDisabled = False
        End With

        Set dsoCol = dsoDMM.Columns.AddNew("Spore Print Color", _
            sbclsRegular)
        With dsoCol
            .ContentType = "DISCRETE"
            .SourceColumn = strFrom & "." & strLQ & _
                "Spore_Print_Color" & strRQ
            .DataType = adWChar
            .IsInput = True
            .IsPredictable = False
            .IsDisabled = False
        End With

        Set dsoCol = dsoDMM.Columns.AddNew("Population", _
            sbclsRegular)
        With dsoCol
            .ContentType = "DISCRETE"
            .SourceColumn = strFrom & "." & strLQ & _
                "Population" & strRQ
            .DataType = adWChar
            .IsInput = True
            .IsPredictable = False
            .IsDisabled = False
        End With

        Set dsoCol = dsoDMM.Columns.AddNew("Habitat", _
            sbclsRegular)
        With dsoCol
            .ContentType = "DISCRETE"
            .SourceColumn = strFrom & "." & strLQ & _
                "Habitat" & strRQ
            .DataType = adWChar
```

```
    .IsInput = True
    .IsPredictable = False
    .IsDisabled = False
End With

' This is the Predictable column. That way, our mushroom
' users can use the model to find the value of this column.
Set dsoCol = dsoDMM.Columns.AddNew("Edibility", _
    sbclsRegular)
With dsoCol
    .ContentType = "DISCRETE"
    .SourceColumn = strFrom & "." & strLQ & _
        "Edibility" & strRQ
    .DataType = adWChar
    .IsInput = True
    .IsPredictable = True
    .IsDisabled = False
End With

' Save the data-mining model.

With dsoDMM

    ' The LastUpdated property of the data-mining model
    ' needs to be set programmatically - it's not an
    ' automatic function.

    .LastUpdated = Now

    ' Save the metadata of the data-mining model.

    .Update

End With

' Train (process) the data-mining model.

With dsoDMM

    ' The model needs to be locked for processing to occur.

    .LockObject olapLockProcess, _
        "Processing mushroom mining model"

    ' It's normal for this to take a while depending on the
    ' number of cases in the data source and the number
    ' of attributes in the model.

    .Process processFull

    ' Unlock the model after the processing is done.
```

(continued)

```
            .UnlockObject
        End With

        Set dsoRole = Nothing
        Set dsoCol = Nothing
        Set dsoDMM = Nothing

        dsoServer.CloseServer

        Set dsoServer = Nothing

    End Sub
```

Creating the OLAP Data-Mining Model Using DSO

This Visual Basic sample demonstrates the creation and training of a new data-mining model based on an OLAP data source. Initially, it's not much different from the previous example with the relational data source. The columns still must be defined and created in exactly the same way. This example uses the Sales cube in the FoodMart 2000 database.

```
Public Sub newOlapDMM()
    Dim dsoServer As New DSO.Server
    Dim dsoDB As DSO.MDStore
    Dim dsoDMM As DSO.MiningModel
    Dim dsoCol As DSO.Column
    Dim dsoRole As DSO.Role

    ' Constants used for DataType property
    ' of the DSO.Column object.
    ' Notice that these constants are identical to
    ' those used in ADO in the DataTypeEnum enumeration.
    Const adInteger = 3
    Const adWChar = 130

    ' Connect to the server on this computer.
    dsoServer.Connect "dataserver"

    ' Select the FoodMart 2000 database.
    Set dsoDB = dsoServer.MDStores("FoodMart 2000")

    ' Check for the existence of the model on this computer.
    If Not dsoDB.MiningModels("CustSalesModelOLAP") Is Nothing Then
        ' If this model exists, delete it.
        dsoDB.MiningModels.Remove "CustSalesModelOLAP"
    End If

    ' Create a new OLAP mining model
    ' called CustSalesModelOLAP.
    Set dsoDMM = dsoDB.MiningModels.AddNew("CustSalesModelOLAP", _
        sbclsOlap)
```

```
' Create a new mining model role called All Users.
Set dsoRole = dsoDMM.Roles.AddNew("All Users")

' Set the needed properties for the new mining model.
With dsoDMM
    .DataSources.AddNew "FoodMart", sbclsRegular
    ' Set the description of the model.
    .Description = "Analyzes the salaries " & _
        "of customers"
    ' Select the algorithm provider for the model.
    .MiningAlgorithm = "Microsoft_Decision_Trees"
    ' Set the source cube for the model to the Sales cube.
    .SourceCube = "Sales"
    ' Set the case dimension for the model to the
    ' Customers shared dimension.
    .CaseDimension = "Customers"
    ' Let DSO define the training query.
    .TrainingQuery = ""
    ' Let DSO add the cube structure to the
    ' data-mining model structure, automatically
    ' creating needed data-mining model columns.
    .Update
End With

' Set the column properties pertinent to the new model.
' Notice that when columns are automatically added to
' the model in this fashion, they are disabled. You
' must choose which columns are to be enabled
' before you can process the model, and at least
' one column must be enabled, or an error will result.

' Enable the Name column. As this column is the
' lowest enabled level on the Customers case dimension,
' it becomes the case level for the data-mining model.
Set dsoCol = dsoDMM.Columns("Name")
dsoCol.IsDisabled = False

' Enable the Gender column as an Input column.
Set dsoCol = dsoDMM.Columns("Gender")
dsoCol.IsInput = True
dsoCol.IsDisabled = False

' Enable the Marital Status column as an Input column.
Set dsoCol = dsoDMM.Columns("Marital Status")
dsoCol.IsInput = True
dsoCol.IsDisabled = False

' Enable the Education column as an Input column.
Set dsoCol = dsoDMM.Columns("Education")
dsoCol.IsInput = True
dsoCol.IsDisabled = False
```

(continued)

```
' Enable the Unit Sales column as a Predictable column.
Set dsoCol = dsoDMM.Columns("Yearly Income")
dsoCol.IsPredictable = True
dsoCol.IsDisabled = False

' Save the data-mining model.
With dsoDMM
    ' Set the LastUpdated property of the new mining model
    ' to the present date and time.
    .LastUpdated = Now
    ' Save the model definition.
    .Update
End With

' Process the data-mining model.
With dsoDMM
    ' Lock the mining model for processing.
    .LockObject olapLockProcess, _
        "Processing the data-mining model in sample code"
    ' Fully process the new mining model.
    ' This may take up to several minutes.
    .Process processFull
    ' Unlock the model after processing is complete.
    .UnlockObject
End With

' Clean up objects and close server connection.
Set dsoRole = Nothing
Set dsoCol = Nothing
Set dsoDMM = Nothing

dsoServer.CloseServer
Set dsoServer = Nothing

End Sub
```

The *DataSource* Object

The *DataSource object* provides access to the data sources associated with a database, a cube, a partition, an aggregation, or a data-mining model source for case data in SQL Server 2000 Analysis Services, under the *DataSources* collection for each DSO object.

The *DataSource* object is used to

- Retrieve data source–specific information such as connection strings and quote characters for use by client applications.

- Determine various states, such as connection state, of the data source in Analysis Services.

Data-Mining Model (Decision Support Objects)

The *MiningModel* object provides support for data-mining models in Analysis Services. To access data-mining models, the *MiningModels* collection of the DSO *Database* object is used instead of the *MDStores* interface. The *MiningModel* object is used to

- Provide access to data-mining columns for a Relational or OLAP data-mining model.
- Construct and modify Relational or OLAP data-mining models.
- Process a Relational or OLAP data-mining model.
- Provide access to data-mining model roles.

Adding a New Data Source

```
Private Sub newDataSource()
    Dim dsoServer As New DSO.Server
    Dim dsoDB As DSO.MDStore
    Dim dsoDS As DSO.DataSource

    Dim strDBName As String
    Dim strDSName As String
    Dim strDSConnect As String

    ' Initialize variables for the database name,
    ' data source name, and the ConnectionString property
    ' for the data source.
    strDBName = "DataMiner"
    strDSName = "Dataserver"
    strDSConnect = "Provider=MSDASQL.1;User ID=sa;" & _
        "Data Source=dataserver;Connect Timeout=15"

    ' Create a connection to the Analysis server.
    dsoServer.Connect "dataserver"

    ' Locate the database first.
    If dsoServer.MDStores.Find(strDBName) Then
        Set dsoDB = dsoServer.MDStores(strDBName)

        ' Check to see whether the data source already exists.
        If dsoDB.DataSources.Find(strDSName) Then
            MsgBox "Data source " & strDSName & _
                " already exists for database " & strDBName
        Else
            ' Create a new data source.
            Set dsoDS = dsoDB.DataSources.AddNew(strDSName)
            ' Add the ConnectionString properties
            dsoDS.ConnectionString = strDSConnect
            ' Update the data source.
```

(continued)

```
                dsoDS.Update
                ' Inform the user
                MsgBox "Data source " & strDSName & _
                    " has been added to database " & strDBName
            End If
        Else
            MsgBox strDBName & " is missing."
        End If

    End Sub
```

A Word About the Repository and Metadata

You have surely noticed by now that some of the code has an *Update* method to apply changes made to the data-mining model. Where do these changes get stored? The answer for the data-mining model and all other objects in Analysis Services is the Microsoft Repository. The properties of the Analysis server objects, such as the names of the databases, the data sources, and the columns of the mining models are referred to as *metadata*, or data about data. Although a full description of the repository is well beyond the scope of this book, I think it's important to know that the *Microsoft Repository* is a specialized database designed to store metadata in such a way that it can be automatically retrieved and applied to objects when instantiated again.

The repository can be stored in either SQL Server's MSDB database, a Jet database, or even in a structured COM file. In the case of Analysis Services, it's stored in a Jet database in ..\OLAP Services\Bin\msmdrep.mdb. If you want, you can assign SQL Server to be the storage mechanism for the repository database by migrating it to a SQL Server. To do this, right-click on the Analysis server, and choose Migrate Repository from the menu. The wizard will then direct you to take the steps needed to migrate the repository. Because it requires that SQL Server always be running and available when working with Analysis Services, you really should refrain from migrating the repository to the SQL Server unless you expect to be managing 50 or more databases. In that case, SQL Server is a more robust and reliable storage facility for your metadata.

Analysis Server Roles

A *database role* is used to assign rights to objects in a single database while they are connected to it from a client application, and it can map to a Microsoft Windows NT or Windows 2000 user account or group. These apply only to client application use and not to administrative use.

Once the database roles are created, they are assigned to cubes or data-mining models. Each assignment grants access to the cube or mining model and creates a cube or mining model role with the same name as the database role. It's important to notice that the database roles apply only to that database, so for a different database, a new set of roles would need to be defined.

Data-Mining Model Roles

Database roles are first created and then assigned to the data-mining models. Each *database role* grants access to the model and automatically creates a mining model role with the same name as the database role. The database role provides default membership for the mining model role, but users can be added or deleted from the default membership of the mining model role. Any changes to role membership in a mining model role cause the database role of the same name to receive the same changes.

Adding a New Data-Mining Model Role

```
Private Sub newMiningModelRole()
    Dim dsoServer As New DSO.Server
    Dim dsoDB As DSO.MDStore
    Dim dsoDMM As DSO.MiningModel
    Dim dsoRole As DSO.Role

    ' Connect to the local server.

    dsoServer.Connect "dataserver"

    ' Connect to the Mushrooms database.

    Set dsoDB = dsoServer.MDStores.Item("Mushrooms")

    ' Connect to the Mushrooms RDBMS mining model.

    Set dsoDMM = dsoDB.MiningModels("MushroomsRDBMS")

    ' Because the mining model is about to be changed, lock the
    ' mining model.

    dsoDMM.LockObject olapLockProcess, "Adding Mining Model Role"

    ' Create a new mining model role named MushroomRole, based on
    ' the database role named MushroomRole.

    Set dsoRole = dsoDMM.Roles.AddNew("MushroomRole", sbclsRegular)

    ' All of the other properties are propagated, such as the
    ' user list, from the TestRole database role.

    ' Confirm the changes by saving them to the metadata repository.

    dsoDMM.Update

    ' Unlock the mining model.

    dsoDMM.UnlockObject

End Sub
```

Summary

Decision support objects were created to provide an interface for programmers for developing applications that perform administrative tasks with Analysis Services. This functionality is important for all of us who want to automate and schedule administrative tasks such as training data-mining models with new cases or reporting on the status of various data-mining objects. Since DSO covers every object available in Analysis Services, it can even be used to create an application similar to Analysis Manager.

Chapter 10
Understanding Data-Mining Structures

The structure of a data-mining model is designed to be similar to a relational database table. It has tables that contain columns and a certain number of rows. It should come as no surprise, then, that the structure and contents of these tables can be retrieved through a SELECT statement, albeit a derivation of the standard SQL statement. This is important because you can develop third-party applications that access the structure and contents of the nodes in a decision tree model and the clusters of a clustering model. In fact, if you were up to it, you could use the information here to create your own node browser like the one in the Analysis Manager data-mining content browser. As we'll see in Chapter 12, this SQL-like statement also allows us to use the models to make predictions against test data.

The Structure of the Data-Mining Model Case

One of the first things we need to do is understand how the structure of these data-mining models is represented when we query their content. The content we want relates to data-mining models, of course, but also to the individual components that make them up. Therefore, a given data-mining model has a certain number of nodes, each with certain characteristics, such as its name and the rule that describes it. But each node also contains a variable number of instances of each attribute that are the basis for the histogram and the distribution count. This panel is located on the right side of the node browser, which contains the percentage of each kind of attribute in the node.

Data-Mining Models Look Like Tables

In order to make it possible to query the model using conventionally available tools and interfaces, such as ADO with Visual Basic, it was necessary to make these objects available in the form of tables, with columns for the attributes and a row for each node. In some cases, there are logical data relationships such as with the node and the table of probability histograms in that node. To make objects available in this form, one of the columns in the node table contains a reference to a table, rather than a scalar value. This is called a *nested table* because of the way the second table appears to be embedded in the first table.

Using Code to Browse Data-Mining Models

First I'll begin with a short program that connects to a data-mining model and queries the contents of a data-mining model only for the sake of getting the names of the fields in the mushrooms model we created in Chapter 5.

> **Note** For the sake of simplicity and practicality, the code samples used in this chapter use VBScript with Windows Scripting Host (WSH). Windows Scripting Host allows you to run scripts that are similar both to the code you would use in a Visual Basic application and to code you would use in an Active Server Pages (ASP) page. Understanding this code requires you to have at least a rudimentary knowledge of the ADO object model and the VBScript syntax.
>
> If you want to run these samples, download them from *http://msdn.microsoft.com/ scripting*. If you happen to be using Windows 2000 or Windows XP, you don't need to do anything because WSH is already installed on your computer. Once you have WSH installed, you only need to create a text file with a .vbs extension and call it from the command line using the following syntax:
>
> C:\>cscript myfile.vbs

Here's the code:

```
Dim cn
Dim rs
Dim ns

Set cn = wscript.CreateObject("adodb.connection")
Set rs = wscript.CreateObject("adodb.recordset")

cn.Provider = "msolap.2"
cn.ConnectionString = _
    "data source=dataserver;initial catalog=mushrooms"
cn.Open

set rs = _
    cn.Execute ("SELECT * from [mushroom analysis rdbms].content")
```

```
For i = 0 to rs.fields.count -1
    wscript.echo cstr(i+1) & ": " & rs.fields(i).name
Next

rs.Close
cn.Close
```

The output from this program should display the following list of fields:

```
Microsoft (R) Windows Script Host Version 5.1 for Windows
Copyright (C) Microsoft Corporation 1996-1999.
All rights reserved.

1: MODEL_CATALOG
2: MODEL_SCHEMA
3: MODEL_NAME
4: ATTRIBUTE_NAME
5: NODE_NAME
6: NODE_UNIQUE_NAME
7: NODE_TYPE
8: NODE_GUID
9: NODE_CAPTION
10: CHILDREN_CARDINALITY
11: PARENT_UNIQUE_NAME
12: NODE_DESCRIPTION
13: NODE_RULE
14: MARGINAL_RULE
15: NODE_PROBABILITY
16: MARGINAL_PROBABILITY
17: NODE_DISTRIBUTION
18: NODE_SUPPORT
19: MSOLAP_MODEL_COLUMN
20: MSOLAP_NODE_SCORE
21: MSOLAP_NODE_SHORT_CAPTION
```

Note that in order to get this list, I used standard ADO with a connection string that specifies MSOLAP as the provider. Other than the choice of providers, the connection and the recordset operations are exactly the same as any ordinary ADO program using SQL Server as the provider.

Note The results of this query will be sorted by the following fields by default:

MODEL_CATALOG
MODEL_SCHEMA
MODEL_NAME
ATTRIBUTE_NAME

The query used is very close to standard Ansi-SQL except for the object of the FROM clause. This clause is [*data mining model*].*content*. The .content specifies that I'm not making a prediction query, but that I'm specifically querying the contents of the mining model in order to browse them. The purpose of each column is discussed in the "MINING_MODELS Schema Rowset" section later in this chapter.

The following program will display all the nodes in the data-mining model. It also shows a representative number of attributes.

```
Dim cn
Dim rs
Dim ns
Dim tmpVal

Set cn = wscript.CreateObject("adodb.connection")
Set rs = wscript.CreateObject("adodb.recordset")
Set ns = wscript.CreateObject("adodb.recordset")

cn.Provider = "msolap.2"
cn.ConnectionString = _
    "data source=dataserver;initial catalog=mushrooms"
cn.Open

set rs = _
    cn.Execute ("SELECT * from [mushroom analysis rdbms].content")
While Not rs.EOF
    For i = 0 to rs.fields.count -1

        ' This field is a nested table that can't be output to the
        ' screen like an ordinary scalar value; therefore, a label
        ' is placed there instead, knowing that there's code a few
        ' lines down, which is designed to list the contents of
        ' this nested table.
        If rs.fields(i).name = "NODE_DISTRIBUTION" Then
            tmpVal = "NESTED TABLE"
        Else
            tmpVal = rs.fields(i).value
        End If

        wscript.echo cstr(i+1) &": "& rs.fields(i).name & _
            " - " & tmpVal

        ' This is a nested table that contains the distribution
        ' histogram of that node for the predictive value.
        If rs.fields(i).name = "NODE_DISTRIBUTION" Then
```

```
' This column actually contains a recordset object!
set ns = rs.fields("node_distribution").value
wscript.echo
While not (ns.eof)

    For j = 0 To ns.Fields.Count - 1
        wscript.echo "        " & _
            ns.Fields(j).name & _
            " "& ns.Fields(j).Value
    Next

    wscript.echo "        ********"
    ns.movenext

Wend
End If

Next
rs.Movenext
wscript.echo "-----------"
Wend
rs.Close
cn.Close
```

Here is a partial listing from the program's output that shows a representative number of attributes. Note the values in the fields:

```
 ⋮
1: MODEL_CATALOG - Mushrooms
2: MODEL_SCHEMA -
3: MODEL_NAME - mushroom analysis rdbms
4: ATTRIBUTE_NAME - Edibility
5: NODE_NAME - 012147483669
6: NODE_UNIQUE_NAME - 012147483669
7: NODE_TYPE - 3
8: NODE_GUID -
9: NODE_CAPTION - Odor = none
10: CHILDREN_CARDINALITY - 2
11: PARENT_UNIQUE_NAME - 2147483669
12: NODE_DESCRIPTION - Odor = none
13: NODE_RULE - <predicate op = "eq" value = "none">
<simple-attribute name = "Odor"/>
</predicate>

14: MARGINAL_RULE - <predicate op = "eq" value = "none">
<simple-attribute name = "Odor"/>
</predicate>
```

(continued)

```
15: NODE_PROBABILITY - 0.434268833087149
16: MARGINAL_PROBABILITY - 0.434268833087149
17: NODE_DISTRIBUTION - NESTED TABLE

     ATTRIBUTE_NAME Edibility
     ATTRIBUTE_VALUE missing
     SUPPORT 0
     PROBABILITY 0.00283205890682526
     VARIANCE 0
     VALUETYPE 1
     ********
     ATTRIBUTE_NAME Edibility
     ATTRIBUTE_VALUE edible
     SUPPORT 3408
     PROBABILITY 0.965448881336732
     VARIANCE 0
     VALUETYPE 4
     ********
     ATTRIBUTE_NAME Edibility
     ATTRIBUTE_VALUE poisonous
     SUPPORT 120
     PROBABILITY 0.0342679127725857
     VARIANCE 0
     VALUETYPE 4
     ********
18: NODE_SUPPORT - 3528
19: MSOLAP_MODEL_COLUMN - Edibility
20: MSOLAP_NODE_SCORE - 262.639862428876
21: MSOLAP_NODE_SHORT_CAPTION - Odor = none
  ⋮
```

The NODE_DISTRIBUTION column contains the distribution histogram nested table with the following fields as you can see from the previous listing.

- **ATTRIBUTE_NAME**   Name of the attribute.
- **ATTRIBUTE_VALUE**   The attribute value represented as a variant.
- **SUPPORT**   The number of cases that support this attribute value.
- **PROBABILITY**   Probability of occurrence of this attribute value.
- **VARIANCE**   Variance of this attribute value.
- **VALUETYPE**   The value type of the attribute. It can be one of the following values that describes the type of attribute that is contained in that column.
  - **VALUETYPE_MISSING = 1**   Missing values, which can occur with cases having incomplete information.
  - **VALUETYPE_EXISTING =**   The value exists and does not fall in categories 3 to 6. This occurs with values that are already discrete.

- **VALUETYPE_CONTINUOUS = 3**   Numerical data that has a sequence, such as time, age, or distance.

- **VALUETYPE_DISCRETE = 4**   Values that have a finite number, such as colors or shapes. In the example above, there are only two discrete values: "Yes" and "No."

- **VALUETYPE_DISCRETIZED = 5**   Numerical values, such as prices that cannot be dealt with unless they are artificially placed in a bin or discrete type. An attribute that contains a wide range of prices or weights, for example, will likely be discretized, or converted to a discrete type by classifying the prices according to four or five price or weight nodes.

- **VALUETYPE_BOOLEAN = 6**   True or False (0 or 1) values.

Using the Schema Rowsets

Another more effective way to retrieve data about data mining is to use the ADO *OpenSchema* method to retrieve the metadata about the data-mining models within Analysis Services. Because the schema type has not been defined yet, the adSchema-ProviderSpecific type needs to be used along with the GUID value of the type of metadata you need to retrieve. Here's the syntax:

```
Connection.OpenSchema(adSchemaProviderSpecific, _
    array(restrictions), guid)
```

MINING_MODELS Schema Rowset

This schema rowset describes all the data-mining models present within the database. The order of the results is sorted by

- MODEL_CATALOG
- MODEL_SCHEMA
- MODEL_NAME

Available restriction keys are

- MODEL_CATALOG
- MODEL_SCHEMA
- MODEL_NAME
- MODEL_TYPE
- SERVICE_NAME
- SERVICE_TYPE_ID

The column names are as follows:

- **MODEL_CATALOG**   Name of the database that contains the data-mining model.
- **MODEL_SCHEMA**   Schema name. Most often it's NULL unless the provider supplies or supports the use of schema names.
- **MODEL_NAME**   Name of the data-mining model.
- **MODEL_TYPE**   Model type, a provider-specific string usually containing NULL.
- **SERVICE_NAME**   A provider-specific name that describes the algorithm used to generate the model.
- **MODEL_GUID**   Unique identifier of the model used internally by Analysis Services. It serves as the unique GUID value for that model.
- **DESCRIPTION**   Description of the model, if one was specified at creation time.
- **MODEL_PROPID**   Property ID of the model. Usually NULL because data-mining models do not make use of this value.
- **DATE_CREATED**   Date when the model was created.
- **DATE_MODIFIED**   Date when the model definition was last modified.
- **CREATION_STATEMENT**   This is the creation statement used to build the data-mining model.
- **PREDICTION_ENTITY**   A comma-delimited list indicating which columns the model can predict.
- **SERVICE_TYPE_ID**   A bitmask that serves as the ID for the algorithm used to build the model. Even though the first two algorithms are the only ones currently supported, the other values were already added to provide support for possible future implementations. Any new third-party algorithms that get added to Analysis Services will require that a field be added in Table 10-1.

Table 10-1. Service Type IDs

DM_SERVICETYPE_CLASSIFICATION	0x0000001
DM_SERVICETYPE_CLUSTERING	0x0000002
DM_SERVICETYPE_ASSOCIATION	0x0000004
DM_SERVICETYPE_DENSITY_ESTIMATE	0x0000008
DM_SERVICETYPE_SEQUENCE	0x0000010

- **IS_POPULATED**   Boolean VARIANT_TRUE if the model is populated; VARIANT_FALSE if the model is not populated as would be the case in an empty model with a defined structure that has not been trained with data.

A restriction column serves as a filter to limit the types of rows that get returned. This gets defined as an array placed as a second parameter. For example:

```
connection.OpenSchema(adSchemaProviderSpecific,_
    Array(EMPTY,EMPTY,EMPTY,"Microsoft_Decision_Trees"),_
    DMSCHEMA_MINING_MODELS)
```

This restriction would limit the rows to those models that were created using decision trees.

To retrieve information about all the data-mining models in my Mushrooms database with the structure of Table 10-1, you can use the following program:

```
dim cn
dim rs


Set cn = wscript.CreateObject("adodb.connection")
set rs = wscript.CreateObject("adodb.recordset")


cn.Provider = "msolap.2"
cn.ConnectionString = _
    "data source=dataserver;initial catalog=mushrooms"
cn.Open


Const DMSCHEMA_MINING_MODELS = _
    "{3add8a77-d8b9-11d2-8d2a-00e029154fde}"
Const adSchemaProviderSpecific = -1


Set rs = cn.OpenSchema(adSchemaProviderSpecific, _
    ,DMSCHEMA_MINING_MODELS)


while rs.eof = 0

    For j = 0 To rs.fields.count - 1
        wscript.echo CStr(j+1) & ": " &_
            rs.fields(j).name & " - " & rs.fields(j).value
    Next
    wscript.echo "*******************"
    rs.movenext
wend
```

This program will generate the following output:

```
Microsoft (R) Windows Script Host Version 5.1 for Windows
Copyright (C) Microsoft Corporation 1996-1999.
All rights reserved.

1: MODEL_CATALOG - Mushrooms
2: MODEL_SCHEMA -
3: MODEL_NAME - Census cluster
4: MODEL_TYPE -
5: MODEL_GUID - {902FB4D2-EA1F-4E06-A2F4-AA6D9B5427BA}
6: DESCRIPTION -
7: MODEL_PROPID -
8: DATE_CREATED - 12/17/2000 1:52:35 PM
9: DATE_MODIFIED - 12/17/2000 2:05:10 PM
10: SERVICE_TYPE_ID - 2
11: SERVICE_NAME - Microsoft_Clustering
12: CREATION_STATEMENT - CREATE MINING MODEL [Census cluster'S]
  ([Id] TEXT    KEY  , [Age] LONG    DISCRETIZED() PREDICT, [Workclass]
  TEXT    DISCRETE  PREDICT, [Fnlwgt] TEXT    DISCRETE  PREDICT,
  [Education] TEXT    DISCRETE  PREDICT, [Education num] LONG
  CONTINUOUS  PREDICT, [Marital status] TEXT    DISCRETE  PREDICT,
  [Occupation] TEXT    DISCRETE  PREDICT, [Relationship] TEXT    DISCRETE
  PREDICT, [Race] TEXT    DISCRETE  PREDICT, [Sex] TEXT    DISCRETE
  PREDICT, [Capital gain] DOUBLE    CONTINUOUS  PREDICT,
  [Capital loss] DOUBLE    CONTINUOUS  PREDICT, [Hours per week]
  LONG    CONTINUOUS  PREDICT, [Native country] TEXT    DISCRETE
  PREDICT, [Class] TEXT    DISCRETE  PREDICT) USING
  Microsoft_Clustering
13: PREDICTION_ENTITY - Age,Workclass,Fnlwgt,Education,
  Education num,Marital status,Occupation,Relationship,Race,
  Sex,Capital gain,Capital loss,Hours per week,Native country,
  Class
14: IS_POPULATED - True
15: MSOLAP_MODEL_SOURCE -
********************
1: MODEL_CATALOG - Mushrooms
2: MODEL_SCHEMA -
3: MODEL_NAME - census
```

```
 4: MODEL_TYPE - OLAP
 5: MODEL_GUID - {11F7DA3B-365D-4CC4-97D3-991DA8FEE188}
 6: DESCRIPTION -
 7: MODEL_PROPID -
 8: DATE_CREATED - 12/14/2000 2:57:14 AM
 9: DATE_MODIFIED - 12/14/2000 2:57:17 AM
10: SERVICE_TYPE_ID - 1
11: SERVICE_NAME - Microsoft_Decision_Trees
12: CREATION_STATEMENT - CREATE OLAP MINING MODEL [census'S]
 FROM [Census] (CASE DIMENSION [Occupation] LEVEL [Workclass]  ,
 LEVEL [Occupation]  , DIMENSION [Relationship]
 LEVEL [Relationship]  , DIMENSION [Class] PREDICT LEVEL [(All)]
 , LEVEL [Class]  , DIMENSION [Country]  LEVEL [Native country]
 , DIMENSION [race]  LEVEL [Race]  , DIMENSION [Education]
 LEVEL [Education]  , LEVEL [Educationnum]  ,
 DIMENSION [Hours per week]  LEVEL [Hours per week]  ,
 MEASURE [Capital gain] , MEASURE [Capital loss] )
 USING Microsoft_Decision_Trees
13: PREDICTION_ENTITY - Class,Class.Class.Class
14: IS_POPULATED - True
15: MSOLAP_MODEL_SOURCE - Census
********************
 1: MODEL_CATALOG - Mushrooms
 2: MODEL_SCHEMA -
 3: MODEL_NAME - CensusCluster
 4: MODEL_TYPE -
 5: MODEL_GUID - {8A626ECD-46CB-47BF-9C4C-8B9F9A4F02E6}
 6: DESCRIPTION -
 7: MODEL_PROPID -
 8: DATE_CREATED - 12/25/2000 2:18:37 PM
 9: DATE_MODIFIED - 12/25/2000 2:29:37 PM
10: SERVICE_TYPE_ID - 2
11: SERVICE_NAME - Microsoft_Clustering
12: CREATION_STATEMENT - CREATE MINING MODEL [CensusCluster'S]
 ([Id] TEXT   KEY  , [Age] LONG   CONTINUOUS  PREDICT, [Workclass]
 TEXT   DISCRETE  PREDICT, [Fnlwgt] TEXT   DISCRETE  PREDICT,
 [Education] TEXT   DISCRETE  PREDICT, [Education num] LONG
```

(continued)

CONTINUOUS PREDICT, [Marital status] TEXT   DISCRETE PREDICT,
[Occupation] TEXT   DISCRETE PREDICT, [Relationship] TEXT
DISCRETE PREDICT, [Race] TEXT   DISCRETE PREDICT, [Sex] TEXT
DISCRETE PREDICT, [Capital gain] DOUBLE   CONTINUOUS PREDICT,
[Capital loss] DOUBLE   CONTINUOUS PREDICT, [Hours per week]
LONG   CONTINUOUS PREDICT, [Native country] TEXT   DISCRETE
PREDICT, [Class] TEXT   DISCRETE PREDICT) USING
Microsoft_Clustering
13: PREDICTION_ENTITY - Age,Workclass,Fnlwgt,Education,Education
num,Marital status,Occupation,Relationship,Race,Sex,
Capital gain,Capital loss,Hours per week,Native country,Class
14: IS_POPULATED - True
15: MSOLAP_MODEL_SOURCE -
****
1: MODEL_CATALOG - Mushrooms
2: MODEL_SCHEMA -
3: MODEL_NAME - Mushroom Analysis RDBMS
4: MODEL_TYPE -
5: MODEL_GUID - {499D525B-13EC-4B4C-918F-F75E73E01AC4}
6: DESCRIPTION -
7: MODEL_PROPID -
8: DATE_CREATED - 1/29/2001 10:45:25 PM
9: DATE_MODIFIED - 1/29/2001 10:45:33 PM
10: SERVICE_TYPE_ID - 1
11: SERVICE_NAME - Microsoft_Decision_Trees
12: CREATION_STATEMENT - CREATE MINING MODEL
 [Mushroom Analysis RDBMS'S] ([Id] LONG   KEY , [Cap Shape]
 TEXT   DISCRETE , [Cap Surface] TEXT   DISCRETE , [Cap Color]
 TEXT   DISCRETE , [Bruises] TEXT   DISCRETE , [Odor] TEXT
 DISCRETE , [Gill Attachment] TEXT   DISCRETE , [Gill Spacing]
 TEXT   DISCRETE , [Gill Size] TEXT   DISCRETE , [Gill Color]
 TEXT   DISCRETE , [Stalk Shape] TEXT   DISCRETE , [Stalk Root]
 TEXT   DISCRETE , [Stalk Surface Above Ring] TEXT   DISCRETE ,
 [Stalk Surface Below Ring] TEXT   DISCRETE ,
 [Stalk Color Above Ring] TEXT   DISCRETE ,
 [Stalk Color Below Ring] TEXT   DISCRETE , [Veil Type] TEXT
 DISCRETE , [Veil Color] TEXT   DISCRETE , [Ring Number] TEXT
 DISCRETE , [Ring Type] TEXT   DISCRETE , [Spore Print Color]
 TEXT   DISCRETE , [Population] TEXT   DISCRETE , [Edibility]
 TEXT   DISCRETE PREDICT, [Habitat] TEXT   DISCRETE PREDICT)
 USING Microsoft_Decision_Trees

```
13: PREDICTION_ENTITY - Edibility,Habitat
14: IS_POPULATED - True
15: MSOLAP_MODEL_SOURCE -
*********************
1: MODEL_CATALOG - Mushrooms
2: MODEL_SCHEMA -
3: MODEL_NAME - Mushrooms Cluster
4: MODEL_TYPE -
5: MODEL_GUID - {074F9AE0-D0DE-4925-A231-21265E564F9B}
6: DESCRIPTION -
7: MODEL_PROPID -
8: DATE_CREATED - 12/17/2000 12:48:19 PM
9: DATE_MODIFIED - 12/17/2000 12:48:57 PM
10: SERVICE_TYPE_ID - 2
11: SERVICE_NAME - Microsoft_Clustering
12: CREATION_STATEMENT - CREATE MINING MODEL
 [Mushrooms Cluster'S] ([Id] TEXT    KEY  , [Edibility]
 TEXT    DISCRETE  PREDICT_ONLY, [Cap Shape] TEXT    DISCRETE  ,
 [Cap Surface] TEXT    DISCRETE  , [Cap Color] TEXT    DISCRETE  ,
 [Bruises] TEXT    DISCRETE  , [Odor] TEXT    DISCRETE  ,
 [Gill Attachment] TEXT    DISCRETE  , [Gill Spacing] TEXT
 DISCRETE  , [Gill Size] TEXT    DISCRETE  , [Gill Color] TEXT
 DISCRETE  , [Stalk Shape] TEXT    DISCRETE  , [Stalk Root] TEXT
 DISCRETE  , [Stalk Surface Above Ring] TEXT    DISCRETE  ,
 [Stalk Surface Below Ring] TEXT    DISCRETE  ,
 [Stalk Color Above Ring] TEXT    DISCRETE  ,
 [Stalk Color Below Ring] TEXT    DISCRETE  , [Veil Type] TEXT
 DISCRETE  , [Veil Color] TEXT    DISCRETE  , [Ring Number] TEXT
 DISCRETE  , [Ring Type] TEXT    DISCRETE  , [Spore Print Color]
 TEXT    DISCRETE  , [Population] TEXT    DISCRETE  , [Habitat]
 TEXT    DISCRETE  ) USING Microsoft_Clustering (CLUSTER_COUNT=6)
13: PREDICTION_ENTITY - Edibility
14: IS_POPULATED - True
15: MSOLAP_MODEL_SOURCE -
*********************
```

MINING_COLUMNS Schema Rowset

The MINING_COLUMNS schema rowset describes the individual columns of all defined
data-mining models known to the provider. This schema rowset can be viewed as an
enhanced form of the COLUMNS rowset for data-mining models. Many of the entries are
derived from the COLUMNS schema rowset and are optional.

The columns are sorted in the following order:

- MODEL_CATALOG
- MODEL_SCHEMA
- MODEL_NAME
- COLUMN_NAME

The available restriction columns are:

- MODEL_CATALOG
- MODEL_SCHEMA
- MODEL_NAME
- COLUMN_NAME

The column names are as follows:

- **MODEL_CATALOG**   Catalog name. NULL if the provider does not support catalogs. In the case of Microsoft Data Mining, it refers to the name of the database that contains the mining model.
- **MODEL_SCHEMA**   Unqualified schema name. NULL if the provider does not support schemas.
- **MODEL_NAME**   Mining model name. This column is a required field.
- **COLUMN_NAME**   The name of the column; this might not be unique. If this cannot be determined, a NULL is returned.

   By itself, this column is not enough to uniquely identify a column. For that you need to use a combination of the COLUMN_GUID and COLUMN_PROPID, which then becomes the ID of the column. Since one of the columns is always NULL, combining the two ensures that you will reference a GUID that serves as a unique key.
- **COLUMN_GUID**   Providers that do not use GUIDs to identify columns should eturn NULL in this column.
- **COLUMN_PROPID**   Providers that do not associate PROPIDs with columns should return NULL in this column.
- **ORDINAL_POSITION**   The ordinal of the column. Columns are numbered starting from one. The value will be NULL if there is a way to apply a numerical value to the order of the column.

- **COLUMN_HASDEFAULT**

    - **VARIANT_TRUE**   The column has a default value.

    - **VARIANT_FALSE**   The column does not have a default value, or it is unknown whether the column has a default value.

- **COLUMN_DEFAULT**   Default value of the column. If the default value is the NULL value, COLUMN_HASDEFAULT is VARIANT_TRUE and the COLUMN_DEFAULT column is a NULL value.

- **COLUMN_FLAGS**   A bitmask that describes column characteristics. The DBCOLUMNFLAGS enumerated type specifies the bits in the bitmask. This column cannot contain a NULL value.

- **IS_NULLABLE**

    - **VARIANT_TRUE**   The column might be nullable.

    - **VARIANT_FALSE**   The column is known not to be nullable.

- **DATA_TYPE**   The indicator of the column's data type. Table 10-2 is an example.

Table 10-2. Column Data Types

"TABLE"	DBTYPE_HCHAPTER
"TEXT"	DBTYPE_WCHAR
"LONG"	DBTYPE_I8
"DOUBLE"	DBTYPE_R8
"DATE"	DBTYPE_DATE

- **TYPE_GUID**   The GUID of the column's data type. Providers that do not use GUIDs to identify data types should return NULL in this column.

- **CHARACTER_MAXIMUM_LENGTH**   The maximum possible length of a value in the column. For character, binary, or bit columns, this is one of the following:

    - The maximum length of the column in characters, bytes, or bits, respectively, if the length is defined. For example, a CHAR (5) column in an SQL table has a maximum length of 5.

    - The maximum length of the data type in characters, bytes, or bits, respectively, if the column does not have a defined length.

    - Zero (0) if neither the column nor the data type has a defined maximum length.

    - NULL for all other types of columns.

- **CHARACTER_OCTET_LENGTH** Maximum length in octets (bytes) of the column if the type of the column is character or binary. A value of zero means the column has no maximum length. NULL for all other types of columns.
- **NUMERIC_PRECISION** If the column's data type is of a numeric data type other than VARNUMERIC, this is the maximum precision of the column. The precision of columns with a data type of DBTYPE_DECIMAL or DBTYPE_NUMERIC depends on the definition of the column. If the column's data type is not numeric or is VARNUMERIC, this is NULL.
- **NUMERIC_SCALE** If the column's type indicator is DBTYPE_DECIMAL, DBTYPE_NUMERIC, or DBTYPE_VARNUMERIC, this is the number of digits to the right of the decimal point. Otherwise, this is NULL.
- **DATETIME_PRECISION** Datetime precision (number of digits in the fractional seconds portion) of the column if the column is a datetime or interval type. If the column's data type is not datetime, this is NULL.
- **CHARACTER_SET_CATALOG** Catalog name in which the character set is defined. NULL if the provider does not support catalogs or different character sets.
- **CHARACTER_SET_SCHEMA** Unqualified schema name in which the character set is defined. NULL if the provider does not support schemas or different character sets.
- **CHARACTER_SET_NAME** Character set name. NULL if the provider does not support different character sets.
- **COLLATION_CATALOG** Catalog name in which the collation is defined. NULL if the provider does not support catalogs or different collations.
- **COLLATION_SCHEMA** Unqualified schema name in which the collation is defined. NULL if the provider does not support schemas or different collations.
- **COLLATION_NAME** Collation name. NULL if the provider does not support different collations.
- **DOMAIN_CATALOG** Catalog name in which the domain is defined. NULL if the provider does not support catalogs or domains.
- **DOMAIN_SCHEMA** Unqualified schema name in which the domain is defined. NULL if the provider does not support schemas or domains.
- **DOMAIN_NAME** Domain name. NULL if the provider does not support domains.
- **DESCRIPTION** Human-readable description of the column. For example, the description for a column named Name in the Employee table might be "Employee name." NULL if there is no description associated with the column.

- **DISTRIBUTION_FLAG**   Table 10-3 is a list of DISTRIBUTION_FLAGs.

Table 10-3. DISTRIBUTION_FLAG Values

NORMAL	Distribution of data in which a majority of the continuous values are in the middle of the distribution curve, with a relatively equal number of variances in the high and low end. (See "Distribution Types" sidebar.)
LOG_NORMAL	The distribution of continuous data suggests that there are a majority of values on the high end with a lower number of continuous variables skewed toward one end of the curve (high or low end).
UNIFORM	All the values are the same.
BINOMIAL	The values in the distribution curve are distributed among two possibilities only, such as a Boolean true-false value or, as in our case "Yes" or "No", to designate edibility.
MULTINOMIAL	Distribution of data among a fixed number of variables, usually from a discrete set.
POISSON	Distribution used when there is a limited number of variables, perhaps even only two, but where the case count is high and the probability of one occurring and opposed to the other is extremely skewed.
HEAVYTAIL (also known as Pareto)	This is the source of the "80-20 rule" where 80 percent of a given activity can be explained by 20 percent of the factors. The key is to zero in on those 20 percent of the factors.
MIXTURE	This concerns modeling a statistical distribution by a weighted sum of other distributions. It forms the basis for clustering.

Provider-specific flags may also be defined.

- **CONTENT_TYPE**   Table 10-4 is a list of CONTENT_TYPEs.

Table 10-4. CONTENT_TYPE Values

KEY	This denotes a discrete key value used to identify the case. This value actually never gets used for aiding in predictions. It simply helps Analysis Services keep track of cases internally. It's also useful if an operator seeks to tie cases together with the original data source for debugging purposes.
DISCRETE	Contains a discrete set of values, such as the edibility or the color values. The values are finite in number and have no relationship to each other.
CONTINUOUS	Contains a numerical value that has quantitative meaning such as age or weight. In addition, the values have measurable differences between them that have value so that one age is measurably higher or lower than another age.

(continued)

Table 10-4. *(continued)*

DISCRETIZED([value])	A set of values, usually numbers, that are converted over to a smaller number of discrete values because the algorithm is unable to use them as inputs or prediction fields. To be able to analyze them, the values are converted to discrete values for the sake of training the model.
	There are four possible parameters that can be provided to this function to direct this process:
	• **AUTOMATIC** The default method for the algorithm is chosen.
	• **EQUAL_AREAS** Tries to create bins of data that contain equal numbers of values in each. This works well when there are many different types of values with relatively even counts in each. In a situation where there are small numbers of different types of values and high numbers favored for any one type, the results may be questionable. This is designed for data that fits in a normal distribution curve.
	• **THRESHOLDS** Looks for data that has high levels of distinctive values as compared to other values in the group. This shows up as inflection points on a distribution curve. This generally is used for continuous data with irregular high and low values.
	• **CLUSTERS** Applies an algorithm very similar to the clustering algorithm used in building a data-mining model. Because of the complexity of the algorithm, the processing takes longer, but the results tend to be better since the algorithm can adapt to any distribution curve.
ORDERED	Contains a set of values that have a hierarchical value relationship to each other. Examples include tax brackets or earning levels. There is a rank associated to their value but unlike age, for example, there is no relative values between those levels.
SEQUENCE_TIME	The column contains time-related values that have a sequential relationship to each other, such as dates and years.
CYCLICAL	These are discrete, but ordered, values that have to repeat themselves in a cyclical fashion, such as the months of the year or the days of the week. Functionally, these values act as both discrete and ordered values at the same time.
PROBABILITY	This is the probability of this value occurring in a node. It's expressed as a decimal between 0 and 1.
VARIANCE	The statistical variance of the associated value in this column.
STDEV	The standard deviation of the associated value in this column.
SUPPORT	The number of occurrences of this value in the node.
PROBABILITY_VARIANCE	The statistical variance of the probability of the associated value in this column. This is not yet supported by Analysis Services.
PROBABILITY_STDEV	The standard deviation of the probability of the associated value in this column. This is not yet supported by Analysis Services.
ORDER	Used to order the columns in this table. This is the order in which this row is placed.

Distribution Types

When we work with continuous data, such as used automobile prices, we see three types of statistical distribution—*normal, log_normal,* and *uniform.* For example, if you were to sample the prices of the cars in a large used car lot, assuming the cars are of basically the same type and mileage, you would expect to find a few very cheaply priced cars because they have unusually high mileage or a few dents, and you would also expect to find a few very expensive cars because they were only driven by the proverbial "little old lady who only drove the car on Sundays to church." Generally, the bulk of the cars in the lot will fall within a similar price range, give or take a few hundred dollars. Graphing the prices of these cars shows a normal distribution curve that should look something like the one shown here.

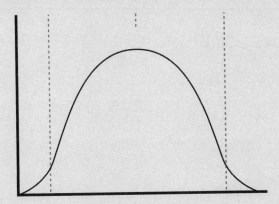

Normal distribution curve.

If this were an atypical car lot with average priced cars and a few cheap ones, you could draw a log_normal curve like the one shown here.

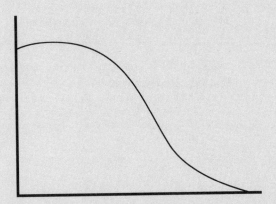

Log_Normal distribution curve.

If by chance all the cars were priced exactly the same, the curve would be uniform like this one.

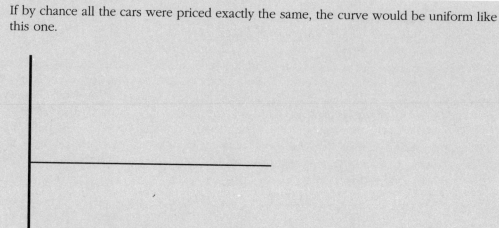

Uniform distribution curve.

Provider-specific flags may also be defined. Those listed here provide additional information or hints that Analysis Services uses to build the model.

- **MODELING_FLAG** A comma-delimited list of flags. The defined flags are listed and defined in Table 10-5.

Table 10-5. MODELING_FLAG Values

MODEL_EXISTENCE_ONLY	Denotes that a column is important not because of the value that it contains, but because a value exists at all. It can be more important to know that a mushroom has a value for "Spore Color", rather than the value itself, because the fact that the mushroom has spores is an important predictor of edibility.
NOT_NULL	This column must have a value. The absence of a value is considered an anomaly.
IGNORE_NULL	If a column contains a null value, it won't provide any statistical information about the model.
NULL_INFORMATIVE	Null values are counted, but considered missing. The fact that the value is null can have high significance. Consider data-mining ballots—missing values are important in that they signify a refusal to vote or even a miscount.

Provider-specific flags may also be defined.

- **IS_RELATED_TO_KEY**   VARIANT_TRUE if this column is related to the key. If the key is a single column, the RELATED_ATTRIBUTE field optionally may contain its column name.

- **RELATED_ATTRIBUTE**   The name of the target column that the current column either relates to or is a special property of.

- **IS_INPUT**   VARIANT_TRUE if this is an input column.

- **IS_PREDICTABLE**   VARIANT_TRUE if the column is predictable.

- **CONTAINING_COLUMN**   Name of the TABLE column containing this column. NULL if any table does not contain the column.

- **PREDICTION_SCALAR_FUNCTIONS**   A comma-delimited list of scalar functions that may be performed on the column. The functions will be discussed in Chapter 12, where we'll look at how to make predictions with code.

- **PREDICTION_TABLE_FUNCTIONS**   A comma-delimited list of functions that may be applied to the column, returning a table. The list has the following format:

  <function name>(<column1> [, *<column2>*], ...)

  The format allows the client to determine which columns will be present in the table returned by any given function.

- **IS_POPULATED**   VARIANT_TRUE if the column has learned a set of possible values and VARIANT_FALSE if the column is not populated.

- **PREDICTION_SCORE**   The score of the model on the predicting column. Score is used to measure the accuracy of a model as it relates to the value to be predicted. The higher the number, the more accurate this prediction will be. This function forms part of the OLEDB specification for data mining, but is not yet implemented in Analysis Services.

  ```
      ⋮
  Const DMSCHEMA_MINING_COLUMNS = _
          "{3add8a78-d8b9-11d2-8d2a-00e029154fde}"
  Const adSchemaProviderSpecific = -1

  Set rs = cn.OpenSchema(adSchemaProviderSpecific,_
          array(empty,empty,"mushroom analysis rdbms","edibility"),_
          DMSCHEMA_MINING_COLUMNS)
  ```

  (continued)

...

Microsoft (R) Windows Script Host Version 5.1 for Windows
Copyright (C) Microsoft Corporation 1996-1999.
All rights reserved.

```
 1: MODEL_CATALOG - Mushrooms
 2: MODEL_SCHEMA -
 3: MODEL_NAME - mushroom analysis rdbms
 4: COLUMN_NAME - Edibility
 5: COLUMN_GUID -
 6: COLUMN_PROPID -
 7: ORDINAL_POSITION - 23
 8: COLUMN_HAS_DEFAULT - False
 9: COLUMN_DEFAULT -
10: COLUMN_FLAGS - 0
11: IS_NULLABLE - True
12: DATA_TYPE - 130
13: TYPE_GUID -
14: CHARACTER_MAXIMUM_LENGTH - 0
15: CHARACTER_OCTET_LENGTH - 0
16: NUMERIC_PRECISION -
17: NUMERIC_SCALE -
18: DATETIME_PRECISION -
19: CHARACTER_SET_CATALOG -
20: CHARACTER_SET_SCHEMA -
21: CHARACTER_SET_NAME -
22: COLLATION_CATALOG -
23: COLLATION_SCHEMA -
24: COLLATION_NAME -
25: DOMAIN_CATALOG -
26: DOMAIN_SCHEMA -
27: DOMAIN_NAME -
28: DESCRIPTION -
29: DISTRIBUTION_FLAG - NONE
30: CONTENT_TYPE - DISCRETE
31: MODELING_FLAG -
32: IS_RELATED_TO_KEY - False
33: RELATED_ATTRIBUTE -
34: IS_INPUT - True
```

```
35: IS_PREDICTABLE - True
36: CONTAINING_COLUMN -
37: PREDICTION_SCALAR_FUNCTIONS -Predict,PredictAdjustedProbability,
 PredictProbability,PredictScore,PredictStddev,PredictStdev,
 PredictSupport,PredictVariance
38: PREDICTION_TABLE_FUNCTIONS - PredictHistogram
39: IS_POPULATED - True
40: PREDICTION_SCORE - 0
```

MINING_MODEL_CONTENT Schema Rowset

This schema rowset allows browsing of the content of a data-mining model. The user can employ special tree-operation restrictions to navigate the contents in a manner that facilitates the creation of a decision tree graph or a cluster graph.

The results are ordered by the following fields by default:

- MODEL_CATALOG
- MODEL_SCHEMA
- MODEL_NAME
- ATTRIBUTE_NAME

The following are the available restriction columns:

- MODEL_CATALOG
- MODEL_SCHEMA
- MODEL_NAME
- ATTRIBUTE_NAME
- NODE_NAME
- NODE_UNIQUE_NAME
- NODE_TYPE
- NODE_GUID
- NODE_CAPTION

There is an additional restriction called the *tree operation* that isn't on any particular column of the MINING_MODEL_CONTENT rowset; rather, it specifies a tree operator. The idea is that the application specified a NODE_UNIQUE_NAME restriction and the tree operator (ANCESTORS, CHILDREN, SIBLINGS, PARENT, DESCENDANTS, SELF) to obtain the desired set of members. The SELF operator includes the row for the node itself in the list of returned rows. The following constants are defined in Table 10-6.

Table 10-6. NODE_UNIQUE_NAME Restrictions

DMTREEOP_ANCESTORS	0x00000020
DMTREEOP_CHILDREN	0x00000001
DMTREEOP_SIBLINGS	0x00000002
DMTREEOP_PARENT	0x00000004
DMTREEOP_SELF	0x00000008
DMTREEOP_DESCENDANTS	0x00000010

The columns are as follows:

- **MODEL_CATALOG** This is the name of the database that the data-mining model belongs to. In this case it happens to be "Mushrooms".

- **MODEL_SCHEMA** It's supposed to contain the unqualified name of the schema, but since it's currently not supported, it always contains a NULL value.

- **MODEL_NAME** The name of the data-mining model. In this case it's "mushroom analysis rdbms".

- **ATTRIBUTE_NAME** For every predictable field, a separate model is created. Every created model is contained in the same table but is differentiated by this field. The model we created in Chapter 5 used the edibility field to determine whether a mushroom is poisonous, and we also used the habitat field to determine where the mushroom would most likely be found given its characteristics. Both of these fields generate a separate tree model. So in this case we'll find either Edibility or Habitat as the value for this field. That value will tell us what model uses this node.

- **NODE_NAME** This contains a numerical string that serves as a unique name for the node. It has no real descriptive use in an application. In a future release, this name may contain a unique alphanumeric word.

- **NODE_UNIQUE_NAME** The exact same value as NODE_NAME.

- **NODE_TYPE** This denotes the type of node. There can be six possible values for this node represented by an integer from 1 to 6:

  1. DM_NODE_TYPE_MODEL
  2. DM_NODE_TYPE_TREE
  3. DM_NODE_TYPE_INTERIOR
  4. DM_NODE_TYPE_DISTRIBUTION
  5. DM_NODE_TYPE_CLUSTER
  6. DM_NODE_TYPE_UNKNOWN

- **DM_NODE_TYPE_MODEL**   A model node is the topmost node in any data-mining model, regardless of the actual structure of the model. All models start with a model node. It contains no data or distribution histograms. You never even see this node in the Analysis Manager because it's actually the node before the ALL node.

- **DM_NODE_TYPE_TREE**   For all tree-based models, this node serves as the root node of the tree. A data-mining model may have many trees that make up the whole; but for each tree, there is only one tree node that all other nodes are related to. A decision tree-based model always has one model node and at least one tree node. This is the ALL node.

- **DM_NODE_TYPE_INTERIOR**   An interior node represents a generic interior node of a model. For example, in a decision tree, this node usually represents a split in the tree.

- **DM_NODE_TYPE_DISTRIBUTION**   A distribution node is guaranteed to have a valid link to a nested distribution table. A distribution node describes the distribution of values for one or more attributes according to the data represented by this node. A good example of a distribution node is the leaf node of a decision tree.

- **DM_NODE_TYPE_CLUSTER**   A cluster node stores the attributes and data for the abstraction of a specific cluster. In other words, it stores the set of distributions that constitute a cluster of cases for the data-mining model. A clustering-based model always has one model node and at least one cluster node.

- **DM_NODE_TYPE_UNKNOWN**   The unknown node type is used when a node does not fit any of the other node types provided and the algorithm cannot resolve the node type.

- **NODE_GUID**   It contains a NULL value and is currently not supported.

- **NODE_CAPTION**   A label or a caption associated with the node. This property is used primarily for display purposes. If a caption does not exist, the contents of the NODE_NAME column are returned.

- **CHILDREN_CARDINALITY**   Gives an estimate of how many immediate children emanate from a particular node. Leaf nodes have a 0 value.

- **PARENT_UNIQUE_NAME**   The unique name of the node's parent. NULL is returned for any nodes at the root level.

- **NODE_DESCRIPTION**   A user-friendly description of the node.

- **NODE_RULE**   An XML description of the rule that is embedded in the node.

- **MARGINAL_RULE**   An XML description of the rule that is moving to the node from the parent node.

- **NODE_PROBABILITY**   The probability associated with this node.
- **MARGINAL_PROBABILITY**   The probability of reaching the node from the parent node.
- **NODE_DISTRIBUTION**   A nested table that contains the probability histogram for each of the attributes that make up the node.
- **NODE_SUPPORT**   Total number of cases that make up the node.
- **MSOLAP_MODEL_COLUMN**   The name of the column from the model definition that this node pertains to.
- **MSOLAP_NODE_SCORE**   The score that was computed for this node.
- **MSOLAP_NODE_SHORT_CAPTION**   A short caption for the node that can be used for display purposes to improve readability.

MINING_SERVICES Schema Rowset

This rowset exposes the data-mining algorithms available from the provider. It can be used to determine the prediction capabilities, complexity, and similar information about the algorithm. Third-party providers need to supply the values of their algorithms in this table.

The columns are sorted by SERVICE_NAME.

Column restrictions available are

- SERVICE_NAME
- SERVICE_TYPE_ID

The column descriptions are as follows:

- **SERVICE_NAME**   The name of the algorithm. Provider-specific. This will be used as the service identifier in the language. (It is not localizable.)
- **SERVICE_TYPE_ID**   A bitmask that describes mining service types. The following list includes known popular mining service values:
  - DM_SERVICETYPE_CLASSIFICATION (0x0000001)
  - DM_SERVICETYPE_CLUSTERING (0x0000002)
  - DM_SERVICETYPE_ASSOCIATION (0x0000004)
  - DM_SERVICETYPE_DENSITY_ESTIMATE (0x0000008)
  - DM_SERVICETYPE_SEQUENCE (0x0000010)

- **SERVICE_DISPLAY_NAME**   The localizable display name of the algorithm. Provider-specific.
- **SERVICE_GUID**   GUID for the algorithm. NULL if no GUID.
- **DESCRIPTION**   Description of the algorithm.
- **PREDICTION_LIMIT**   The maximum number of predictions the model and algorithm can provide; 0 means no limit.
- **SUPPORTED_DISTRIBUTION_FLAGS**   A comma-delimited list of one or more of the following:
  - "NORMAL"
  - "LOG_NORMAL"
  - "UNIFORM"

Provider-specific flags may also be defined.

- **SUPPORTED_INPUT_CONTENT_TYPES**   A comma-delimited list of one or more of the following:
  - KEY
  - DISCRETE
  - CONTINUOUS
  - DISCRETIZED
  - ORDERED
  - SEQUENCE_TIME
  - CYCLICAL
  - PROBABILITY
  - VARIANCE
  - STDEV
  - SUPPORT
  - PROBABILITY_VARIANCE
  - PROBABILITY_STDEV
  - ORDER
  - SEQUENCE

Provider-specific flags may also be defined.

- **SUPPORTED_PREDICTION_CONTENT_TYPES** A comma-delimited list of one or more of the following:
  - DISCRETE
  - CONTINUOUS
  - DISCRETIZED
  - ORDERED
  - SEQUENCE_TIME
  - CYCLICAL
  - PROBABILITY
  - VARIANCE
  - STDEV
  - SUPPORT
  - PROBABILITY_VARIANCE
  - PROBABILITY_STDEV

Provider-specific flags may also be defined.

- **SUPPORTED_MODELING_FLAGS** A comma-delimited list of one or more of the following:
  - MODEL_EXISTENCE_ONLY
  - NOT NULL

Provider-specific flags may also be defined.

- **SUPPORTED_SOURCE_QUERY** The <source_data_query> types that the provider supports. This is a comma-delimited list of one or more of the following syntax descriptions that can be used as the source of data for INSERT INTO or that can be PREDICTION JOINED to a DMM for SELECT:
  - SINGLETON_CONSTANT
  - SINGLETON_SELECT
  - OPENROWSET
  - SELECT
  - SHAPE

- **TRAINING_COMPLEXITY** Indication of expected time for training. Table 10-7 provides the estimated run time.

Table 10-7. TRAINING_COMPLEXITY Values

DM_TRAINING_COMPLEXITY_LOW	Running time is proportional to input and is relatively short.
DM_TRAINING_COMPLEXITY_MEDIUM	Running time may be long but is generally proportional to input.
DM_TRAINING_COMPLEXITY_HIGH	Running time is long and may grow exponentially in relationship to input.

- **PREDICTION_COMPLEXITY** Indication of expected time for prediction (same as for TRAINING_COMPLEXITY).
- **EXPECTED_QUALITY** Indication of expected quality of model produced with this algorithm:
  - DM_EXPECTED_QUALITY_LOW
  - DM_EXPECTED_QUALITY_MEDIUM
  - DM_EXPECTED_QUALITY_HIGH
- **SCALING** Indication of the scalability of the algorithm:
  - DM_SCALING_LOW
  - DM_SCALING_MEDIUM
  - DM_SCALING_HIGH
- **ALLOW_INCREMENTAL_INSERT** VARIANT_TRUE if additional INSERT INTO statements are allowed after the initial training.
- **ALLOW_PMML_INITIALIZATION** VARIANT_TRUE if the creation of a DMM (including both structure and content) based on an XML string is allowed.
- **CONTROL** One of the following:
  - DM_CONTROL_NONE
  - DM_CONTROL_CANCEL
  - DM_CONTROL_SUSPENDRESUME
  - DM_CONTROL_SUSPENDWITHRESULT
- **ALLOW_DUPLICATE_KEY** TRUE if cases may have duplicate key.

SERVICE_PARAMETERS Schema Rowset

This schema rowset provides a list of parameters that can be supplied when generating a mining model with the CREATE MINING MODEL statement. The client will generally restrict by SERVICE_NAME to obtain the parameters supported by the provider and applicable to the type of mining model being generated.

The default sort order is

- SERVICE_NAME
- PARAMETER_NAME

The available restriction columns are

- SERVICE_NAME
- PARAMETER_NAME

Column descriptions are as follows:

- **SERVICE_NAME**   The name of the algorithm. Provider-specific.
- **PARAMETER_NAME**   The name of the parameter.
- **PARAMETER_TYPE**   Data type of parameter (DBTYPE).
- **IS_REQUIRED**   If true, the parameter is required.
- **PARAMETER_FLAGS**   A bitmask that describes parameter characteristics. The following values (or a combination thereof) may be used:
  - DM_PARAMETER_TRAINING (0x0000001)—for training
  - DM_PARAMETER_PREDICTION (0x00000002)—for prediction
- **DESCRIPTION**   Text describing the purpose and format of the parameter.

Example Listing of Algorithms Available Using Code

```
...

Const DMSCHEMA_MINING_SERVICES = _
    "{3add8a95-d8b9-11d2-8d2a-00e029154fde}"
Const adSchemaProviderSpecific = -1

Set rs = cn.OpenSchema(adSchemaProviderSpecific,, _
    DMSCHEMA_MINING_SERVICES)

...
```

The following results are output from the code above:

```
Microsoft (R) Windows Script Host Version 5.1 for Windows
Copyright (C) Microsoft Corporation 1996-1999.
All rights reserved.

1: SERVICE_NAME - Microsoft_Clustering
2: SERVICE_TYPE_ID - 2
3: SERVICE_DISPLAY_NAME - Microsoft Clustering
4: SERVICE_GUID - {181CB1C9-C7F5-11D3-8BF9-00C04F68DDC2}
5: DESCRIPTION - Clustering finds natural groupings of data in a
 multidimensional space. Clustering is useful when you want to
 see general groupings in your data.
6: PREDICTION_LIMIT - 0
7: SUPPORTED_DISTRIBUTION_FLAGS - NORMAL,UNIFORM
8: SUPPORTED_INPUT_CONTENT_TYPES - CONTINUOUS,CYCLICAL,
 DISCRETE,DISCRETIZED,ORDERED,SEQUENCE_TIME,TABLE
9: SUPPORTED_PREDICTION_CONTENT_TYPES - CONTINUOUS,CYCLICAL,
 DISCRETE,DISCRETIZED,SEQUENCE_TIME,TABLE
10: SUPPORTED_MODELING_FLAGS - MODEL_EXISTENCE_ONLY, NOT NULL
11: SUPPORTED_SOURCE_QUERY - OPENROWSET,SHAPE,SINGLETON SELECT
12: TRAINING_COMPLEXITY - 1
13: PREDICTION_COMPLEXITY - 0
14: EXPECTED_QUALITY - 2
15: SCALING - 1
16: ALLOW_INCREMENTAL_INSERT - False
17: ALLOW_PMML_INITIALIZATION - True
18: CONTROL - 1
19: ALLOW_DUPLICATE_KEY - False
*******************
1: SERVICE_NAME - Microsoft_Decision_Trees
2: SERVICE_TYPE_ID - 1
3: SERVICE_DISPLAY_NAME - Microsoft Decision Trees
4: SERVICE_GUID - {181CB1C8-C7F5-11D3-8BF9-00C04F68DDC2}
5: DESCRIPTION - The Microsoft Decision Trees algorithm chooses
 significant characteristics in the data and narrows sets of
 data based on those characteristics until clear correlations
 are established. Decision trees are useful when you want to
 make specific predictions based on information in the source
 data.
6: PREDICTION_LIMIT - 0
7: SUPPORTED_DISTRIBUTION_FLAGS - NORMAL,UNIFORM
```

(continued)

```
 8: SUPPORTED_INPUT_CONTENT_TYPES - CONTINUOUS,CYCLICAL,
    DISCRETE,DISCRETIZED,KEY,ORDERED,TABLE
 9: SUPPORTED_PREDICTION_CONTENT_TYPES - DISCRETE,DISCRETIZED,
    TABLE
10: SUPPORTED_MODELING_FLAGS - MODEL_EXISTENCE_ONLY, NOT NULL
11: SUPPORTED_SOURCE_QUERY - OPENROWSET,SHAPE,SINGLETON SELECT
12: TRAINING_COMPLEXITY - 1
13: PREDICTION_COMPLEXITY - 0
14: EXPECTED_QUALITY - 1
15: SCALING - 1
16: ALLOW_INCREMENTAL_INSERT - False
17: ALLOW_PMML_INITIALIZATION - True
18: CONTROL - 1
19: ALLOW_DUPLICATE_KEY - False
******************
```

MODEL_CONTENT_PMML Schema Rowset

This rowset stores the XML representation of the content of each model. The format of the XML string follows the PMML standard.

The default sort order of these results is

- MODEL_NAME
- MODEL_SCHEMA
- MODEL_NAME

The available restriction columns are

- MODEL_CATALOG
- MODEL_SCHEMA
- MODEL_NAME
- MODEL_TYPE

The columns descriptions are as follows:

- **MODEL_CATALOG**   Catalog name. NULL if the provider does not support catalogs.
- **MODEL_SCHEMA**   Unqualified schema name. NULL if the provider does not support schemas.
- **MODEL_NAME**   Model name. This column cannot contain NULL.
- **MODEL_TYPE**   Model type, a provider-specific string—can be NULL.

- **MODEL_GUID**   GUID that uniquely identifies the model. Providers that do not use GUIDs to identify tables should return NULL in this column.
- **MODEL_PMML**   An XML representation of the model's content with PMML format.
- **SIZE**   Number of bytes of the XML string size.
- **LOCATION**   The location of the XML file. NULL if the file is stored in the default directory.

Summary

Almost all structural aspects of the data-mining models are exposed through the OLEDB for data-mining provider, which stored all the data about them in table-like structures. This information is complete; thus it's possible not only to understand the internal parameters at work that derived the model, but also to browse the content of these models in sufficient detail to create your own version of the Analysis Services browser if you choose to do so.

For the most part, this interface is more about reporting on the data in the model and understanding the models themselves than it is about manipulating them. In the next chapter, we'll be looking more at the role of PivotTable and how this service helps read the contents of a model and even make local mining models that can be stored on your computer and used offline.

Chapter 11
Data Mining Using PivotTable Service

PivotTable Service is an OLE DB provider that serves as a bridge between the server side of Analysis Services and the client. Whenever a data-mining query is issued, regardless of whether the data-mining model resides on the server or—as we'll see in this chapter—on the local disk, it goes through PivotTable Service. As a desktop version of Analysis Services, PivotTable Service also performs other functions that allow you to create local data-mining models, which reside locally in your memory space or in a file on your local disk. These local data-mining models contain all the predictive and analytical information that a server-side model would contain. With the exception of those management applications that use DSO, most client applications that will interact with the data from Analysis Services will use PivotTable Service. The PivotTable Service architecture is shown in Figure 11-1.

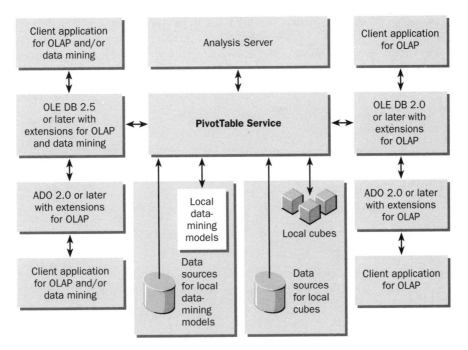

Figure 11-1. *PivotTable Service architecture.*

In many cases, the processing power of a local machine is more than enough to process data-mining models that can then be used locally. The ability to perform data-mining tasks while disconnected from the network is one of the main benefits of this service. This makes possible a scenario in which an office creates a data-mining model using their local data and then e-mails the whole model to a distant office that might be interested in testing their cases against this model to make predictions.

Since PivotTable Service has a Data Definition Language (DDL), it's possible to create client applications that create the data-mining models locally and then query them without having to centralize the data in a remote server somewhere.

As we'll see in this chapter, PivotTable Service is accessible to any language that is able to instantiate COM objects, such as Visual Basic, Visual FoxPro, VBScript, and Perl. The main focus of this chapter is to show how PivotTable Service is used as a local data-mining server. We'll use it to create local data-mining models complete with cases and model training. As an added bonus, we'll use the local data-mining models to see how XML is applied to data mining—another subject we'll cover shortly.

Redistributing Components

Because PivotTable Service is an important component of a client-based application that needs to use Analysis Services functions, it's important to know what files need to be provided as part of your distribution. For that reason, I'm going to spend a little time familiarizing you with the installation and redistribution process. PivotTable Service includes a number of dynamic-link libraries (DLLs) that you may need to ship with a client application. Any individual client application may need a combination of these components, depending on which PivotTable Service features it uses. The services and files needed per service use are listed here:

- To communicate with the Analysis Services server using TCP/IP or HTTP and to read local cube files, add the following files.
  - Msolap80.dll
  - Msolui80.dll
  - Msolap80.rll
  - Olapuir.rll
  - Microsoft Data Access Components (MDAC)

- To create and refresh local cubes, add the following files.
  - Msmdcb80.dll
  - Msmdgd80.dll
  - OLE DB tabular data provider
- To read OLAP and relational data-mining models, add the following files.
  - Msdmine.dll
  - Msmdun80.dll
  - Msdmine.rll
  - Msdmeng.dll

Note   If you are installing PivotTable Service, you must first install Microsoft Data Access Components (MDAC). If you're performing the installation on Windows 95, Windows 98, or Windows Me, you must first install the DCOM.

Installing and Registering Components

By using InstallShield or another automated installation package builder, you can provide your own setup program. This is a likely scenario if you are also distributing custom or shrink-wrapped software that performs Analysis Services client functions as part of your application. You can also use the installation options present in the SQL Server 2000 installation CD to install the proper files. Later in this section, we'll discuss how to do both.

After the required components have been installed, the following components must also be registered using Regsvr32.exe or their own *DLLSelfRegister* functions. This is because they function as ActiveX server components and must be registered before they can be seen by other applications.

- Msolap80.dll
- Msolui80.dll
- Msmdgd80.dll
- Msmdcb80.dll
- Msmdun80.dll
- Msdmine.dll
- Msdmeng.dll

File Locations

The files must be placed in the following locations, with some variances depending on the language version of the product being used:

- **C:\Program Files\Common Files\System\OLE DB** All the dynamic-link library files (.dll) go in this directory.

- **C:\Program Files\Common Files\System\OLE DB\Resources\1033** All the resource files (.rll) go in here. This assumes that you're distributing the English language version of the product. If you are installing another language version of the product, use the appropriate subdirectory under the Resources folder with the appropriate language code. The codes are provided in Table 11.1.

Table 11-1. Language Codes

Language	Code
Arabic	1025
British English	2057
Czech	1029
Danish	1030
German	1031
Estonian	1061
Spanish	3082
French	1036
Croatian	1050
Italian	1040
Latvian	1062
Lithuanian	1063
Hungarian	1038
Dutch	1043
Norwegian	2068
Polish	1045
Portuguese	2070
Brazilian	1046
Romanian	1048
Slovak	1051
Slovenian	1060
Finnish	1035
Swedish	1053

Language	Code
Turkish	1055
English	1033
Greek	1032
Bulgarian	1026
Russian	1049
Thai	1054
Korean	1042
Japanese	1041
Simplified Chinese	2052
Traditional Chinese	1028

Installation Registry Settings

For the purposes of installing and uninstalling, all PivotTable Service files should be considered shared files. Create a registry value for each PivotTable Service file under the following registry key:

```
HKEY_LOCAL_MACHINE\SOFTWARE\Microsoft\Windows\CurrentVersion-
\SharedDLLs
```

If by chance the registry key already exists for the given shared DLL, increment the number by 1. This ensures that Windows knows that the same file is being used by more than one application. This way, if someone decides to uninstall one of the programs, it will simply decrement the number by 1 and not remove the file altogether.

Redistribution Setup Programs

If these instructions sound a bit tedious, two utilities provided in the SQL Server 2000 CD in the \Msolap\Install\Pts folder offer some relief:

- **PTSLITE.EXE**   Installs the needed service files to run PivotTable Service and assumes that you already have the necessary MDAC files installed.
- **PTSFULL.EXE**   Installs both PivotTable Service files and the MDAC components needed for connectivity.

Ptslite.exe installs the following PivotTable Service files:

- atl.dll
- msdmeng.dll
- msdmine.dll

- msmdcb80.dll
- mdmdgd80.dll
- msolap80.dll
- msolui80.dll
- msmdcube.dll
- msmdgdrv.dll
- msolap.dll
- msolapui.dll
- msdmine.rll
- msolap80.rll
- olapuir.rll
- msvbvm60.dll
- msmdun80.dll
- msolapr.dll

Ptsfull.exe installs the same files as Ptslite.exe, and MDAC.

Connecting to the PivotTable Service

PivotTable Service, included as part of Analysis Services, provides methods for data-mining analysis of multidimensional data and relational data. It is the primary interface for your applications to interact with Analysis Services.

You can connect to Analysis Services using PivotTable Service either locally through the OLE DB provider by using ADO, for example, or you can establish a connection over the Web using HTTP.

Connect to Analysis Services Using PivotTable Service

When you use the PivotTable Service to connect to a data-mining model in Analysis Services on the server, the interaction is greatly simplified because the entire communication protocol sequence and cache management is hidden from the client implementation. This makes it very easy to query the models and to create new local data-mining models that are based on the models stored on the server without being concerned about network connectivity issues.

When the mining model is local, PivotTable Service takes on all the functionality of the server, allowing a user to query, create, modify, and delete local models without having to interact with Analysis Services features on the server side.

I know I've mentioned this before, but I'll repeat it again because it's very important: If you want to create a data-mining model on the server, managed by Analysis Services, you can only do so by using DSO as detailed in Chapter 10. If you want to create a local mining model that will reside on your disk, you must use the DDL available through PivotTable Service.

Connect to a mining model using VBScript with Windows Scripting Host (WSH) in the following manner:

```
dim rs
dim cn
dim tt

set cn = wscript.createobject("adodb.connection")
set rs = wscript.createobject("adodb.recordset")

cn.ConnectionString = _
    "provider=MSOLAP.2;" &_
    "Data Source=dataserver;" &_
    "Initial Catalog=mushrooms"

cn.properties.item("Mining Location") = ":\DMM\LOCALMODELS"
cn.open
```

Notice the inline reference to *cn.properties.item(<property name>)*. You may use either the name enclosed in quotes or the numerical value it represents. The possible connection properties are listed in Table 11-2.

Table 11-2. Connection Properties

Property	Value	Description
Integrated Security	0	Determines whether Integrated Security is being used with Windows NT or 2000.
Password	1	Specifies the password to use when connecting using HTTP.
Persist Security Info	2	Determines whether logins supplied to the server are cached locally to prevent the user from being prompted for a username and password for each new connection.
User ID	3	Specifies a valid username, such as a valid domain logon or local logon.
Data Source	4	The name of the server computer or local data-mining file.

(continued)

Table 11-2. *(continued)*

Property	Value	Description
Window Handle	5	Not used.
Location	6	Not used.
Mode	7	Not used.
Prompt	8	Not used.
Connect Timeout	9	Determines the maximum amount of time the client application will take attempting to connect to the server before timing out.
Extended Properties	10	Not used.
Locale Identifier	11	The locale ID of preference for the client application.
Asynchronous Initialization	12	Not used.
Initial Catalog	13	The name of the initial database (catalog).
CREATECUBE	14	The CREATE CUBE statement to create a local cube file.
INSERTINTO	15	The INSERT INTO statement used to populate a local cube file created with the CREATE CUBE statement.
SOURCE DSN	16	The OLE DB connection string, ODBC connection string, or ODBC data source name (DSN) for the source relational database; used only when creating a local cube file.
USEEXISTINGFILE	17	Determines whether a local cube file is overwritten if the connection string contains CREATE CUBE and INSERT INTO statements.
ARTIFICIALDATA	18	Not used.
Client Cache Size	19	Controls the amount of memory used by the client cache.
SOURCE DSN SUFFIX	20	Used to specify DSN properties for creating local cubes that should not be stored as part of the local cubes structure, such as the user ID and password for the local cube's data source.
Auto Synch Period	21	Controls the frequency (in milliseconds) of client/server synchronization.
Cache Policy	22	Not used.
Execution Location	23	Determines the location of query resolution: the client application, server, or a combination of both.

Property	Value	Description
Writeback Timeout	24	Determines the maximum amount of time the client application will attempt to communicate updates to a writeback table on the server before timing out.
Default Isolation Mode	25	Controls whether the isolation level is isolated or determined by the cursor type requested by the rowset properties.
CompareCaseSensitiveStringFlags	26	Adjusts case-sensitive string comparisons for a specified locale.
CompareCaseNotSensitiveStringFlags	27	Adjusts case-sensitive string comparisons for a specified locale.
Large Level Threshold	28	Determines the definition of large level for client/server handling of level members.
Read Only Session	29	Not used.
Secured Cell Value	30	Determines the type of return value that results from a reference to a secured cell.
Roles	31	Specifies a comma-delimited string of the role names by which a client application connects to the server.
MDX Compatibility	32	Determines how empty members are treated for ragged and unbalanced hierarchies.
SQL Compatibility	33	Not used.
SSPI	34	Determines the security package to use during the session, such as: Negotiate Kerberos NTLM Anonymous user
MDX Unique Name Style	35	Determines the technique for generating unique names.
Distinct Measures By Key	36	Not used.
Do Not Apply Commands	37	Not used.
Default MDX Visual Mode	38	Determines the default behavior of the "visual totals" MDX clause.
MDX Calculated Members Mode	39	Not used.
Mining Location	40	Path where a local mining model will be stored. If left blank, the model is kept in memory and is lost once the session is over.

Connect to Analysis Services Using HTTP

Using a URL as the data source property of the connection, you can connect directly to the Analysis server through a firewall using the proper port over the Internet as shown in Figure 11-2. This connection is accomplished with a special Active Server Pages (ASP) page, Msolap.asp, which is found in C:\Program Files\Microsoft Analysis Services\Bin.

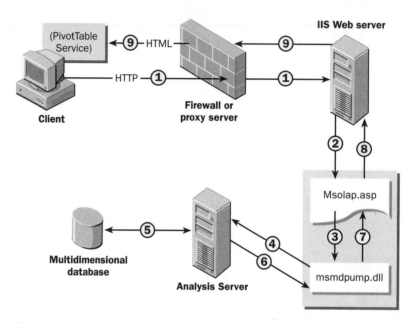

Figure 11-2. *Establishing an HTTP connection.*

Building a Local Data-Mining Model

Unlike the case with Analysis Services on the server side, local mining models are not created and trained using DSO—instead a DDL is used. As you can see from the following example, this DDL is somewhat similar to the one used when creating SQL Server tables, aside from some data-mining specific clauses:

```
CREATE MINING MODEL <new model name>
(
    <comma separated list of column definitions>
)
USING <algorithm name> [(<parameter list>)]
```

or

```
CREATE MINING MODEL <new model name> FROM PMML <xml definition>
```

or

```
CREATE OLAP MINING MODEL <new model name>
    FROM <cube name> <olap definition>
    USING <algorithm name> [(<parameter list>)]
```

The CREATE MINING MODEL statement creates a new mining model based on the column definition list or on the structure of a given cube. A column definition is one of the following forms:

```
<column name> <type> [<content flags>] [<column relation>]
    [<prediction flag>]
```

or

```
<column name> TABLE [<prediction flag>] (
    <non-table column definition list>
)
```

The *<column name>* can be any valid name that begins with an alphanumeric character and does not contain any invalid characters such as [ ]\-*.&%$@. The *<type>* can be any valid SQL type, such as LONG, DOUBLE, DATE, TEXT, and TABLE (for nested tables, which will be discussed later in this chapter).

The *<content flags>*, shown in Table 11-3, are additional, optional parameters that provide further instructions to PivotTable Service to tell it how to treat that column. For the descriptions of these flags, please refer to Chapter 10, where these are discussed in detail.

Table 11-3. Content Flags for Column Definitions

Distribution flags	NORMAL
	LOG_NORMAL
	UNIFORM
Type flags	KEY
	CONTINUOUS
	DISCRETE
	DISCRETIZED
	ORDERED
	CYCLICAL
	SEQUENCE TIME
	SEQUENCE
Modeling flags	MODEL_EXISTENCE_ONLY
	NOT NULL

(continued)

Table 11-3. *(continued)*

Special Property Flags	PROBABILITY
	VARIANCE
	STDEV
	PROBABILITY_VARIANCE
	PROBABILITY_STDEV
	SUPPORT
Prediction Flags	PREDICT
	PREDICT_ONLY
Relation	OF
	RELATED TO

Because the Relation flag in Table 11-3 is the first time we've come across the notion of related tables when creating a mining model, I need to explain what a relation flag is. In the first case, a column may simply be the result of the probability, a variance, or any such other special property flag that depends on another column. In that case, we use the OF clause to specify the dependent field. For example, a possible column could be SupportHabitat Double SUPPORT of Habitat. This column will contain the support number for any given value in the Habitat column.

A data-mining model is not designed to work within the structure of a relational database engine; however, it's very possible for a column to contain a link to a list of other values. Case information for a data-mining model may not reside in a single case table, but may have supporting tables supplying additional information to define the case. The data-mining model can take advantage of nested data-mining columns to process this supporting information and create additional rules and patterns for the case based on the data in the supporting tables.

To accommodate this need, Analysis Services and PivotTable Service use a mechanism known as the *nested table*, which allows a column to be of a type TABLE and have its own list of column definitions. The target of a RELATED TO column can be a Key column in a nested table, a Discretely Valued column on the case row, or another column with a RELATED TO clause.

This example uses VBScript to create a local mining model based on the results of a content query.

```
dim rs
dim cn
dim tt
```

```
set cn = wscript.createobject("adodb.connection")
set rs = wscript.createobject("adodb.recordset")

cn.ConnectionString = "provider=MSOLAP.2;Data Source=dataserver;
    Initial Catalog=mushrooms"

cn.properties.item("Mining Location") = "c:\pscripts"
cn.open

strDdl = "CREATE MINING MODEL [MushroomLocal] " &_
    "([Id]                       LONG KEY  , "        &_
    "[Cap Shape]                 TEXT  DISCRETE , "   &_
    "[Cap Surface]               TEXT  DISCRETE , "   &_
    "[Cap Color]                 TEXT  DISCRETE , "   &_
    "[Bruises]                   TEXT  DISCRETE , "   &_
    "[Odor]                      TEXT  DISCRETE , "   &_
    "[Gill Attachment]           TEXT  DISCRETE , "   &_
    "[Gill Spacing]              TEXT  DISCRETE , "   &_
    "[Gill Size]                 TEXT  DISCRETE , "   &_
    "[Gill Color]                TEXT  DISCRETE , "   &_
    "[Stalk Shape]               TEXT  DISCRETE , "   &_
    "[Stalk Root]                TEXT  DISCRETE , "   &_
    "[Stalk Surface Above Ring]  TEXT DISCRETE  , "   &_
    "[Stalk Surface Below Ring]  TEXT DISCRETE  , "   &_
    "[Stalk Color Above Ring]    TEXT DISCRETE  , "   &_
    "[Stalk Color Below Ring]    TEXT DISCRETE  , "   &_
    "[Veil Type]    TEXT DISCRETE  , "                &_
    "[Veil Color]   TEXT DISCRETE  , "                &_
    "[Ring Number]  TEXT DISCRETE  , "                &_
    "[Ring Type]    TEXT DISCRETE  , "                &_
    "[Spore Print Color] TEXT DISCRETE  , "           &_
    "[Population] TEXT DISCRETE  , "                  &_
    "[Edibility] TEXT DISCRETE   PREDICT, "           &_
    "[Habitat] TEXT DISCRETE   PREDICT) "             &_
    "USING Microsoft_Decision_Trees"

'set rs = cn.execute(strDdl)
```

Tip In data-mining models with a fairly large number of rows like this one, it can be advantageous to query the actual MINING_MODELS schema rowset, copy the value from the CREATION_STATEMENT field, and use that value as the creation statement for the local mining model, provided you want it to be like the original in structure. This trick can save you quite a bit of typing!

Storage of Local Mining Models

Although the use of XML will be discussed in more detail later in the chapter, it's important to note that if you execute the CREATE MINING MODEL statement from the example above, you'll find that a file named mushroomslocal.dmm.xml has been created in the location specified in the Mining Location connection parameter. If you have Microsoft Internet Explorer 5.0 or later installed, and you double-click on this file, it will open up the XML structure of the model. Here is a listing of that model:

```
<?xml version="1.0" ?>
- <pmml name="MushroomsLocal"
    GUID="{4A30AD32-4A13-4FE2-AC3C-67647D7ED4C1}"
    creation-time="2001-02-12T10:59:27"
    modified-time="2001-02-12T10:59:27">
- <statements>
  <statement type="CREATE" value="CREATE MINING MODEL [MushroomsLocal]
    ([Id] LONG KEY , [Cap Shape] TEXT DISCRETE ,
    [Cap Surface] TEXT DISCRETE , [Cap Color] TEXT DISCRETE ,
    [Bruises] TEXT DISCRETE , [Odor] TEXT DISCRETE ,
    [Gill Attachment] TEXT DISCRETE , [Gill Spacing] TEXT DISCRETE ,
    [Gill Size] TEXT DISCRETE , [Gill Color] TEXT DISCRETE ,
    [Stalk Shape] TEXT DISCRETE , [Stalk Root] TEXT DISCRETE ,
    [Stalk Surface Above Ring] TEXT DISCRETE ,
    [Stalk Surface Below Ring] TEXT DISCRETE ,
    [Stalk Color Above Ring] TEXT DISCRETE ,
    [Stalk Color Below Ring] TEXT DISCRETE ,
    [Veil Type] TEXT DISCRETE , [Veil Color] TEXT DISCRETE ,
    [Ring Number] TEXT DISCRETE , [Ring Type] TEXT DISCRETE ,
    [Spore Print Color] TEXT DISCRETE ,
    [Population] TEXT DISCRETE ,
    [Edibility] TEXT DISCRETE PREDICT,
    [Habitat] TEXT DISCRETE PREDICT)
    USING Microsoft_Decision_Trees" />
</statements>
- <data-dictionary>
    <key name="Id" datatype="LONG" isinput="true" />
    <categorical name="Cap Shape" isinput="true"
        datatype="TEXT" />
    <categorical name="Cap Surface" isinput="true"
        datatype="TEXT" />
    <categorical name="Cap Color" isinput="true"
        datatype="TEXT" />
    <categorical name="Bruises" isinput="true"
        datatype="TEXT" />
    <categorical name="Odor" isinput="true"
        datatype="TEXT" />
```

```
        <categorical name="Gill Attachment" isinput="true"
            datatype="TEXT" />
        <categorical name="Gill Spacing" isinput="true"
            datatype="TEXT" />
        <categorical name="Gill Size" isinput="true"
            datatype="TEXT" />
        <categorical name="Gill Color" isinput="true"
            datatype="TEXT" />
        <categorical name="Stalk Shape" isinput="true"
            datatype="TEXT" />
        <categorical name="Stalk Root" isinput="true"
            datatype="TEXT" />
        <categorical name="Stalk Surface Above Ring"
            isinput="true" datatype="TEXT" />
        <categorical name="Stalk Surface Below Ring"
            isinput="true" datatype="TEXT" />
        <categorical name="Stalk Color Above Ring" isinput="true"
            datatype="TEXT" />
        <categorical name="Stalk Color Below Ring" isinput="true"
            datatype="TEXT" />
        <categorical name="Veil Type" isinput="true"
            datatype="TEXT" />
        <categorical name="Veil Color" isinput="true"
            datatype="TEXT" />
        <categorical name="Ring Number" isinput="true"
            datatype="TEXT" />
        <categorical name="Ring Type" isinput="true"
            datatype="TEXT" />
        <categorical name="Spore Print Color" isinput="true"
            datatype="TEXT" />
        <categorical name="Population" isinput="true"
            datatype="TEXT" />
        <categorical name="Edibility" isinput="true"
            ispredict="true" datatype="TEXT" />
        <categorical name="Habitat" isinput="true"
            ispredict="true" datatype="TEXT" />
    </data-dictionary>
    <tree-model />
</pmml>
```

If you have a file like this one available, you can use it to create a new mining model with the FROM PMML clause by reading the content of the text file into a variable and using it as the XML definition parameter.

Later in the chapter, we'll expand this strategy using Microsoft Data Mining Models in conjunction with those of other vendors.

SELECT INTO Statement

The SELECT INTO statement creates a new mining model by copying schema and other information from an existing mining model. If the existing model is trained, the new model will automatically be trained with the same query. If the existing model is not trained, the new model will be empty.

```
SELECT * INTO <new model>
USING <algorithm> [(<parameter list>)]
FROM <existing model>
```

INSERT INTO Statement

The INSERT INTO statement inserts training data into the model. The columns from the query are mapped to model columns through the <mapped model columns> section. The keyword SKIP is used to instruct the model to ignore columns that appear in the source data query that are not used in the model. The format of the statement is as follows:

```
INSERT INTO <new model name> (<mapped model columns>)
    <source data query>
```

or

```
INSERT INTO <model> (<mapped model columns>)
    VALUES <constant list>
```

or

```
INSERT INTO <model>.COLUMN_VALUES(
    <mapped model columns>
) <source data query>
```

or

```
INSERT INTO <model>
```

The INSERT INTO <model>.COLUMN_VALUES form inserts data directly into the model's columns without training the model's algorithm. This allows you to provide column data to the model in a concise, ordered manner that is useful when dealing with data sets containing hierarchies or ordered columns. The "." operator is used to specify columns that are part of a nested table. When you use this form, columns that are part of a relation (either through RELATE TO or by being a KEY in a nested table) cannot be inserted individually and must be inserted together with all the columns in the relation.

The <mapped model columns> section has the following form:

```
<column identifier> | <table identifier>(<column identifier>
    | SKIP), …
```

OPENROWSET Syntax

You can train the local mining model with the contents of a SQL Server table or an OLAP cube by using the OPENROWSET function. This function establishes a connection with a remote data source, performs the query, and returns the data set. The condition, of course, is that the returned rows match the order and number of rows in the destination data-mining model.

```
OPENROWSET('provider_name'
    {
        'datasource';'user_id';'password'
        | 'provider_string'
    },
    {
        'query'
    })
```

- **provider_name**   A character string that represents the friendly name of the OLE DB provider as specified in the registry. It has no default value. If the source were SQL Server, for example, then the provider name would be SQLOLEDB.

- **datasource**   A string constant that corresponds to a particular OLE DB data source object. Typically, this string includes the name of the database file, the name of a database server, or a name that the provider understands to locate the data source.

- **user_id**   Needed for those data source providers, such as SQL Server, that have a security mechanism that requires a logon name.

- **password**   The password to authenticate the logon.

- **provider_string**   A provider-specific connection string that contains all the parameters needed to establish a connection to the data source. This is used as an alternative to and not in conjunction with the first three parameters.

- **query**   A string constant that is sent to and executed by the provider.

Here is an example of OPENROWSET that uses the INSERT INTO statement to insert rows into a mining model:

```
strIns = "insert into [mushroomslocal] (" &_
"[Id]                      , "        &_
"[Cap Shape]               , "        &_
"[Cap Surface]             , "        &_
"[Cap Color]               , "        &_
"[Bruises]                 , "        &_
"[Odor]                    , "        &_
"[Gill Attachment]         , "        &_
"[Gill Spacing]            , "        &_
"[Gill Size]               , "        &_
"[Gill Color]              , "        &_
"[Stalk Shape]             , "        &_
"[Stalk Root]              , "        &_
"[Stalk Surface Above Ring]    , "  &_
"[Stalk Surface Below Ring]    , "  &_
"[Stalk Color Above Ring]      , "  &_
"[Stalk Color Below Ring]      , "  &_
"[Veil Type]    , "                   &_
"[Veil Color]   , "                   &_
"[Ring Number] , "                    &_
"[Ring Type]    , "                   &_
"[Spore Print Color] , "              &_
"[Population] , "                     &_
"[Edibility] , "              &_
"[Habitat] ) openrowset("                &_
"'sqloledb'," &_
"'dataserver';'dtsuser';''," &_
"'SELECT DISTINCT " &_
"[ID] AS [Id]," &_
"cap_shape AS [Cap Shape]," &_
"cap_surface AS [Cap Surface]," &_
"cap_color AS [Cap Color]," &_
"bruises AS [Bruises]," &_
"odor AS [Odor]," &_
"gill_attachment AS [Gill Attachment]," &_
"gill_spacing AS [Gill Spacing]," &_
"gill_size AS [Gill Size]," &_
"gill_color AS [Gill Color]," &_
"stalk_shape AS [Stalk Shape]," &_
"stalk_root AS [Stalk Root]," &_
"stalk_surface_above_ring AS [Stalk Surface Above Ring]," &_
"stalk_surface_below_ring AS [Stalk Surface Below Ring]," &_
"stalk_color_above_ring AS [Stalk Color Above Ring]," &_
"stalk_color_below_ring AS [Stalk Color Below Ring]," &_
"veil_type AS [Veil Type]," &_
```

```
"veil_color AS [Veil Color]," &_
"ring_number AS [Ring Number]," &_
"ring_type AS [Ring Type]," &_
"spore_print_color AS [Spore Print Color]," &_
"population AS [Population]," &_
"edibility AS [Edibility]," &_
"habitat AS [Habitat] " &_
"FROM dataminer..mushrooms &_
"')"

'set rs = cn.execute(strIns)
```

Tip If you ever wanted to see the syntax of the training query used to populate your data-mining model from a SQL Server source, open a trace to SQL Server using the Profiler utility to capture all the SQL statements issued against the server. Then process the mining model. This will generate the query that Analysis Services uses to query the server, and this query is stored in the profiler for use. This query can be used to help create the query that is used to populate the local mining model.

Nested Tables and the SHAPE Statement

The SHAPE statement permits you to retrieve all the data needed for the cases from multiple queries and "shape" them into a single table with nested tables structures that can be used to train the DMM.

```
SHAPE {<master query>}
   APPEND ({<child table query>}
   RELATE <master column> TO <child column>)
      AS <column table name>
   [
      APPEND ({<child table query>}
      RELATE <master column> TO <child column>)
         AS <column table name>
      ⋮
   ]
```

The SHAPE statement allows the addition of table columns to a master query by specifying the child table rows and the way to match between the row in *<master query>* and its child rows in the *<child query>*.

Note If you reopen the mushroomslocal.dmm.xml XML file, you'll now notice that the file has become considerably larger because of the addition of the new cases. If you open the XML file that represents the local mining model, you'll now notice that there is a series of XML tags for each case entered.

Using XML in Data Mining

Extensible Markup Language (XML) is used to store the local mining models, but even the mining models that reside on the server contain schema rowsets with the XML definition of the model.

The PMML Standard

Predictive Model Markup Language (PMML) provides applications with a vendor-independent method of creating and storing data-mining models so that all data-mining vendor applications can share the models among themselves for the purpose of visualizing, manipulating, or enriching them with new cases. Because a standard format can be used, the integration of all of these different source models is relatively transparent to the data-mining applications themselves. As of the publication of this book, the Document Type Definition (DTD) for data-mining models exists in PMML form. Notice that the following list contains only the definitions for those models provided by Microsoft data mining. For the complete PMML Document Type Definition specification, please refer to http://www.dmg.org/html/dtd_v1_1.html.

```
<?xml version='1.0' encoding='ISO-8859-1' ?>

<!ENTITY % A-PMML-MODEL '(TreeModel | ClusteringModel)' >

    <!ELEMENT PMML  (Header,  DataDictionary,
        (%A-PMML-MODEL;)+,  Extension*)>

    <!ATTLIST PMML
        version CDATA #REQUIRED
    >

    <!ELEMENT Extension ANY>
    <!ATTLIST Extension
        extender CDATA #IMPLIED
        name CDATA #IMPLIED
        value CDATA #IMPLIED
    >

    <!ENTITY  % NUMBER  "CDATA">
    <!ENTITY  % INT-NUMBER  "CDATA">
        <!-- content must be an integer,
            no fractions or exponent -->
```

```
<!ENTITY  % REAL-NUMBER "CDATA">
    <!-- content can be any number
        covers C/C++ types 'float','long','double'
        scientific notation, eg 1.23e4, is allowed -->
<!ENTITY  % PROB-NUMBER "CDATA">
    <!-- a REAL-NUMBER between 0.0 and 1.0
        usually describing a probability -->
<!ENTITY  % PERCENTAGE-NUMBER "CDATA">
    <!-- a REAL-NUMBER between 0.0 and 100.0  -->

<!ENTITY % FIELD-NAME  "CDATA">
<!ELEMENT Array (#PCDATA)>
<!ATTLIST Array
    n   %INT-NUMBER; #IMPLIED
    type (int| real | string) #IMPLIED
>

<!ENTITY  % NUM-ARRAY "Array">
    <!-- an array of numbers -->
<!ENTITY  % INT-ARRAY "Array">
    <!-- an array of integers -->
<!ENTITY  % REAL-ARRAY  "Array">
    <!-- an array of reals -->
<!ENTITY  % STRING-ARRAY  "Array">
    <!-- an array of strings -->

<!-- =========     Header      ============================
======= -->

<!ELEMENT Header (Application?, Annotation*, Timestamp?)>

<!ATTLIST Header
    copyright   CDATA #REQUIRED
    description CDATA #IMPLIED
>

<!-- describes the software application that
    generated the PMML-->
<!ELEMENT Application EMPTY>

<!ATTLIST Application
    name        CDATA #REQUIRED
    version     CDATA #IMPLIED
>
```

(continued)

```
<!ELEMENT Annotation (#PCDATA)>

<!-- a timestamp in the format YYYY-MM-DD hh:mm:ss
    GMT +/- xx:xx -->
<!ELEMENT Timestamp (#PCDATA)>

<!-- =========    Data Dictionary    ====================
======== -->

<!ELEMENT DataDictionary (Extension*, DataField+)>
<!ATTLIST DataDictionary
    numberOfFields   %INT-NUMBER; #IMPLIED
>
<!ELEMENT DataField  (Extension*, (Interval*| Value*))>
<!ATTLIST DataField
    name          %FIELD-NAME;  #REQUIRED
    displayName  CDATA           #IMPLIED
    optype       (categorical | ordinal | continuous)  #REQUIRED
    isCyclic      (0 | 1)      "0"
>

<!ELEMENT Value (Extension*)>
<!ATTLIST Value
    value        CDATA #REQUIRED
    displayValue CDATA #IMPLIED
    property      (valid | invalid | missing) "valid"
>

    <!ELEMENT Interval  EMPTY>
    <!ATTLIST Interval
        closure      (openClosed | openOpen | closedOpen
            | closedClosed) #REQUIRED
        leftMargin %NUMBER;   #IMPLIED
        rightMargin %NUMBER;   #IMPLIED
    >

<!-- =========    Mining Schema    =====================
====== -->

<!ELEMENT MiningSchema (Extension*, MiningField+)>

<!ENTITY % FIELD-USAGE-TYPE "(active | predicted
    | supplementary)">

<!ENTITY % OUTLIER-TREATMENT-METHOD "(asIs
    | asMissingValues | asExtremeValues)">
```

```
<!ELEMENT MiningField (Extension*)>
<!ATTLIST MiningField
    name            %FIELD-NAME;                    #REQUIRED
    usageType       %FIELD-USAGE-TYPE;              "active"
    outliers        %OUTLIER-TREATMENT-METHOD;      "asIs"
    lowValue        %NUMBER;                        #IMPLIED
    highValue       %NUMBER;                        #IMPLIED
>
<!-- =========      Statistics     =========================
== -->

<!ELEMENT ModelStats    (UnivariateStats+)>

<!ENTITY % AGGREGATE "(Counts?, NumericInfo?)">

<!ELEMENT UnivariateStats ((%AGGREGATE;)?, DiscrStats?,
    ContStats?)>
<!ATTLIST UnivariateStats
    field   %FIELD-NAME; #IMPLIED
>

<!ELEMENT Counts EMPTY>
<!ATTLIST Counts
    totalFreq           %NUMBER; #REQUIRED
    missingFreq         %NUMBER; #IMPLIED
    invalidFreq         %NUMBER; #IMPLIED
>

<!ELEMENT NumericInfo (Quantile*)>
<!ATTLIST NumericInfo
    minimum             %NUMBER; #IMPLIED
    maximum             %NUMBER; #IMPLIED
    mean                %NUMBER; #IMPLIED
    standardDeviation   %NUMBER; #IMPLIED
    median              %NUMBER; #IMPLIED
    interQuartileRange  %NUMBER; #IMPLIED
>

<!ELEMENT Quantile EMPTY>
<!ATTLIST Quantile
    quantileLimit  %PERCENTAGE-NUMBER;  #REQUIRED
    quantileValue  %NUMBER; #REQUIRED
>

<!ELEMENT DiscrStats (Extension*, (%STRING-ARRAY;)?,
    (%INT-ARRAY;)?)>
<!ATTLIST DiscrStats
    modalValue              CDATA    #IMPLIED
>
```

(continued)

```
<!ELEMENT ContStats (Extension*, Interval*,
    (%INT-ARRAY;)?, (%NUM-ARRAY;)?, (%NUM-ARRAY;)?)>
<!ATTLIST ContStats
    totalValuesSum %NUMBER;    #IMPLIED
    totalSquaresSum %NUMBER;    #IMPLIED
>


<!ELEMENT Partition (PartitionFieldStats+)>
<!ATTLIST Partition
    name   CDATA    #REQUIRED
    size   %NUMBER; #IMPLIED
>


<!ELEMENT PartitionFieldStats (%AGGREGATE;,
    (%NUM-ARRAY;)*)>
<!ATTLIST PartitionFieldStats
    field           %FIELD-NAME; #REQUIRED
>


<!-- =========      Normalization    =======================
==== -->


<!ENTITY % NORM-INPUT "(NormContinuous | NormDiscrete)">


<!ELEMENT NormContinuous (Extension*, LinearNorm*)>
<!ATTLIST NormContinuous
    field   %FIELD-NAME; #REQUIRED
>


<!ELEMENT LinearNorm EMPTY>
<!ATTLIST LinearNorm
    orig    %NUMBER;   #REQUIRED
    norm    %NUMBER;   #REQUIRED
>


<!ELEMENT NormDiscrete (Extension*)>
<!ATTLIST NormDiscrete
    field %FIELD-NAME;  #REQUIRED
    method          (indicator | thermometer) #FIXED "indicator"
    value CDATA #REQUIRED
>


<!ELEMENT ClusteringModel
    (Extension*, MiningSchema, ModelStats?,
        ComparisonMeasure, ClusteringField*, CenterFields?,
        Cluster+)>
<!ATTLIST ClusteringModel
    modelName                    CDATA           #IMPLIED
    modelClass (centerBased | distributionBased)   #REQUIRED
    numberOfClusters                %INT-NUMBER;   #REQUIRED
>
```

```
<!ELEMENT CenterFields ((%NORM-INPUT;)+)>
<!ELEMENT Cluster (Extension*, (%NUM-ARRAY;)?, Partition?,
    Covariances?)>
<!ATTLIST Cluster
    name                CDATA           #IMPLIED
>

<!-- =========      Tree Classification =====================
====== -->

<!ENTITY % PREDICATES
    "(Predicate | CompoundPredicate | True | False)"
    >
    <!ELEMENT TreeModel (Extension*, MiningSchema, ModelStats?, Node)>
    <!ATTLIST TreeModel
    modelName CDATA #IMPLIED
    >

    <!ELEMENT Node (Extension*, (%PREDICATES;), Node*,
        ScoreDistribution*)>

        <!ATTLIST Node

        score CDATA #REQUIRED
        recordCount %NUMBER; #IMPLIED
        >

        <!ELEMENT Predicate EMPTY>
        <!ATTLIST Predicate
            field %FIELD-NAME; #REQUIRED
            operator (equal | lessThan | notEqual | lessOrEqual
                | greaterThan | greaterOrEqual) #REQUIRED
            value CDATA #REQUIRED
        >

        <!ELEMENT CompoundPredicate ( %PREDICATES; ,
            (%PREDICATES;)+)>
        <!ATTLIST CompoundPredicate
            booleanOperator (or | and | xor | cascade) #REQUIRED

        >
        <!ELEMENT True EMPTY>
        <!ELEMENT False EMPTY>
        <!ELEMENT ScoreDistribution EMPTY>
        <!ATTLIST ScoreDistribution
            value CDATA #REQUIRED
            recordCount %NUMBER; #REQUIRED
        >
```

Summary

In addition to the powerful server functions provided by Analysis Services, PivotTable Service exists (in the form of an OLE DB provider) to supply the same functionality on the client side. Thanks to this service, it's possible to create, train, modify, and query data-mining models that exist locally. Interestingly, the data-mining models created locally adhere to the PMML standard recently adopted by many data-mining vendors. This standardization lets the models you create with Analysis Services be distributed among vendors of data-mining products.

In the next chapter, we'll take a close look at querying the data-mining models using code both with mining models that reside on the server and with those created with PivotTable Service.

Chapter 12
Data-Mining Queries

The usefulness of data-mining models, particularly those that use decision trees, comes from the ability to predict the values of the missing attributes in new cases. To be able to make a prediction, you need to have a fully populated data-mining model as well as your test cases that have the missing attributes. The test cases are simple cases with missing attributes that need to be predicted. In our sample mushrooms database, the cases contain as many attributes about the mushrooms as we can identify in hopes of finding out whether the missing attribute, "Edibility," can be found. The reason we will be concentrating on the decision trees algorithm in this instance is because it is the only algorithm that offers the possibility of predicting missing values. As we've discussed, clustering creates a model that is browsed to find records that are similar to each other.

> **Note** Remember that it's not a good idea to use the same cases for predictions that were used to train the model because this method will invariably lead to seemingly perfect predictions and any inaccuracies in the model will be missed.

The prediction queries are issued against the Analysis server's model or a local data-mining model created with PivotTable Service. The connection and the query itself are issued through OLE DB, usually using the ADO wrapper as with a typical SQL Server or Jet Engine connection.

Components of a Prediction Query

The statement used to execute a data-mining query is the SELECT statement that appears to be very similar to the standard SQL Select statement. There are, however, some very specific key words and constructs that exist only in the data-mining query.

The Basic Prediction Query

The basic syntax of the SELECT statement needed to make a basic prediction query is shown here. For the moment we're concentrating on the column references, so the reference to the test case table may seem a bit oversimplified, but I'll explain how to join a case table.

```
SELECT
*
FROM
    <data mining model> as DM PREDICTION JOIN <cases table> as TC
ON  DM.column1 = TC.column1
    DM.column2 = TC.column2
```

Specifying the Test Case Source

Typically, the test cases are going to reside in a table or a flat file structure such as an Excel spreadsheet. Because this structure is never stored as a data-mining model, the query needs to connect to a source outside the data-mining environment for the duration of the query. The OPENROWSET function returns a table structure based on OLE DB connection options and the query passed on to that connection. If I had a SQL Server table containing test cases in a SQL Server table, I would have to specify the connectivity options for a remote connection as shown in the code sample that follows. We can dispense with this only if the test cases happen to be in an OLAP cube on the same server, in which case it's only necessary to issue an MDX query to retrieve the data source.

```
SELECT
*
FROM
    <mushroom analysis rdbms> as DM PREDICTION JOIN
OPENROWSET
    (
        'SQLOLEDB.1',
        'Provider=SQLOLEDB.1;user=dtsuser;password=;' &_
        'Initial Catalog=DataMiner;Data Source=dataserver', &_
        'SELECT * FROM "mushrooms_test" '
    ) as TC
ON
    DM.column1 = TC.column1
    DM.column2 = TC.column2
⋮
```

Singleton Queries

Although test cases are often stored in table structures for retrieval, there is an easier way to retrieve them with the singleton query. In the case of mushrooms, you may want to test the edibility of a single mushroom case without having to go through the trouble to insert that record in a table and use OPENROWSET to retrieve it for the query. A *singleton query* allows you to place hard-coded values in the source query without establishing a connection to a remote data source, as you can see from the following listing:

```
SELECT FLATTENED
[TC].[mushroom_name],
    ( SELECT
        edibility ,
        $Probability,
        $support FROM
        PredictHistogram( [edibility])
    ) AS [EdibilityStats]
FROM
[Mushroom Analysis RDBMS]
NATURAL PREDICTION JOIN
    (
        select
        'Test Mushroom' as [Mushroom_Name],
        'Convex' as [Cap Shape],
        'Smooth' as [Cap Surface],
        'White' as [Cap Color],
        '' as [Bruises],
        'None' as [Odor],
        '' as [Gill Attachment],
        '' as [Gill Spacing],
        '' as [Gill Size],
        'White' as [Gill Color],
        '' as [Stalk Shape],
        '' as [Stalk Root],
        '' as [Stalk Surface Above Ring] ,
        '' as [Stalk Surface Below Ring] ,
        '' as [Stalk Color Above Ring],
        '' as [Stalk Color Below Ring],
        '' as [Veil Type] ,
        '' as [Veil Color] ,
        '' as [Ring Number] ,
        '' as [Ring Type] ,
        '' as [Spore Print Color] ,
        '' as [Population] ,
        '' as [Habitat]
    )
    AS [TC]
```

This is especially convenient for applications that allow a user to enter ad hoc attributes of a test case on a Web page, for example, and retrieve the prediction values on the fly.

Specifying Columns

Instead of specifying columns with the asterisk (*), you can specify the columns from the data-mining model, from the cases table, from functions, and from scalar variables. To select specific columns, the syntax is similar to standard SQL syntax as you can see from this listing.

```
SELECT
    TC.[Mushroom Name],
    DM.[Habitat],
    DM.[Edibility]
FROM
    <mushroom analysis rdbms> as DM PREDICTION JOIN
OPENROWSET
    (
        'SQLOLEDB.1',
        'Provider=SQLOLEDB.1;user=dtsuser;password=;' &_
        'Initial Catalog=DataMiner;Data Source=dataserver', &_
        'SELECT * FROM "mushrooms_test" '
    ) as TC
ON
    DM.[odor] = TC.[odor]
    DM.[cap shape] = TC.[cap shape]
    ⋮
```

The PREDICTION JOIN Clause

The SELECT statement is composed of a join between two data sources, the data-mining model and the test cases. Because of its predictive function, this type of join is called a PREDICTION JOIN. When constructing this join, the actual cases from the test cases source are matched with the set of all possible cases from the mining model with the PREDICTION JOIN operator. The PREDICTION JOIN differs from the JOIN in a standard SQL SELECT statement in that all the attributes in the data-mining model are matched with all the known attributes of the test cases. The PREDICTION JOIN is used to find records that match, and these matches enable the mining model to provide the known attribute and provide the missing values to the test cases. The PREDICTION JOIN will take the case from the test set that's presented and, using the values in the ON clause, will find all the matching sets of cases from the data-mining model. The matching sets are then collapsed into an aggregated set that contains the probability of the resulting values.

Tip   You can use the NATURAL PREDICTION JOIN when you know that the columns in the model and the columns in the source data have the same names. This allows you to dispense with the need for lengthy ON clauses because the columns will be automatically joined based on their common names. (See the singleton query listing above for an example of this clause.) Just remember that the data-mining model replaces all underscores with spaces in the column names, so your natural prediction join may not work if your test cases still have columns with underscores in the name. The query will still run without errors, but many of the attributes will have been missed, and therefore the queries may be far less accurate than they could be.

The Key columns identified during the building of the model serve no purpose for the query itself; therefore, they should not be involved in the ON clause. Remember that the test cases need to come from a source different from the cases used to train the model, so there should be no possible join condition on the Key columns.

Let's suppose that you went mushroom picking and came home with a number of different varieties. Before cooking them, you decide to play it safe and consult the data-mining model. You enter all the characteristics you know about them including the name of the mushrooms, and you issue a prediction query. Here is an example of a query used to find the edible mushrooms among those contained in Figure 12-1:

Mushroom Name	Cap Shape	Cap Texture	Cap Color	Odor	Gill Attach-ment	Gill Spacing	Stalk Surface Below Ring	Stalk Shape	Stalk Color	Ring Type	Veil Color	Rings	Spore Print Color
Agaricus Cothurnata	convex	smooth	white	NULL	free	crowded	NULL	enlarged	white	NULL	white	NULL	white
Agaricus Bisporigera	convex	smooth	white	NULL	free	crowded	NULL	NULL	white	NULL	white	NULL	white
Agaricus Ocreata	NULL	smooth	white	NULL	free	NULL	NULL	NULL	white	NULL	white	NULL	white
Agaricus Muscaria	flat	smooth	red	NULL	free	crowded	NULL	NULL	white	NULL	white	NULL	white
Agaricus Pantherina	flat	smooth	brown	NULL	free	crowded	NULL	enlarged	white	NULL	white	NULL	white
Agaricus Phalloides	convex	smooth	yellow	pungent	free	close	NULL	NULL	white	NULL	white	NULL	white
Agaricus Tenufolia	convex	smooth	white	NULL	free	crowded	NULL	NULL	white	NULL	white	NULL	white
Agaricus Verna	convex	smooth	white	NULL	attached	crowded	NULL	NULL	white	NULL	white	one	white
Agaricus Virosa	convex	smooth	white	NULL	free	crowded	NULL	NULL	white	NULL	white	one	NULL
Agaricus A1	NULL	NULL	NULL	none	NULL	NULL	scaly	NULL	NULL	NULL	NULL	NULL	red
Agaricus A2	NULL	NULL	NULL	none	NULL	NULL	scaly	NULL	NULL	NULL	NULL	NULL	red

Figure 12-1. *Mushroom test cases.*

Using the data above, we'll issue the following prediction query to fill in the missing, but crucial, "Edibility" column:

```
SELECT FLATTENED
[TC].[Mushroom_name],
[DM].[Edibility]
FROM
[Mushroom Analysis RDBMS] as DM
PREDICTION JOIN
    OPENROWSET
    (
    'SQLOLEDB.1',
    'Provider=SQLOLEDB.1;Persist Security Info=False;
        User ID=dtsuser;Initial Catalog=DataMiner;
        Data Source=DATASERVER',
    'SELECT  [mushroom_name],
        [cap_shape] AS [Cap Shape],
        [cap_surface] AS [Cap Surface],
        [cap_color] AS [Cap Color],
        [bruises] AS [Bruises],
        [odor] AS [Odor],
        [gill_attachment] AS [Gill Attachment],
        [gill_spacing] AS [Gill Spacing],
        [gill_size] AS [Gill Size],
        [gill_color] AS [Gill Color],
        [stalk_shape] AS [Stalk Shape],
        [stalk_root] AS [Stalk Root],
        [stalk_surface_above_ring] AS
            [Stalk Surface Above Ring],
        [stalk_surface_below_ring] AS
            [Stalk Surface Below Ring],
        [stalk_color_above_ring] AS
            [Stalk Color Above Ring],
        [stalk_color_below_ring] AS
            [Stalk Color Below Ring],
        [veil_type] AS [Veil Type],
        [veil_color] AS [Veil Color],
        [ring_number] AS [Ring Number],
        [ring_type] AS [Ring Type],
        [spore_print_color] AS [Spore Print Color],
        [population] AS [Population],
        [habitat] AS [Habitat]
    FROM [mushrooms_test]'
    )
```

```
AS [TC]
ON
    [TC].[Cap Shape] = [TC].[Cap Shape] AND
    [TC].[Cap Surface] = [TC].[Cap Surface] AND
    [TC].[Cap Color] = [TC].[Cap Color] AND
    [TC].[Bruises] = [TC].[Bruises] AND
    [TC].[Odor] = [TC].[Odor] AND
    [TC].[Gill Attachment] = [TC].[Gill Attachment] AND
    [TC].[Gill Spacing] = [TC].[Gill Spacing] AND
    [TC].[Gill Size] = [TC].[Gill Size] AND
    [TC].[Gill Color] = [TC].[Gill Color] AND
    [TC].[Stalk Shape] = [TC].[Stalk Shape] AND
    [TC].[Stalk Root] = [TC].[Stalk Root] AND
    [TC].[Stalk Surface Above Ring] =
        [TC].[Stalk Surface Above Ring] AND
    [TC].[Stalk Surface Below Ring] =
        [TC].[Stalk Surface Below Ring] AND
    [TC].[Stalk Color Above Ring] =
        [TC].[Stalk Color Above Ring] AND
    [TC].[Stalk Color Below Ring] =
        [TC].[Stalk Color Below Ring] AND
    [TC].[Veil Type] = [TC].[Veil Type] AND
    [TC].[Veil Color] = [TC].[Veil Color] AND
    [TC].[Ring Number] = [TC].[Ring Number] AND
    [TC].[Ring Type] = [TC].[Ring Type] AND
    [TC].[Spore Print Color] = [TC].[Spore Print Color] AND
    [TC].[Population] = [TC].[Population] AND
    [TC].[Habitat] = [TC].[Habitat]
```

The results of the query are listed in Table 12-1.

Table 12-1. Prediction Query Results

Agaricus Cothurnata	poisonous
Agaricus Bisporigera	poisonous
Agaricus Ocreata	poisonous
Agaricus Muscaria	poisonous
Agaricus Pantherina	poisonous
Agaricus Phalloides	poisonous
Agaricus Tenufolia	poisonous
Agaricus Verna	poisonous
Agaricus Virosa	poisonous
Agaricus A1	edible
Agaricus A2	poisonous

It's probably good that you checked these before eating them! We did not have as many characteristics in our test cases as there are in the model, so some of the mushrooms have a higher probability of being poisonous than others. Because we made a simple prediction join, the result set contains only the highest probability scenarios. The question is, how do we find out more information about the results? Specifically, what are the odds that the edible mushroom, Agaricus A2, is poisonous? In the next section, we'll explore some of the functions of a prediction query, which bring more precision in our result sets.

Using Functions as Columns

A function can be used as a column to provide additional information about an attribute. This type of column is known as a *qualifier* and can contain information related to the probability associated to a predicted value or information related to the distribution of the predicted value. There are several such functions, which will be described in detail later in this chapter. This listing shows the use of a function as a column that returns the number of cases supporting that particular prediction.

```
SELECT
    TC.[Mushroom Name],
    DM.[Habitat],
    DM.[Edibility],
    PREDICTSUPPORT(dm.[Edibility]) as Edibility_Support
FROM
    <mushroom analysis rdbms> as DM PREDICTION JOIN
    ⋮
```

Using Tabular Values as Columns

Data-mining queries support the notion of nested tables, or tables within tables. This is done by issuing a subquery as a column as in the query listing above.

In Chapter 5, when we built our data-mining models, we had the option of using more than one table as long as they were related. This relationship gets translated into a nested table as the model is built. That means the foreign key value in the parent table becomes a table type column, which contains the related items from the parent table. This simplifies the structure because the notion of relations, as in an RDBMS engine, no longer needs to be maintained because the multiple tables have been transformed into a single structure. This level of simplicity allows data-mining clients to use the data without having to also retrieve information about the relational rules governing the tables—the rules are simply embedded inside the related fields.

The end result is a model made from multiple tables that is the same as a model created from a single flat table. However, the queries make use of the notion of nested tables when constructing queries and formatting the results. In other words, you can have a field contain the results of a subquery that returns multiple rows. Analysis Services will create a nested tables structure as the result set. Again, this makes it easy for any client to use the results without having to know how to interpret relational rules about related tables. In order for most clients to be able to make use of this nested table, the results need to be "flattened" so as to appear as a single table. For this, the SELECT syntax provides the FLATTENED option, as in the example listing that follows. The FLATTENED option turns the SELECT result table from a hierarchical table to a flat table structure, with a results set that contains one row for each predicted value, simplifying the processing of the prediction results. The result is actually similar to the flattening that occurs in standard SQL when issuing a SELECT statement, which joins two tables in a one-to-many relationship. The result contains as many iterations of the "one" side as there are corresponding records in the "many" side.

```
SELECT FLATTENED
[TC].[mushroom_name],
(SELECT
    edibility,
    $Probability,
    $support
FROM PredictHistogram([edibility])) AS [EdibilityDetails]
FROM
[Mushroom Analysis RDBMS] PREDICTION JOIN
⋮
```

This query yields a result set like the one shown in Table 12-2.

Table 12-2. Results with a Nested Table

Mushroom Name	Edibility	Probability	Support
Agaricus Cothurnata	poisonous	99.65%	576
Agaricus Cothurnata	missing	0.17%	0
Agaricus Cothurnata	edible	0.17%	0
Agaricus Bisporigera	poisonous	99.65%	576
Agaricus Bisporigera	missing	0.17%	0
Agaricus Bisporigera	edible	0.17%	0
Agaricus Ocreata	poisonous	99.65%	576
Agaricus Ocreata	missing	0.17%	0
Agaricus Ocreata	edible	0.17%	0
Agaricus Muscaria	poisonous	99.65%	576

(continued)

Table 12-2. *(continued)*

Mushroom Name	Edibility	Probability	Support
Agaricus Muscaria	missing	0.17%	0
Agaricus Muscaria	edible	0.17%	0
Agaricus Pantherina	poisonous	99.65%	576
Agaricus Pantherina	missing	0.17%	0
Agaricus Pantherina	edible	0.17%	0
Agaricus Phalloides	poisonous	99.23%	256
Agaricus Phalloides	missing	0.39%	0
Agaricus Phalloides	edible	0.39%	0
Agaricus Tenufolia	poisonous	99.65%	576
Agaricus Tenufolia	missing	0.17%	0
Agaricus Tenufolia	edible	0.17%	0
Agaricus Verna	poisonous	99.65%	576
Agaricus Verna	missing	0.17%	0
Agaricus Verna	edible	0.17%	0
Agaricus Virosa	poisonous	99.65%	576
Agaricus Virosa	missing	0.17%	0
Agaricus Virosa	edible	0.17%	0
Agaricus A1	edible	89.47%	16
Agaricus A1	missing	5.26%	0
Agaricus A1	poisonous	5.26%	0
Agaricus A2	poisonous	69.49%	40
Agaricus A2	edible	28.81%	16
Agaricus A2	missing	1.69%	0

The WHERE Clause

The WHERE clause in a prediction query is used in almost exactly the same way as in standard SQL—to filter the results of the query. In the query below, the prediction results are limited to only those mushrooms for which the edibility can be determined with greater than 90 percent accuracy.

```
SELECT
    TC.[Mushroom Name],
    DM.[Habitat],
    DM.[Edibility],
    PREDICTSUPPORT(DM.[Edibility]) as Edibility_Support
FROM
    <mushroom analysis rdbms> as DM PREDICTION JOIN
    ⋮
WHERE PredictProbability(DM.Edibility) > .90
```

Prediction Functions

By default, the prediction query tries to find the best fit for the missing values in the test data to provide a best-case scenario. You can derive extra information from the query by using built-in functions in the data-mining component of Analysis Services.

Some of these functions will return a number as a scalar column value, while others will return entire tables that contain rows of detail concerning the prediction.

By using these functions with a subquery, we can get special nested-table values that contain specific information related to probabilities and distributions. We can also tailor the results to fit the type of prediction we need.

Predict

```
Predict(<scalar or table column reference>, option1, option2, …)
```

The *Predict* function returns either a scalar or table value depending on which type of column this function is applied to. The options in Table 12-3 can be applied to the function, with each option having an effect on how the predicted values are returned.

Table 12-3. Options for the *Predict* Function

Option	Data Type	Description
EXCLUDE_NULL (default)	Scalar	Does not take missing values in the test cases into account.
INCLUDE_NULL	Scalar	Missing values in the test cases are considered significant and should be taken as a measure. This can be useful in cases where the fact that a value is missing in an attribute means something, such as in the example of a customer who has not made payments on a loan.
INCLUSIVE	Table	Includes the information from the test cases as part of the resulting prediction and combines it with the results in the model.
EXCLUSIVE (default)	Table	Does not include the information from the test cases as part of the resulting prediction.
INPUT_ONLY	Table	This ensures that the resulting prediction contains only the rows that were supplied from the test cases.
INCLUDE_STATISTICS	Table	This causes some scalar values $Probability and $Support to become automatically available as a column that can be included in a column list.

PredictProbability

```
PredictProbability(<column>)
```

The *PredictProbability* function returns the percentage of cases that a given prediction represents. This percentage is returned for the row that contains the highest probability value and is therefore considered to be the predicted value. In the listing below, this function is used in a WHERE clause.

```
SELECT
    TC.[Mushroom Name],
    DM.[Habitat],
    DM.[Edibility],
    PREDICTSUPPORT(DM.[Edibility]) as Edibility_Support
FROM
    <mushroom analysis rdbms> as DM PREDICTION JOIN
    ⋮
WHERE PredictProbability(DM.Edibility)  > .90
```

PredictSupport

```
PredictSupport(<column>)
```

The *PredictSupport* function returns the support value for the entry that has the highest probability. It provides information on how many records represent the given probability prediction. The listing below uses the *Predict* and *PredictSupport* functions.

```
SELECT FLATTENED
    [TC].[mushroom_name],
    Predict([edibility]) as PredictionValue,
    PredictSupport([edibility]) as SupportValue
FROM
    [Mushroom Analysis RDBMS] AS DM
PREDICTION JOIN …
```

This code yields the result set shown in Table 12-4.

Table 12-4. Query Results Using *Predict* and *PredictSupport*

Mushroom Name	PredictionValue	SupportValue
Agaricus Cothurnata	Poisonous	576
Agaricus Bisporigera	Poisonous	576
Agaricus Ocreata	Poisonous	576
Agaricus Muscaria	Poisonous	576
Agaricus Pantherina	Poisonous	576
Agaricus Phalloides	Poisonous	256
Agaricus Tenufolia	Poisonous	576
Agaricus Verna	Poisonous	576
Agaricus Virosa	Poisonous	576
Agaricus A1	Edible	16
Agaricus A2	Poisonous	40

PredictVariance

```
PredictVariance(<column>)
```

The *PredictVariance* function returns a number that represents a statistical variance for the row that contains the highest probability for being true. This is relevant to continuous data values (numbers).

> **Note**   *PredictVariance, PredictStdev, PredictProbabilityStdev,* and *PredictProbability-Variance* functions are only relevant to continuous attributes. Remember that continuous attributes in Microsoft Data Mining are binned into mean values for the node in which they are contained. These functions provide insight into what those numbers represent in relation to the overall population of cases in that node. Knowing the standard deviation and variance of a number tells you how far away that mean value is from the high and low numbers for the cases in that node, which in turn determines the accuracy of that figure. It's important to keep in mind that the functions are not aggregate functions like those you would find in SQL Server or OLAP; instead, they represent the range of values that can be found in a given node. It's for that reason that each returned row from a prediction query can return a different return value for the function.

PredictStdev

```
PredictStdev(<column>)
```

The *PredictStdev* function returns a number that represents a statistical standard deviation value for the row that contains the highest probability for being true. This is relevant to continuous data values (numbers).

PredictProbabilityVariance

```
PredictProbabilityVariance(<column>)
```

The *PredictProbabilityVariance* function returns the variance of the probability for the histogram entry with the highest probability.

PredictProbabilityStdev

```
PredictProbabilityStdev(<scalar column reference>)
```

The *PredictProbabilityStdev* function returns the standard deviation of the probability for the histogram entry with the highest probability.

PredictHistogram

```
PredictHistogram(<scalar column reference>)
PredictHistogram(<cluster column reference>)
```

The *PredictHistogram* function returns a table representing a histogram for prediction of the given column. When you look at a node in the Analysis manager, you'll notice the predicted value Id, broken down to all its possible values and the statistical probability of each. A histogram generates statistics columns. For any given predictive column, a histogram consists of the following seven columns:

- $Probability
- $ProbabilityStdev
- $ProbabilityVariance
- $Support
- $Stdev (standard deviation)
- $Variance
- Column being predicted

And when the query involves a cluster, the following columns are returned:

- $Distance
- $Probability
- $Support
- Cluster to represent the cluster identifier

It's important to remember that this function returns a nested table with one record for each possible value for the predicted column. The following listing is an example of a query that uses the *PredictHistogram* function:

```
SELECT FLATTENED
[T1].[mushroom_name],
( SELECT
edibility ,
$Probability,
$support FROM
    PredictHistogram( [edibility] )
    ) AS [EdibilityStats]
FROM
    [Mushroom Analysis RDBMS]
PREDICTION JOIN
    OPENROWSET
    (
        'SQLOLEDB.1',
        'Provider=SQLOLEDB.1;Persist Security Info=False;
            User ID=dtsuser;Initial Catalog=DataMiner;
            Data Source=DATASERVER',
        'SELECT * FROM "mushrooms_test" ORDER BY "mushroom_name"'
    )
    AS [T1]
ON
    [Mushroom Analysis RDBMS].[Cap Shape] = [T1].[Cap_Shape] AND
        [Mushroom Analysis RDBMS].[Cap Surface] =
            [T1].[Cap_Surface] AND
        [Mushroom Analysis RDBMS].[Cap Color] =
            [T1].[Cap_Color] AND
        [Mushroom Analysis RDBMS].[Bruises] = [T1].[Bruises] AND
        [Mushroom Analysis RDBMS].[Odor] = [T1].[Odor] AND
        [Mushroom Analysis RDBMS].[Gill Attachment] =
            [T1].[Gill_Attachment] AND
        [Mushroom Analysis RDBMS].[Gill Spacing] =
            [T1].[Gill_Spacing] AND
        [Mushroom Analysis RDBMS].[Gill Size] =
            [T1].[Gill_Size] AND
        [Mushroom Analysis RDBMS].[Gill Color] =
            [T1].[Gill_Color] AND
        [Mushroom Analysis RDBMS].[Stalk Shape] =
            [T1].[Stalk_Shape] AND
```

(continued)

```
[Mushroom Analysis RDBMS].[Stalk Root] =
    [T1].[Stalk_Root] AND
[Mushroom Analysis RDBMS].[Stalk Surface Above Ring] =
    [T1].[Stalk_Surface_Above_Ring] AND
[Mushroom Analysis RDBMS].[Stalk Surface Below Ring] =
    [T1].[Stalk_Surface_Below_Ring] AND
[Mushroom Analysis RDBMS].[Stalk Color Above Ring] =
    [T1].[Stalk_Color_Above_Ring] AND
[Mushroom Analysis RDBMS].[Stalk Color Below Ring] =
    [T1].[Stalk_Color_Below_Ring] AND
[Mushroom Analysis RDBMS].[Veil Type] =
    [T1].[Veil_Type] AND
[Mushroom Analysis RDBMS].[Veil Color] =
    [T1].[Veil_Color] AND
[Mushroom Analysis RDBMS].[Ring Number] =
    [T1].[Ring_Number] AND
[Mushroom Analysis RDBMS].[Ring Type] =
    [T1].[Ring_Type] AND
[Mushroom Analysis RDBMS].[Spore Print Color] =
    [T1].[Spore_Print_Color] AND
[Mushroom Analysis RDBMS].[Population] =
    [T1].[Population] AND
[Mushroom Analysis RDBMS].[habitat] = [T1].[habitat]
```

This query yields the results shown in Table 12-5.

Table 12-5. Query Results Using *PredictHistogram* Function

Mushroom Name	Edibility	Support	Probability
Agaricus A1	edible	16	0.895
Agaricus A1	missing	0	0.053
Agaricus A1	poisonous	0	0.053
Agaricus A2	poisonous	40	0.695
Agaricus A2	edible	16	0.288
Agaricus A2	missing	0	0.017
Agaricus Bisporigera	poisonous	576	0.997
Agaricus Bisporigera	missing	0	0.002
Agaricus Bisporigera	edible	0	0.002
Agaricus Cothurnata	poisonous	576	0.997
Agaricus Cothurnata	missing	0	0.002
Agaricus Cothurnata	edible	0	0.002

Table 12-5 *(continued)*

Mushroom Name	Edibility	Support	Probability
Agaricus Muscaria	poisonous	576	0.997
Agaricus Muscaria	missing	0	0.002
Agaricus Muscaria	edible	0	0.002
Agaricus Ocreata	poisonous	576	0.997
Agaricus Ocreata	missing	0	0.002
Agaricus Ocreata	edible	0	0.002
Agaricus Pantherina	poisonous	576	0.997
Agaricus Pantherina	missing	0	0.002
Agaricus Pantherina	edible	0	0.002
Agaricus Phalloides	poisonous	256	0.992
Agaricus Phalloides	missing	0	0.004
Agaricus Phalloides	edible	0	0.004
Agaricus Tenufolia	poisonous	576	0.997
Agaricus Tenufolia	missing	0	0.002
Agaricus Tenufolia	edible	0	0.002
Agaricus Verna	poisonous	576	0.997
Agaricus Verna	missing	0	0.002
Agaricus Verna	edible	0	0.002
Agaricus Virosa	poisonous	576	0.997
Agaricus Virosa	missing	0	0.002
Agaricus Virosa	edible	0	0.002

TopCount

```
TopCount(<table expression>, <rank expression>, <n-items>)
```

TopCount is a table-returning expression that includes *<table column reference>* and functions that return a table. This function returns the first *<n-items>* rows in a decreasing order of *<rank expression>*.

TopSum

```
TopSum(<table expression>, <rank expression>, <sum>)
```

TopSum is a table-returning expression that includes *<table column reference>* and functions that return a table. This function returns the first N rows in a decreasing order of *<rank column reference>*, such that the sum of the *<rank expression>* values is at least *<sum>*. *TopSum* returns the smallest number of elements possible while still meeting that criterion.

TopPercent

```
TopPercent(<table expression>, <rank expression>, <percent>)
```

The *TopPercent* function returns the first N rows in a decreasing order of *<rank expression>*, such that the sum of the *<rank column reference>* values is at least the given percentage of the total sum of *<rank column reference>* values. *TopPercent* returns the smallest number of elements possible while still meeting that criterion.

RangeMin

```
RangeMin(<column>)
```

When a numerical column gets placed in a bin, the number represents a mean value for that node. The *RangeMin* function finds the minimum value present in the cases used to build that binned or discretized value.

RangeMid

```
RangeMid(<column>)
```

The *RangeMid* function finds the middle value of the predicted bucket that was discovered for a discretized column.

RangeMax

```
RangeMax(<column>)
```

RangeMax is like the *RangeMin* function except that it finds the highest value in the bin instead of the lowest value.

PredictScore

```
PredictScore(<scalar column reference>)
PredictScore(<table column reference>)
```

The *PredictScore* function returns the prediction score of the specified column.

> **Note** The *PredictScore* function exists in OLE DB for data-mining specification but is not implemented by Microsoft Data Mining. The complete OLE DB for Data Mining specification can be downloaded from *http://www.microsoft.com/data/oledb/dm.htm*.

PredictNodeId

```
PredictNodeId(<column>)
```

The *PredictNodeId* function returns the node ID of the tree leaf node that the case is identified with. This function is especially useful in decision trees to find out how far down the tree the case was able to go (and therefore how accurate the prediction is) before the attributes could no longer be matched to a node.

Prediction Queries with Clustering Models

Unlike decision trees, clustering can't determine missing values directly by filling in the missing attribute columns, and yet it is available as a target for prediction queries. What can we use a cluster for if not to predict missing values? Given that you have identified clusters of cases with common characteristics, you may be able to indirectly predict something about your test cases by knowing what cluster your test cases *would have belonged to* if they had been used as part of a training set! For example, you might find that your cluster node #8 contains the most Gold credit card members and those members also happen to be single females who make more than $50,000 per year. If you find out which of your test cases belong in node #8, this information can be used to persuade members of this group to upgrade their cards. In this example, we're not using clustering to fill missing values; we're looking for cluster node identifiers for the test cases.

> **Note** In clustering models, each node in a cluster has an associated number. When you browse through a clustering model in the Analysis manager, you'll notice that each node is named with a number such as "Cluster 1," "Cluster 2," and so on. The number in that name is actually that node's ID value.

The *Cluster*, *ClusterDistance*, and *ClusterProbability* functions are used only with clustering models. They return crucial information related to the node IDs.

Cluster

The *Cluster* function takes no arguments and returns the identifier of the cluster for which the input case has the highest probability of belonging. It also can be used as a column reference for the *PredictHistogram* function.

ClusterProbability

```
ClusterProbability(([<ClusterNode ID>]))
```

The *ClusterProbability* function returns the probability that the input case belongs to the cluster that has the highest probability. If the cluster node ID is given, the cluster is identified by the evaluation of the expression. The following example queries the FoodMart 2000 database using a singleton query as the data source.

```
SELECT
    [T1].[yearly income],
    [T1].[marital status],
    [T1].[gender],
    cluster() as [cluster node],
    clusterprobability() as [cluster probability]
FROM
    [Member Card Cluster]
    PREDICTION JOIN
        (
            select '$50K - $70K' as [yearly income],
            'S' as [marital status], 'F' as [gender]
        )
    AS [T1]
    ON
        [Member Card Cluster].[yearly income] =
            [T1].[yearly income] AND
        [Member Card Cluster].[marital status] =
            [T1].[marital status] AND
        [Member Card Cluster].[gender] = [T1].[gender]
```

This returns the cluster with the highest probability, as shown in Table 12-6:

Table 12-6. Record Containing the Cluster Node and Probability of Belonging.

Yearly Income	Marital Status	Gender	Cluster Node	Cluster Probability
$50K - $70K	S	F	8	0.30

Cluster node #8 shows that 89 percent of the members of that node have Bronze credit cards, and based on the cluster probability, we can assume that this person has a 30 percent chance of belonging to that group. Again, it's not a prediction in the most direct sense, but it is a form of classification and generalization.

ClusterDistance

```
ClusterDistance([<ClusterNode ID>])
```

The *ClusterDistance* function returns the distance between the input case and the center of the cluster that has the highest probability. The closer the case is to the center, the more accurately it is represented by the node it's contained in. Unlike decision trees, clusters contain records that have varying degrees of relevance to their nodes because they might have some characteristics that identify them with a given node but also have others that do not. Some records are borderline cases that are so close to their node border that they almost belong to another node. Two good examples of borderline cases are the fish and mammal classifications. If our records contain primarily lions, tigers, monkeys, bass, sharks, and barracuda, then a test case containing a leopard will clearly fall in the center of the mammals node because of the leopard's characteristics. However, a dolphin, although a mammal, will be pulled away from the center toward the fish node because of characteristics a dolphin shares with fish. The number returned by the function determines how far from the center a given record is from a given node.

Note   The *ClusterDistance* function is not implemented yet and only returns a NULL value.

Using DTS to Run Prediction Queries

DTS is not only a tool used to generate new mining models—it can also be used to create queries and store the results in a SQL Server table, Microsoft Access database, or an ODBC-compliant database. In the DTS canvas, there is a toolbar on the bottom left with a Data Mining Prediction Task button (the miner's pickaxe). This button serves to create the queries, run them, and store them on another machine. Clicking on this button opens the Data Mining Prediction Query Task Wizard as shown in Figure 12-2.

Figure 12-2. *Data Mining Prediction Query Task Wizard.*

You can alter the name and the description of the task if you want. You must enter the server name where the data-mining model resides. Once you do, the drop-down menu below the server field will let you choose from all the Analysis Services databases. Pick the one that contains the model that you wish to query. The mining-models panel on the lower left contains the available mining models in the database you have chosen. The panel on the lower right provides some statistics that tell you which algorithm has been chosen and whether or not it has been processed. Once you're done, click on the Query tab and move to the next screen. On this screen, you must enter the connection string needed to access the data source where the test cases are stored. You may manually enter the string, or you can click on the button with three dots and build the string with the Data Link Properties dialog box, as shown in Figure 12-3.

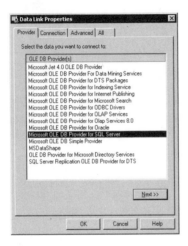

Figure 12-3. *Data Link Properties dialog box.*

You may type your prediction query manually in the text box provided, or you can make use of the assistance provided by the Prediction Query Builder dialog box, which is accessed by clicking on the New Query button. (See Figure 12-4.)

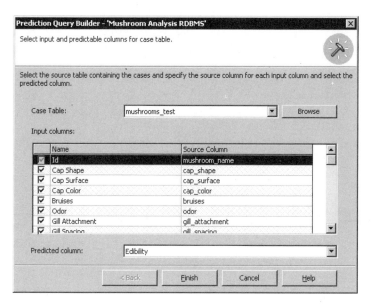

Figure 12-4. *Prediction Query Builder dialog box.*

On the left panel of this dialog box, you'll find the available columns for the data-mining model, and on the right side, you'll find the automatically matched columns from the test data source. Those columns that are not matched automatically can be selected from drop-down menus on the right.

Caution   When you work with the Prediction Query Builder, there are some features to be aware of. First, the Prediction Query Builder will automatically and irrevocably choose the case ID of the data-mining model that is to be part of the query even though the case almost never should be part of the model. Usually the test cases come from samples that are not used to build the model (as should be the case); therefore, it's highly unlikely that you'll find a match between the ID values in the model and the ID values in the test cases. The builder also forces you to supply a matching column in the test case for the ID in the model before you can leave the window. I suggest that you go ahead and supply an arbitrary column as the matching column and that you edit the generated query later to eliminate references to joins involving those two columns. The columns in the model are automatically matched for you when the names are the same; however, the data-mining model replaces all underscores in column names with spaces, so you'll find the only columns that automatically match are those that contain no underscores in the test set. You will need to manually match the columns by picking them from the list on the right.

At the bottom of the window, you can select the attribute to be predicted. Click on the Finish button when you're done to generate the query in the Prediction Query editor as shown in Figure 12-5.

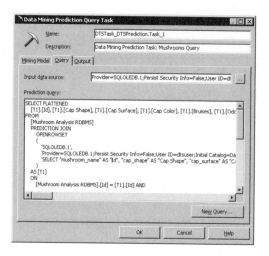

Figure 12-5. *Prediction Query editor with generated code.*

You can make any manual adjustments to the code including any special functions you wish to add in the Prediction Query editor. (See Figure 12-6.)

Figure 12-6. *Prediction Query editor with modified code.*

To modify the code, click on the Output tab to go to the Output selection window. (See Figure 12-7.)

Figure 12-7. *Prediction Query Builder Output selection window.*

The Output selection window is simple to use and requires only the connection string and table name of the location where the results will be stored. Again, you can either type in the connection string or use the Data Link dialog box.

Note   The generated table will overwrite any existing table with the same name.

Now you can click on the Execute button at the top of the DTS designer canvas and run the task until it's finished. (See Figure 12-8.)

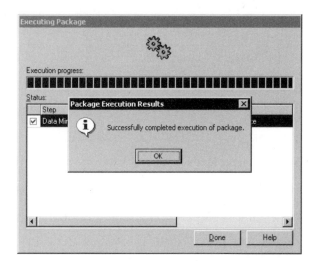

Figure 12-8. *Prediction Query Builder: Running the task.*

Notice how simple it is to run the task because all connections, queries, and output designations are stored in one task. Now you can go to the location of the table and query the results in the same way you would any table. (See Figure 12-9.)

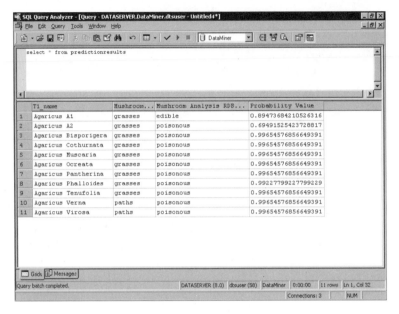

Figure 12-9. *Querying the results.*

Summary

The culmination of all the efforts to build a data-mining model centers around the ability to query it and thus use it to predict missing values from test cases. These cases can be on the topics of mushrooms, credit cards, or consumer product preferences. Microsoft Data Mining provides the prediction query syntax to allow a user or programmer to find missing prediction values from a decision tree with the same relative ease of querying a relational table. In this chapter, we covered DTS tasks to make these predictions.

Because the syntax of data-mining queries is so similar to that of standard SQL, the technical aspects of prediction queries are easily understood by thousands of SQL programmers.

The additional functions and special join features help gain an advantage from the statistical foundations that data mining is based on. With these functions, you generate predictions that come with additional information regarding the strength of those pre-dictions in terms of degree of probability and support by number of cases. We also looked at using prediction queries to gather information from test cases as they relate to Microsoft Clustering. Although these are not prediction queries in the sense that we can predict the value of missing attributes, it does tell you what group any particular case is likely to belong to by using functions specific to clustering models.

Microsoft Data Mining provides tight integration with other Microsoft tools such as DTS, but also serves as an OLE DB provider, which allows third-party products to easily inte-grate prediction queries into their applications using PERL, C++, Visual Basic, or any other language capable of connecting through OLE DB.

Appendix
Regression Analysis

As you have noticed from reading this book, Microsoft Analysis Services provides data-mining algorithms that are primarily suited for classifying cases into groups and predicting missing values from discrete sets. With Microsoft Data Mining, it's easy to find whether a given mushroom is edible based on its characteristics or what film genre a given customer is likely to rent based on their past behavior, but it's virtually impossible to predict specific continuous (numerical) data values, such as the price of a car based on its make, model, and condition.

Other data-mining algorithms, such as regression analysis, are well suited to this type of data mining. Unfortunately, Microsoft Data Mining doesn't support regression analysis at this time. However, this shouldn't stop you from using Microsoft SQL Server 2000 to apply such algorithms to make predictions. The rich array of tools and functions available in SQL Server 2000 makes it possible to use other algorithms. In this appendix, I'll show you how the regression analysis algorithm works and one way to apply it directly to OLAP and relational data without using data-mining components from Analysis Services. This serves two purposes—one, it provides you with a solid understanding of the underlying processes of a data-mining algorithm and two, it suggests an alternative way to mine data using your programming knowledge and the SQL Server tools. As soon as Analysis Services allows third-party algorithms, you will be able to use variations of the formulas described in this appendix to add the algorithm to the list of algorithms available in the data-mining tools.

What Is Regression Analysis?

Regression analysis is the application of statistical formulas to two sets of numbers to determine the degree to which one set of numbers affects the second set of numbers. The purpose of regression analysis is to improve our ability to predict the next occurrence of our dependent variable based on past experience. Regression analysis is also the mathematical relationship between two variables expressed in an equation. One variable can be predicted using what we know about the other variable. The variable whose value is to be predicted is called the *dependent variable*. The variable about which knowledge is available is called the *independent variable*. The relationships between variables may be linear or curvilinear. By *linear*, we mean that the functional relationship can be described graphically (on a common X-Y coordinate system) with a straight line and mathematically by the common form: y = mx + b. By *curvilinear*, we mean that the relationship is defined by a curved line, which incidentally happens to be more complex to calculate.

There are many situations in which the value of one numerical variable has an effect on the numerical value of another variable. Our example will use regression analysis to find out whether the size of a house has a direct effect on the cost of electricity. If the results show a relationship, regression analysis can also help predict how much the cost increases per square foot.

Predicting Continuous Attributes: An Example

The best way to grasp how regression analysis works is to actually work through an example. Table A-1 lists the square footage and average annual electric costs of 12 homes:

Table A-1. House Size vs. Observed Electricity Costs

House Size (sq. ft.)	Annual Electricity Costs
1900	$600
2000	$660
2525	$900
1300	$480
3500	$1,680
4100	$1,710
2870	$1,200
1700	$540
2300	$1,500
2450	$1,080
2890	$1,200
1890	$540

Imagine that you are going to buy a home that you intend to live in for at least five years. Before deciding which home to buy, you need to know how much it will cost per month. Besides the mortgage, the costs include maintenance, taxes, insurance, and utilities. Because the homes are located in a warm climate, you will have the added expense of air conditioning.

Correlation

The idea that there is a correlation between the size of a home and the cost to live in it sounds reasonable. To test the hypothesis, the first thing you need to do is establish that there is a link between home size and electricity costs. This link, or *correlation*, is expressed as a number between −1 and 1. The closer to 1 the number is, the higher the *positive correlation*. Therefore, the larger the home, the higher the electricity costs. The closer to −1 this number is, the higher the *negative correlation* is. If there was a negative correlation in this relationship, a larger home would use less electricity. If the correlation number is 0, it is unlikely that there is any link between home size and energy consumption. The number that describes the correlation is known as the *correlation coefficient*. I'll show you the actual equation for calculating the correlation coefficient in a moment, but first I'll build out the table of sums and means that we'll need to plug into the equation. Table A-2 contains all the numbers needed to calculate both the correlation coefficients and the regression line that I'll discuss later in the section. The column of numbers containing the independent variables is commonly referred to as the X column or the column of x values. The dependent variables are commonly referred to as the y values.

Table A-2. x and y Value Computations for Correlation and Regression Equations

	X	Y	X²	Y²	XY
1	1900	600	3,610,000	360,000	1,140,000
2	2000	660	4,000,000	435,600	1,320,000
3	2525	900	6,375,625	810,000	2,272,500
4	1300	480	1,690,000	230,400	624,000
5	3500	1680	12,250,000	2,822,400	5,880,000
6	4100	1710	16,810,000	2,924,100	7,011,000
7	2870	1200	8,236,900	1,440,000	3,444,000
8	1700	540	2,890,000	291,600	918,000
9	2300	1500	5,290,000	2,250,000	3,450,000
10	2450	1080	6,002,500	1,166,400	2,646,000
11	2890	1200	8,352,100	1,440,000	3,468,000
12	1890	540	3,572,100	291,600	1,020,600

	X	Y	X²	Y²	XY
Sum	Σx=29,425	Σy=12,090	Σx^2=79,079,225	Σy^2=14,462,100	Σxy=33,194,100
Mean	$\bar{x}$=2452	$\bar{y}$=1007.50	$\bar{x}^2$=6,012,712.67	$\bar{y}^2$=1,015,056.25	$\bar{x}\,\bar{y}$=2,766,175

Now that we've calculated the sums and the means of each column, we can move on to the equations. Figure A-1 shows the equation used to calculate the correlation coefficient. To simplify the explanation, I've divided the computation into the three main components. These are the covariance of the x and y values divided by the product of the standard deviations of x and the standard deviations of y.

$$r = \frac{cov_{xy}}{std_x std_y}$$

Figure A-1. *Correlation coefficient equation.*

The covariance is calculated with the formula in Figure A-2.

$$cov_{xy} = \frac{\Sigma xy}{n} - \overline{xy}$$

Figure A-2. *The covariance of x and y equation.*

By now some of you are probably wishing you had never fallen asleep in high school precalculus. No need to worry; I'll explain this process step by step just to show you how simple it is.

First we get the covariance by substituting the numbers:

Cov_{xy} = (33,194,100 / 12) – (2452 × 1007.5)

Cov_{xy} = 295,701

Then we calculate the standard deviations of the X and Y columns, starting with the X column. (See Figure A-3.)

$$std_x = \sqrt{\frac{\Sigma x^2}{n} - \overline{x}^2}$$

Figure A-3. *The standard deviation of x equation.*

Substituting the numbers for x gives us the following result. (See Figure A-4.)

Std_x = square_root((79,079,225 / 12) –6,012,712.67)

Std_x = 759.75

$$std_x = \sqrt{\frac{\Sigma y^2}{n} - \overline{y}^2}$$

Figure A-4. *The standard deviation of y equation.*

Substituting the numbers for y gives us the following result:

Std_y = square_root((14,462,100 / 12) − 1,015,056.25)

Std_y = 436.02

Substituting all the numbers gives us the following result:

r = 295,701 / (759.75 × 436.02)

r = .89 or 89 %

This number, because it is close to 1, or 100 percent, shows a very strong positive correlation. In other words, there is a direct link to home size and electricity consumption. The next question is how much will an x-sized house consume in electricity per year? To get this information, we first need to calculate the regression line.

How to Interpret the Correlation Coefficient Value

Generally, anything above 50 percent correlation is considered significant. However, that depends heavily on the size of the sample. An 80 percent correlation when there are only five rows of data in the sample is largely insignificant compared to a 54 percent correlation when there are 150 rows of data in the sample. The larger the sample, the lower the correlation can be and the smaller the sample, the higher we need the correlation to be before we can conclude that the data correlation is high enough.

A common misinterpretation of correlation figures is that strong correlations somehow prove that the independent variables (the x values) cause the values of the dependent variables (the y values). To prove that this is not always true, some statisticians have shown strong correlations between the number of Certified Public Accountant (CPA) certifications and the number of prison incarcerations for a given year. There are coincidental factors that contribute to those figures but no causal link between the two. There are various statistical tests that can be done to investigate the significance of the correlation, but these are beyond the scope of this appendix.

To find out whether there is a causal effect between two values, the correlation coefficient is squared to come up with a coefficient of determination. The squaring of the correlation coefficient causes the number to be smaller, so if your correlation coefficient for a given analysis is .80, then the coefficient of determination will be .64.

The Regression Line

In this case, the independent variable is the square footage of the house. We assume that this number (x value) is not influenced by any other variables. The electricity cost is the dependent variable (y value) because it is the direct result of the independent variable.

Before we discuss the statistical formulas, look at the numbers from Table A-2 when transferred to a graph. (See Figure A-5.)

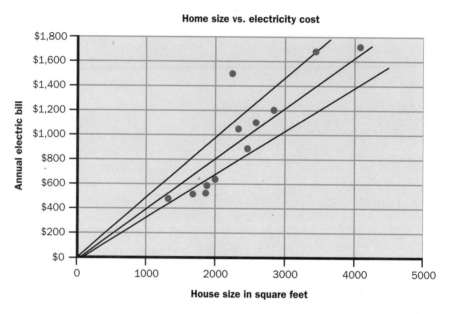

Figure A-5. *Scatter chart representation of the home size vs. electricity costs.*

As you can see from Figure A-5, the algorithm looks for a straight line that best describes the highest possible correlation by making the points fall as close to the line as possible. Regression looks for the slope and intercept of the line closest to all the points on the graph. The *slope* is a number that describes the steepness of the line as it moves up or down the Y axis of the graph. The *intercept* is the number that denotes the point on the Y axis when $x = 0$. Because of this goal, this line is known as the *best fit line* or *regression line*.

Note This section uses a straight line to find this best fit. However, it's often more accurate to establish relationships between numbers using curved lines, especially when the numbers show trends indicating that they go through predictable or seasonal changes. A curved line could follow this trend far more accurately than a straight line, but for the sake of simplicity, we'll use the straight line. Once you understand linear regression, I urge you to explore the use of nonlinear regression for data sets that do not necessarily follow a linear trend.

If a = the intercept and b = the slope, the basic equation that best describes linear regression is as follows:

$y = bx + a$

If we can calculate the value for a and b, thereby providing a value for a given house price (x), we should be able to solve the equation and get the expected electric bill (y).

Finding the Slope

The equation for the calculation of the slope is shown in Figure A-6.

$$b = \frac{n\Sigma xy - \Sigma x \Sigma y}{n\Sigma x^2 - (\Sigma x)^2}$$

Figure A-6. *Regression line slope equation.*

By substituting the numbers, we get the following result:

b = [(12 × 33,194,100) − (29,425 × 12,090)] / (12 × 79,079,225) − 29,425²

b = 42,580,950 / 83,120,075

b = 0.512

We now have one variable of the equation set. The next step is to find the intercept, which we'll do with the help of the slope.

Finding the Intercept

The formula for finding the intercept is shown in Figure A-7.

$$a = \bar{y} - b\bar{x}$$

Figure A-7. *The intercept of the regression line equation.*

Table A-2 provides the numbers we plug in to the equation:

a = 1007.50 − (0.512 × 2452.08)

a = -248

The Regression Coefficient

Now that we have computed the numbers, we know that the regression formula is $y =$ $(0.512 \times x) - 248$. By replacing x with a proposed home size, we can predict the expected annual electric bill. This coefficient is a two-way street—if we wanted to predict the size of the house, we could simply replace y with a proposed electric bill!

Using Regression Analysis to Make Predictions

Imagine you have seen several homes, and you want to find the annual electric bill. By substituting the home size in square feet for x, you'll get the y value, or the expected cost of electricity per year. (See Table A-3.)

Table A-3. Using x to predict y

Square Footage of Home (X)	Expected Cost of Electricity (Y)
1150	$340.80
1875	$712.00
2247	$902.46
3324	$1,453.89
3754	$1,674.05
4120	$1,861.44
4621	$2,117.95

In addition to the dangers associated with making predictions based on data that might have high coincidental correlations, there is also the danger of making predictions that go beyond the range of values present in the sample. In our house size vs. electricity bills example, our house size was between 1300 and 4100 square feet. It might be tempting to predict values for x and y where x is outside the range, as I did in Table A-3. Notice that I have one home with 1150 square feet in the first row and another with 4621 square feet on the last row. These two values fall outside the range of house sizes in the sample. These values make it risky to act on the calculated results or predictions. The ranges fall outside our experience and the assumption is that the results will remain linear. Making predictions based on numbers that do not fall within the sample is called *extrapolation*. This is in contrast to *interpolation*, a process that generates predictions based on the range of values contained in the model.

Cause and Effect

Regression and correlation analysis cannot determine cause and effect. It's up to the analyst to do a logic check, determine an appropriate hypothesis, and test the hypothesis against the data. For example, a correlation value of .95 relates the number of new CPAs in a city to the number of people arrested for drunk driving in the same city in one year. Clearly there is no cause and effect involved here. A deeper variable, population, is the true independent variable that drives both the number of CPAs and the number of arrests made for drunk driving. As analysts, we must choose data sets that are related and check that they influence one another.

Using extrapolation to predict energy costs with small homes is less risky than doing so with a sample of small and large homes combined in the same sample. For example, large houses will show a major increase in electricity use simply because they have proportionately higher ceilings than smaller homes, which causes the air-conditioning bills to be higher than in a house with lower ceilings. The predicted values will be false because they were based on the proportions measured with the smaller homes.

Analyzing the Accuracy of the Regression Line

The slope and the intercept of the regression line tells us very little about how well the line actually fits the points on the graph. Although the correlation coefficient mentioned previously in the chapter tells us about the strength of the relationships between the numbers, we still need a way to quantify the accuracy of our predictions. Ideally, for every prediction of Y, we would get an error range that tells us how far off the mark we are. For example, it would be nice to know that a prediction for a house of x size consumes y dollars in electricity give or take v dollars. To calculate our margin of error, we use the formula in Figure A-8.

$$\hat{m} = \frac{\overline{xy} - (\overline{x}\,\overline{y})}{\overline{x^2} - \overline{x}^2}$$

$$\hat{b} = \overline{y} - \hat{m}\overline{x}$$

$$MSE = \frac{\Sigma[\,y_i - (\hat{m}x_i + \hat{b})]^2}{n-2}$$

$$V = MSE\left[1 + \frac{1}{n} + \frac{(x_{current} - \overline{x})^2}{\Sigma(x_i - \overline{x})^2}\right]$$

Figure A-8. *The formula for testing the error range of* y *for a value of* x.

Use Table A-4 for the following formulas.

Table A-4. x and y Values for Correlation and Regression Equations with Additional Columns for Variance Analysis

X	Y	X²	Y²	XY	Y'	(Y–Y')²	(X–AVG(X))
1900	600	3,610,000	360,000	1,140,000	$724.80	$15,575.04	304796.01
2000	660	4,000,000	435,600	1,320,000	$776.00	$13,456.00	204379.34
2525	900	6,375,625	810,000	2,272,500	$1,044.80	$20,967.04	5316.84
1300	480	1,690,000	230,400	624,000	$417.60	$3,893.76	1327296.01
3500	1680	12,250,000	2,822,400	5,880,000	$1,544.00	$18,496.00	1098129.34
4100	1710	16,810,000	2,924,100	7,011,000	$1,851.20	$19,937.44	2715629.34
2870	1200	8,236,900	1,440,000	3,444,000	$1,221.44	$459.67	174654.34
1700	540	2,890,000	291,600	918,000	$622.40	$6,789.76	565629.34
2300	1500	5,290,000	2,250,000	3,450,000	$929.60	$325,356.16	23129.34
2450	1080	6,002,500	1,166,400	2,646,000	$1,006.40	$5,416.96	4.34
2890	1200	8,352,100	1,440,000	3,468,000	$1,231.68	$1,003.62	191771.01
1890	540	3,572,100	291,600	1,020,600	$719.68	$32,284.90	315937.67
Σx=29,425	ΣY=12,090	Σx^2=79,079,225	Σy^2=14,462,100	Σxy=33,194,100			SUM = 6,926,672.92
$\bar{x}$=2452	$\bar{y}$=1007.50	$\bar{x}^2$=6,012,712.67	$\bar{y}^2$=1,015,056.25	$\bar{x}\bar{y}$=2,766,175		MSE = $46,636.63	

Notice that the first thing we must do is get the value for the prediction based on the x values that we used to build the model. The Y'column contains the predicted values.

1. Apply the regression coefficient using the already existing x values and ignoring the real y values.

2. Square the difference and input the sums in each cell of the $(Y-Y')^2$ column.

3. Sum $(Y-Y')^2$ and then divide by n−2. This gives us the mean squared error (MSE) value. The MSE should equal $466366.36/(12-2) = \$46,636.63$.

4. Apply the last part of the formula to get a variance of Y. $46636.63 \times (1 + 1/n + ((3500_{\text{proposed value}} - 2452.08)^2/ 6,926,672.92)) = 57577.59$. The $x_{\text{proposed value}}$ is the proposed x value that is used to predict a y value. Calculate this value for every prediction. For this example, use 3500 for this value.

5. Take the square root of the variance and multiply it by the t-distribution coefficient that corresponds to the 95 percent confidence level for 12 data points. (See Table A-5.) Looking at the degrees of freedom for 10 (12−2) and the 95 percent confidence column, you get the number 2.228.

6. Multiply the t-distribution coefficient with the square root of the variance and you'll get 534.61. This represents the range of error you can be 95 percent sure your prediction will be within.

Table A-5. T-Distribution Table

T-Distribution Significance Level

Degrees of Freedom (n-2)	90%	95%	98%	99%
1	6.314	12.706	31.821	63.657
2	2.92	4.303	6.965	9.925
3	2.353	3.182	4.541	5.841
4	2.132	2.776	3.747	4.604
5	2.015	2.571	3.365	4.032
6	1.943	2.447	3.143	3.707
7	1.895	2.365	2.998	3.499
8	1.86	2.306	2.896	3.355
9	1.833	2.262	2.821	3.25
10	1.812	2.228	2.764	3.169
11	1.796	2.201	2.718	3.106
12	1.782	2.179	2.681	3.055
13	1.771	2.16	2.65	3.012

(continued)

Table A-5. *continued*

T-Distribution Significance Level

Degrees of Freedom (n-2)	90%	95%	98%	99%
14	1.761	2.145	2.624	2.977
15	1.753	2.131	2.602	2.947
16	1.746	2.12	2.583	2.921
17	1.74	2.11	2.567	2.898
18	1.734	2.101	2.552	2.878
19	1.729	2.093	2.539	2.861
20	1.725	2.086	2.528	2.845
21	1.721	2.08	2.518	2.831
22	1.717	2.074	2.508	2.819
23	1.714	2.069	2.5	2.807
24	1.711	2.064	2.492	2.797
25	1.708	2.06	2.485	2.787
26	1.706	2.056	2.479	2.779
27	1.703	2.052	2.473	2.771
28	1.701	2.048	2.467	2.763
29	1.699	2.045	2.462	2.756
30	1.697	2.042	2.457	2.75
40	1.684	2.021	2.423	2.704
60	1.671	2	2.39	2.66
120	1.658	1.98	2.358	2.617

Using this method, my predictions can now look like those in Table A-6.

Table A-6. Results of Using the x Values to Predict the y Values with Error Values

Square Footage of Home (X)	Expected Cost of Electricity (Y)	Error Interval
1150	$340.80	$0–$893
1875	$712	$201–$1,222
2247	$902.46	$401–$1,402
3324	$1,453.89	$928–$1,977
3754	$1,674.05	$1,121–$2,226
4120	$1,861.44	$1,276–$2,445
4621	$2,117.95	$1,480–$2,753

Note Most statistics books cover other methods for analyzing variance, and these are worth exploring if you're interested in being able to assert accurate levels of confidence in your predictions.

Using OLAP to Create Regression Models

When Microsoft OLAP first entered the market, what many data miners looked for first were the statistical functions. Because statistics depends heavily on the compilation of aggregated data, OLAP is a powerful tool to perform regression analysis. OLAP provides the following MDX functions to perform the same calculations as those we just did.

To calculate the slope and the intercept, we can use the LinRegSlope and LinRegIntercept functions in the following way:

- LinRegSlope (set, y measure, x measure)
- LinRegIntercept (set, y measure, x measure)

  The structures are very straightforward; just remember that the y value must be the first parameter and the x value must be the second.

The correlation to measure the strength of the relationship between the X and Y arrays is just as easy to compute:

- correlation (set, y measure, x measure)

Predictions can be made using the *LinRegPoint* function. The following function predicts a given y value for the proposed x value:

- LinRegPoint (Proposed x value, set, y measure, x measure)

The following listing shows these functions in action. I created a very simple cube that contains a time dimension and the same home size vs. electricity cost measures as in the previous examples. Consequently, I ran this MDX query in the MDX Sample Application provided with Analysis Services with the following result:

```
with member [measures].[correlation]
as 'correlation(
    {descendants([time],[time].[day])},
    [home size],
    [electric])'

member [measures].[slope]
as 'linregslope(
    {descendants([time],[time].[day])},
    [electric],
    [home size])'
```
(continued)

```
member [measures].[intercept]
as 'linregintercept(
    {descendants([time],[time].[day])},
    [electric],
    [home size])'

member [measures].[predict 3500]
as 'linregpoint(3500,
    {descendants([time],[time].[day])},
    [electric],
    [home size])'

select {[time]} on columns,
{
    [correlation],
    [slope],
    [intercept],
    [predict 3500]
} on rows
    from [homes]
```

The MDX regression analysis yields the results shown in Figure A-9.

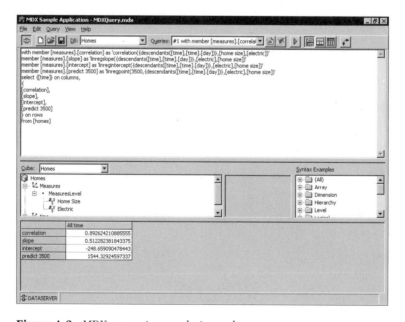

Figure A-9. *MDX regression analysis results.*

An added advantage of OLAP is the ease and speed with which queries are issued. Also, OLAP allows you to navigate across various dimensions, allowing you to drill down levels and have the statistical functions dynamically calculate according to the current aggregation you happen to be in.

Applying Regression to a Relational Database

To make regression analysis even more valuable to data miners, we must be able to apply the algorithm to a table. The most important point to keep in mind when choosing a data source or when building a table is that the logically related pairs of data values must remain grouped together in a row. Using our house example, a logical pair would be the square footage of a house and its annual electricity costs. Regression, as you've probably noticed, makes use of the product of the values in the X and Y columns to generate the regression line.

The house size vs. electricity consumption example is straightforward, but many other real-world regression analysis projects rely on data that has the x values in one table and the y values in another. A SELECT statement is used to join them. For example, if you're going to use the daily interest rates as the x values to predict the price of airline tickets in the Y column, you need to make sure that each row contains an interest rate and a ticket price for the same date, week, or other common measurement level the values share so that the paired values are related.

Getting the values you need from tables using the SQL syntax is more complex because SQL lacks many of the statistical functions available in OLAP. Also, relational tables are designed to return result sets after only one pass through the tables. To get around the set-oriented functions of RDBMS engines, it's possible to take advantage of the richness of the T-SQL syntax to store all the needed numerical elements in variables and perform the calculations with them as we do in the code listing below. The result can then be returned in the form of a table.

Note If this were a real application, tables could be designed to structure the environment for regression in a more sensible manner. The correlation, the slope, and the intercept would obviously be computed once and stored in a table so that the predictions could simply perform calculations based on precomputed data instead of recalculating the same data every time a prediction is made. The stored procedure is structured in this way to demonstrate the use of T-SQL for regression analysis.

```
set nocount on

create table tdist95
    (df int, dist float)

insert into tdist95 values (1, 12.706)
insert into tdist95 values (2, 4.303)
insert into tdist95 values (3, 3.182)
insert into tdist95 values (4, 2.776)
insert into tdist95 values (5, 2.571)
:

-- ***************************************************
-- To fill this table, see the t-distribution table
-- in this document. It's assumed that a permanent
-- t-distribution table will be present to be used
-- by all future regression analysis efforts.
-- ***************************************************

go

create procedure usp_MakeElectricBillPrediction
    @homesize float
as
declare @x float
declare @y float
declare @avgx float
declare @avgy float
declare @xy float
declare @x2 float
declare @y2 float
declare @support int

declare @dist float

declare @correlation float
declare @determination float
declare @slope float
declare @intercept float

declare @sx float
declare @sy float
declare @sxy float

declare @prediction float
```

```
select
    @x = sum([size]) ,
    @y = sum([electricity]),
    @avgx = avg([size]) ,
    @avgy = avg([electricity]) ,
    @xy = sum([size]*[electricity]) ,
    @x2 = sum(square([size])) ,
    @y2 = sum(square([electricity])),
    @support = count(1) as support
        from homeelectric

set @slope = ( (@support * @xy) - (@x * @y) )
    / ( (@support * @x2) - square(@x) )
set @intercept   = ( @y/@support) -
    (@slope * (@x/@support))

set @sxy = (@xy/@support) - (@avgx * @avgy)
set @sx  = sqrt( abs(@x2/@support)-square(@avgx) )
set @sy  = sqrt( abs(@y2/@support)-square(@avgy) )

set @correlation = @sxy/(@sx*@xy)
set @determination = square(@correlation)

-- The t-distribution confidence level is calculated based
-- on the degrees of freedom, which is the support - 2
select @dist = dist from tdist95 where df = (@cnt -2).

if @dist is null
begin
    -- This is in case the support is higher than the highest
    -- degree of freedom value, in which case we use the maximum.
    select @dist = max(dist) from tdist95.
end

-- The expected electric bill is calculated here.
set @prediction = @intercept + (@homesize * @slope)

select
    @errx = sum(X-avgx) as errx,
    @erry = sum(Y-avgy)) as erry,
    @residual = sum(square(y - (intercept + (slope* X)))
    from homeelectric

-- Calculate the error variation.
set @error = (@tdist * @residual) * (square(@prediction -
    @avgx)/@errx) + 1 + (1/@support)
```

(continued)

```
-- Return the results in the form of a table.
select
    @correlation as correlation,
    @support as support,
    @slope as slope,
    @intercept as intercept,
    @prediction as AnnualElectricBill,
    @error as PlusOrMinus
```

Regression with SQL Server vs. Regression Using OLAP

OLAP is able to perform regression functions only with measures in the same fact table. The house size vs. electricity consumption example is ideally suited for this, but if you wanted to perform a regression analysis to see whether the price of two-bedroom houses had any relationship to the price of five-bedroom houses, OLAP couldn't use the regression functions to perform those calculations. This is because the regression functions use the measures that belong to a given set, but to do the house analysis, two sets have to be compared. A big advantage of using SQL Server to perform regression analysis directly with user defined mathematical expressions is that you have the flexibility to perform analysis on data sets in a number of different ways.

Because OLAP tends to include records in a set that may contain 0 values, which you might choose to exclude, the regression analysis can be seriously compromised. For example, if some of the sample houses were uninhabited for some time they would show $0 in electricity consumption. This data would make the correlation as well as the slope of the line inaccurate. As complicated as it would be to eliminate these values from the set when using OLAP, it's easy to exclude records when using SQL Server with a simple WHERE clause.

Using Visual Basic to Perform Regression Analysis

To analyze, regression analysis needs both aggregates and individual rows. Although this analysis can be accomplished with SQL Server user-defined functions, temporary tables, and cursors, you might consider creating a COM+ middle-tier component that does the calculations and returns the slope, intercept, and correlation. The intense mathematics are better left to this component so that CPU cycles are not degraded and taken from the database engine that needs the power to return queries. These calculated values can then be stored in a table for use in subsequent predictions. As you can see from this code listing, using a programming language offers the ultimate in flexibility and power because an application development language is equipped with functions and syntax designed to support complex calculations and data structures. Most languages, such as Microsoft Visual Basic, Microsoft Visual C++, or Perl are designed to easily connect to data sources such as SQL Server, which in our example contains the data needed to perform regression analysis.

> **Note** This code listing was written as a batch script; it wasn't structured using functions or any persistent data storage. This form is not recommended for a real job, but in this example, it makes the code easier to follow and the regression analysis easier to understand.

```
homesize = wcsript.arguments(0)

    dim support
    dim x
    dim y
    dim x2
    dim y2
    dim xy
    dim avgx
    dim avgy
    dim errx
    dim erry
    dim intercept
    dim slope
    dim errorval
    dim correlation
    dim significance
    dim prediction
    dim residual
    dim variance
    dim tDist95[34]

    tdist[1] = 12.706
    tdist[2] = 4.303
    tdist[3] = 3.182
    tdist[4] = 2.776
    tdist[5] = 2.571

    tdist[6] = 2.447
    tdist[7] = 2.365
    tdist[8] = 2.306
    tdist[9] = 2.262
    tdist[10] = 2.228

    tdist[11] = 2.120
    tdist[12] = 2.110
    tdist[13] = 2.101
    tdist[14] = 2.093
    tdist[15] = 2.086

    tdist[16] = 2.080
    tdist[17] = 2.074
    tdist[18] = 2.069
    tdist[19] = 2.064
    tdist[20] = 2.060
```

(continued)

```
          tdist[21] = 2.056
          tdist[22] = 2.052
          tdist[23] = 2.048
          tdist[24] = 2.045
          tdist[25] = 2.042

          tdist[26] = 2.030
          tdist[27] = 2.021
          tdist[28] = 2.014
          tdist[29] = 2.009
          tdist[30] = 2.004

          tdist[31] = 2.000
          tdist[32] = 1.990
          tdist[33] = 1.984
          tdist[34] = 1.980

          Dim oConn as adodb.connection
          Dim oRs as adodb.recordset

          Dim strSql

          Set oConn.ConnectionString = "Provider=sqloledb;
              username=dtsuser;password= ;Data Source=dataserver;
              Initial Catalog=dataminer"
          oConn.Open

          strSql = "select sum([size]) as X," & _
              "sum([electricity]) as Y," & _
              "avg([size]) as AvgX," & _
              "avg([electricity]) as AvgX," & _
              "sum([size]*[electricity]) as XY," & _
              "sum(square([size])) as X2," & _
              "sum(square([electricity])) as Y2," & _
              "count(1) as support" & _
              " from homeelectric"

          Set oRs = oConn.Execute(strSql)

          x =        oRs.x
          y =        oRs.y
          x2 =       oRs.x2
          y2 =       oRs.y2
          avgx =     oRs.avgx
          avgy =     oRs.avgy
          support = oRs.support

          slope  = ( (support * xy) - (x * y) ) / ( (support * x2)
              - square(x) )
          intercept  = (y/support) - (slope * (x/support))
```

```
sxy = (xy/support) - (avg * avgy)
sx  = sqrt( abs(x2/support)-square(avgx) )
sy  = sqrt( abs(y2/support)-square(avgy) )

correlation = sxy/(sx*xy)

oRs.Close

strSql = "select sum(X-" & cstr(avgx) & ") as errx," & _
    "sum(Y-" & cstr(avgy) & "), as erry" & _
    "sum(square(y-(" & cstr(intercept) & " + (" & _
    cstr(slope) & "* X)))) as resid" & _
    " from homeelectric"

Set oRs = oConn.Execute(strSql)

errx = oRs.errx
erry = oRs.erry
residual = oRs.residual

oRs.Close
oConn.Close

prediction = intercept + (slope * homesize)

if support > 35 ' This is so we don't overwrite the array.
    tdist = 1.980
else
    tdist = tDist95[support-2]
end if


MSE = tdist * sqrt( abs(square(residual) / (support-2)  ) )
errorval = MSE * ((square(prediction - avgx)/ errx)) + _
    1 + (1/support)

wscript.echo "Slope : " & cstr(slope)
wscript.echo "Intercept : " & cstr(intercept)
wscript.echo "Correlation : " & cstr(correlation)

wscript.Echo "Prediction"
wscript.Echo "-----------------------------------------------"
wscript.Echo "If house is " & cstr(estimate) & " square feet"
wscript.Echo "You can expect to pay $" & cstr(prediction) & _
            " in for electricity annually"
wscript.Echo " ... give or take $" & cstr(errorval)
```

Creating the Models

We have just seen how to perform the calculations needed to make numerical predictions using linear regression analysis. However, as you've probably noticed, the Microsoft Analysis Services algorithms create a data-mining model that is used to make those predictions. The linear regression algorithm should also generate a data-mining model that can be used for predictions without having to execute the algorithm every time.

Because linear regression is not one of the available data-mining algorithms within Analysis Services, we have only two useful choices to store our models:

- A table created using SQL Server, Visual Foxpro, or Microsoft Access
- A Predictive Modeling Markup Language (PMML) XML file

Unlike the other algorithms we've seen, linear regression needs to store very little data about the cases. It only needs

- **Correlation**   To test the degree to which the data is related.
- **Slope**   A necessary number needed to perform the regression equation.
- **Intercept**   One of the numbers needed to perform the regression equation.
- **Residual value**   This is the difference between the predicted values for y and the actual values for y. The difference exists because we make compromises in the expected values of y to draw a straight line. This helps calculate the variance in the prediction.
- **Variance of x**   This value, combined with the residual value, helps calculate the variance of a prediction.
- **Support**   The number of cases used to create the regression line.

Using a Table

Storing these in a table is easy. A table such as the one shown here is adequate:

```
CREATE TABLE RegressionModel (
    ID int,
    correlation float,
    slope float,
    intercept float,
    residual float,
    -- the error of X (errx) is another name for the variance of X
    errx float,
    support int
    )
```

After the regression line calculation is performed, the numbers are inserted into the model, and all subsequent predictions would simply query the values from the table to build the formula that generates the prediction. Here is a sample query:

```
SELECT intercept + (slope * 1500) as prediction
    FROM RegressionModel
WHERE ID = 10
```

Using PMML

Storing the linear regression mining model in an industry-wide standard structure offers some advantages over storing them in a table. Microsoft has embraced PMML and stores local mining models created with the clustering or decision trees algorithms in a PMML-compliant XML file. By storing the regression model in the same format, there's a good chance you will be able to use today's models within Analysis Services as soon as regression is made available. PMML also provides a way to use other data-mining products that support this algorithm. The downside to this approach, of course, is that until Microsoft supports this model, your applications will have to be designed to read directly from the XML file to make predictions.

> For more information about PMML support for the regression model, go to *http:/ /www.dmg.org/html/generalregression.html*.

Summary

Data mining is a powerful tool, and as of this writing, a new one as well. The decision trees and clustering algorithms available with SQL Server 2000 are ideal for making predictions of discrete attributes. These same algorithms are incapable of supplying specific numeric predictions. Regression analysis is one of the many algorithms used to make predictions on continuous (numeric) data, but it's not currently available as part of the data-mining suite of tools.

Soon you will be able to add your own algorithms or purchase algorithms from third-party vendors to the data-mining tools. The regression analysis algorithm is even hinted at in the OLE DB for data-mining specification. I wanted to demonstrate that the tools that come with SQL Server may be sufficient to apply new algorithms designed to your specifications.

SQL Server does come with powerful tools to perform this regression analysis and numerical predictions, either by using OLAP functions or the SQL Server T-SQL language itself. These tools give you the power to use proven algorithms today and even use the variations that are most appropriate for your data-analysis needs.

Glossary of Data-Mining Terms

A

accuracy When referring to data, accuracy is the percentage of values that can be verified to be correct within the records. In data-mining models, it's the degree to which the data-mining model reflects the values of the underlying data, which should serve to measure how well the model can be used to predict new information.

algorithm Computer logic designed to be used as a framework from which to build computer programs. These are combinations of mathematical formulas and methods designed to solve a particular problem. Data-mining algorithms seek to transform cases into a specific predictive model.

analytical model The logical data structure that is the result of a process, usually an algorithm. Clustering and decision trees are examples of models used for the grouping and classification of data.

anomalous data Case data that contains errors that are generally caused by bad data-entry validation or corrupted processes. These errors can cause inaccurate data-mining models and false or missing predictions.

antecedent When one event is identified as the cause of or link to another event, the original event is described as the antecedent. In a department store, if 45 percent of customers who buy motor oil come back the next day to buy oil stain remover, the purchase of the motor oil is the antecedent. *See also* left-hand side.

API *See* application programming interface

application programming interface (API) Some applications or software tools contain internal functions that can be used by outside programs without the need to delve into the source. In order to provide this functionality, the software exposes these functions through an interface called the API, which allows the outside software developers to incorporate these calls in their own software.

artificial neural network Nonlinear predictive models that learn through training and are designed to imitate the function of biological neural networks in the human brain. Artificial neural networks are used in data-mining processes involving very large quantities of variables that each get analyzed in a separate node of the neural network. This is a directed form of data mining that uses inputs to predict future outcomes.

association algorithm An algorithm that creates rules that identify how often events have occurred together. This fits in with the "beer and diapers" example in which a supermarket finds that the purchase of beer occurs at the same time as the purchase of diapers x percent of times.

B

bias This refers to the inclination of the cases to lean to a particular description because of the way the data was sampled. For instance, if data from a survey was used to build a data-mining model, it might be found that persons who answer surveys have built-in differences from those who don't. This can introduce bias in the results. Bias can also occur when data is extracted from a database using criteria that eliminates the randomness of the sample, such as using zip codes, income brackets, or even dates and names.

binning A process that converts numerical data that would otherwise be continuous into discrete values that are placed in predefined "bins." For instance, if income were to be used as an output variable, the algorithm might need to bin the data because there are too many different values between the highest and the lowest incomes. For efficiency, the algorithm places the incomes in bins of 10,000–30,000, 30,000–50,000, 50,000–80,000, and so on.

bootstrapping When data sets are too large, a process called bootstrapping extracts samples from the original data set and treats each of the samples as the entire population. Because bias can be introduced this way, several samples are then used to create several data models, each of which gets averaged into one.

C

CART *See* classification and regression trees

cases Records containing data that are used to populate a data-mining model. The cases represent the inputs and outputs of the subsequent analysis or predictions that are to be made.

categorical data Categorical data fits into a small number of discrete categories as opposed to continuous, numerical data. Categorical data can either be unordered (nominal), referring to countries or zip codes,

or ordered (ordinal), such as high, medium, or low values.

CHAID *See* Chi-squared Automatic Interaction Detector

chi-squared A statistic that finds the values that are most predominant in a given set. It uses this information to determine the best splits to use in a decision tree, usually created with a CHAID-type algorithm.

Chi-squared Automatic Interaction Detector (CHAID) A decision tree algorithm that uses the chi-squared statistic to identify the most efficient values to use as splits in the data.

classification The process of dividing cases into mutually exclusive groups such that the members of each group are as close as possible to one another, and different groups remain as far as possible from one another. The distance is measured with respect to specific variables you are trying to predict. Classification might seek to divide the entire data sample or population for a credit card company into two groups, those customers with "Good" credit and those with "Bad" credit.

classification and regression trees (CART) A decision tree technique used for classification of a data set. It provides a set of rules that can be applied to new cases to predict which records will have a given outcome. This technique uses two-way splits only, which increases depth, but requires less preparation by the engine.

classification tree A decision tree that places categorical variables into individual classes.

cleansing This is the task that processes the data to be used to build cases in an effort to eliminate all errors and anomalies before the data actually gets used to build a data-mining model. This process can also complete missing information and normalize certain attributes so that they can be treated in the same manner.

clustering algorithm Used to find groups of items with similar attributes. They are used to draw conclusions about the behavior of a given group from which accurate generalizations about the members of the groups are made.

confidence Confidence of a rule is a measure of how likely it is that the rule applies. This is usually based on a number of factors, including the number of cases used to derive that rule as well as the representation of that rule in relation to the others. For instance, the chance of an IRS audit expressed as a rule is 65 percent, and the percent of Gold credit card holders, expressed as a rule, is 85 percent.

confusion matrix A table that compares the actual values vs. the predicted values of a data-mining process. This is most often used to gauge the accuracy of a given data-mining model.

consequent When one event is identified as the cause of or link to another event, the caused event is described as the consequent. In a department store, if 45 percent of customers who buy motor oil come back the next day to buy oil stain remover, the purchase of the oil stain remover is the consequent.

continuous data Refers to numerical values that have relative values to each other. Time data, such as years, and income data are examples of continuous values as opposed to discrete or categorical values.

cross validation A method of estimating the accuracy of a decision tree. The original data set is divided into parts, each playing a specific role in testing the decision tree model against the other parts.

D

data Facts and events gathered through manual or automatic data entry. These facts are usually stored in a database in the form of records. Groups of related records are known as cases.

database management system (DBMS) An application that's designed to manage data, relational, or simple flat file tables.

data format Data format refers to the form of the data in the database. Data items can exist in many formats such as text, integer, and floating-point decimal.

data mining An information extraction activity that uses a combination of machine learning, statistical analysis, modeling techniques, and database technology, data mining finds patterns and subtle relationships in data and infers rules that allow predictions of future results to be made.

data-mining method Procedures and algorithms used to analyze the data in databases.

data navigation The process of viewing different dimensions and levels of detail of a multidimensional OLAP structure. This is often used to confirm or deny assumptions made about the data.

data visualization Visual interpretation of complex relationships in multidimensional data.

data warehouse A database designed for optimizing the storage and delivery of massive quantities of data, oftentimes in a different format than the transactional data.

DBMS *See* database management system

decision tree A tree-shaped structure that represents a set of decisions expressed as nodes that contain rules and descriptions of their members. These nodes generate rules for the classification of a data set.

deduction Deduces information that is a logical and irrefutable consequence of the data. For example if A = B and B = C, then one can deduce that A = C.

degree of fit A measure of how closely the data-mining model fits the training data. Usually a statistical measure known as r-squared is used.

dependent variable The variable derived by the prediction task associated with the data-mining model. It's the outcome or output variable.

deployment The implementation of a trained and completely validated model for use as a base for predictions.

dimension Each attribute of a case or occurrence in the data being mined that affects the value of a given output variable. Usually represented by a field in a flat file record or a column of a relational database table.

discrete A data item that has a finite set of values, such as colors or days of the week. Discrete is the opposite of continuous.

discriminant analysis A statistical method used to determine the location of boundaries between clusters. Used mostly in clustering type processes.

E

entropy A way to measure variability other than with the variance statistic. Depending on the type of decision tree algorithm, this value can be used to decide upon a split in a given node.

exploratory analysis Looking at data to discover relationships not previously detected. This is usually a step done in preparation for data mining because it offers the chance to understand the patterns and trends in the original data.

external data Data not collected by the organization, such as data available from database feeds originating from other companies.

F

feed-forward A neural net in which the signals flow in only one direction, from the inputs to the outputs.

fuzzy logic Applied to fuzzy sets where membership in a fuzzy set is a probability and not necessarily a definite "True" or "False." Fuzzy logic needs to be able to manipulate degrees of probability of truth in addition to true and false.

G

genetic algorithm A method of generating and testing combinations of possible input parameters to find the optimal output. It uses processes based on the principles of natural selection as the criteria for determining truth.

graphical user interface (GUI) An environment in which the user issues commands by clicking buttons and choosing options from menus and lists instead of typing commands on the command line.

GUI *See* graphical user interface

H

hidden nodes The nodes in the hidden layers in a neural network.

I

independent variable The attributes and values used to determine what the prediction or output variables will be.

induction A technique that infers generalizations from the information in the data. The process involves deriving a conclusion based on repetitive patterns rather than irrefutable logical principles.

interaction Two independent variables interact when a change in the value of one changes the effect on the dependent variable of the other.

internal data Data collected by an organization through its own data-entry procedures.

K

k-nearest neighbor A clustering method that classifies a point in space by calculating the distances between the point and points in the training data set. The point is then assigned to the class that is most common among its k-nearest neighbors or clusters.

Kohonen feature map A type of neural network that uses unsupervised learning to find patterns in data. In data mining, it is employed for cluster analysis.

L

layer Nodes in a neural net are usually grouped into layers, with each layer performing an input, output, or hidden function. The input nodes match input variables and the output nodes match output variables.

leaf In a decision tree, a leaf represents the very last node in the tree that has no more branches emanating from it. It's the part of the tree that is used to make the predictions.

learning The process of training a data-mining model with existing data.

least squares A method of training the parameters of a model by choosing the weights that minimize the sum of the squared deviation of the predicted values of the model from the observed values of the data.

left-hand side *See* antecedent

linear model An analytical model that assumes linear relationships between the values of the variables being examined.

linear regression A statistical technique used to find the most accurate linear relationship between a target variable and its input variables.

logistic regression A linear regression that predicts the proportion of categorical target variables, such as the type of customer in a given population. Logistic regression is useful when the observed outcome is restricted to two values, which usually represent the occurrence or non-occurrence of an event.

M

massively parallel processing (MPP) A computer configuration that is able to use hundreds or thousands of CPUs simultaneously. The system usually consists of various computers processing different parts of a program at the same time. Each computer, or node, maintains control of its own resources while maintaining a high level of coordination with the other nodes. This structure is often used for neural networks.

maximum likelihood A training method that finds the maximum likelihood that a parameter is the value that maximizes the probability that the data came from the population defined by the parameter.

mean The arithmetic average value of a collection of numbers.

median The value in the middle of a collection of ordered data. In other words, the value with the same number of items above and below it.

missing data Data values that were not measured, not entered into the system, or were simply unknown. Typically, data-mining methods ignore the missing values, omit any records containing missing values, replace missing values with the mode or mean, or infer missing values from existing values.

mode The most common value in a data set. If more than one value occurs the same number of times, the data is multimodal.

model A logical structure that contains data that represents the patterns discovered in the cases used to build the model. This model is then used for browsing in an effort to better understand the underlying data or as a repository of rules that can be applied to new data in order to predict unknown outcomes.

MPP *See* massively parallel processing

multidimensional database A database designed for OLAP. Structured as a multidimensional cube with aggregates precomputed per dimension.

multiprocessor computer A computer that includes multiple processors that work at the same time.

N

nearest neighbor A clustering technique that makes use of a k-means algorithm. This assumes that the clusters are known in advance, which then allows each record to be evaluated according to its distance from the center of the cluster.

neural network *See* artificial neural network

node A decision point in a decision tree usually containing a specific set of rules governing membership in that node.

noise Nonsensical data or erratic predictions that are often the result of false or even nonexistent patterns. A decision tree that predicts that anybody named Mary is a good credit risk is an example of noise.

nonapplicable data Values that would be logically impossible, such as high-income-earning pets or married plants.

nonlinear model An analytical model that does not attempt to establish any linear relationships between the variables being examined.

normalize The process of culling the cases of all extremes in the data that would adversely affect the predictive ability of the model.

O

object linking and embedding database (OLE DB) *See* OLE DB

OLAP *See* online analytical processing

OLE DB An acronym for object linking and embedding database. A COM interface that allows a program to be written that queries data without having to take the implementation and structure of the underlying data into consideration.

online analytical processing (OLAP) Tools that give the user the capability to browse through multiple levels of aggregation of the data with relative ease.

optimization criterion A function of the difference between predictions and data estimates that are derived and chosen to optimize the predictive capability of the model. Least squares and maximum likelihood are examples of these functions.

outliers Data that falls outside the boundaries of what's normally expected from the value. When predicting income, billionaires might be taken out of the case set because of their unusually large incomes and the low number of billionaires.

overfitting A tendency of some modeling techniques to pursue the training process to the point where patterns contain very few occurrences yet represent very specific predictive recommendations, which because of their low occurrence can cause false outcomes.

overlay Cases from outside sources of data that are combined with the organization's own data.

P

parallel processing The coordination of multiple processors that are used to perform computational tasks with a common goal. Parallel processing can occur either on a multiprocessor computer or on a network of computers, each of which accomplish a part of the task.

pattern A relationship between two or more variables. Data-mining techniques include automatic pattern discovery that makes it possible to detect complicated relationships in data.

precision The measure of variability of a given attribute when arriving at a certain outcome. Although the result might not be accurate, it can be precise in its ability to pinpoint the exact outcome of true or false.

predictability *See* confidence

prediction query A SQL-like syntax that allows a program or a user to input cases with unknown outputs and compare them to a data-mining model, which then "fills in the blanks."

predictive model A structure and process for predicting the values of specified variables in a data set.

prevalence The percentage of times that a given association occurs in a node or a cluster. This can be expressed as "90 percent of members use Gold credit cards in node *xyz*."

prospective data analysis Data analysis that predicts future trends, behaviors, or events based on historical data.

pruning The process of eliminating nodes from a decision tree when it has been determined that those nodes do not reflect accurate predictive descriptions.

R

RAID *See* Redundant Array of Inexpensive Disks

range The difference between the maximum value and the minimum value.

RDBMS *See* Relational Database Management System

Redundant Array of Inexpensive Disks (RAID) A technology for the efficient parallel storage of data for high-performance computer systems.

regression tree A decision tree that predicts values of continuous, numerical variables.

Relational Database Management System (RDBMS) Application that is designed to manage data, but unlike a simple DBMS, it also manages the relations and constraints between tables.

resubstitution error The estimate of error based on the differences between the predicted values of a trained model and the observed values in the training set.

retrospective data analysis Data analysis that provides insights into trends, behaviors, or events that have already occurred in the past in an effort to perform exploratory analysis of the data.

right-hand side *See* consequent

r-squared A number between 0 and 1 that measures how well a model fits its training data. One represents a perfect fit and 0 says the model has no predictive ability. The formula consists of a calculation of the covariance between the predicted and observed values divided by the standard deviations of the predicted and observed values.

rule induction The extraction of useful "if-then rules" from data based on statistical significance.

S

sampling Creating a subset of data from the whole population.

sensitivity analysis Experimenting with the parameters of a model by changing their values and assessing the effects in predictive output.

sequence discovery The same as association algorithm, except that the time sequence of events is also considered. So if an event occurs after another event, the model is also able to predict how long after the first event the second will occur.

significance A probability measure of how strongly the data supports a certain output. For instance, if the significance of a result is said to be 10 percent, it means that there is only a 10 percent chance that the result could have occurred by some coincidence. The lower the significance, the better the output is because it is less likely that the event was unrelated to the input variables.

SMP *See* symmetric multiprocessor

supervised learning Process by which an algorithm trains data and builds a model based on known input parameters. This is used when you know what you are looking for, and you need to apply the model to your data.

support *See* confidence

symmetric multiprocessor (SMP) A type of multiprocessor computer in which simultaneous processing tasks are shared equally among all the processors. Often this feature is a function of the operating system.

T

terabyte One trillion bytes or 1000 gigabytes.

test data A case set that was not used to build the data-mining model. Using this data, it's possible to assess the accuracy of the model.

test error The estimate of error based on the results of applying the test data to the data-mining model.

time series analysis The analysis of a sequence of measurements made at specified time intervals. Time is the most significant dimension in this type of analysis.

time series model A model that forecasts future values of a time series based on past values. The predictions are made based on values as they change over time, so the predictions sought also require time values as a variable.

topology For a neural net, topology refers to the number of layers and the number of nodes in each layer.

training The process of creating the initial data-mining model is referred to as "training the model." The end result is a model that accurately represents the trends and patterns as they exist in the population of data.

training data The set of cases used to train the model.

transformation A structuring and re-expressing of data such as aggregating it, normalizing it, changing its unit of measure, or cleansing it.

U

unsupervised learning Refers to the collection of techniques in which groupings of the data are defined without the use of a dependent variable. This type of process is used when the outputs are essentially unknown. Cluster analysis is an example.

V

validation The process of testing the models with a data set other than the set from the original training cases. By using a different set of cases, the model is put to the test of accurately predicting values that were not initially known at training time.

variance A statistical measure of dispersion. The initial deviations of a data item from its average value are squared, and then the average of those squared deviations is obtained to get the overall measure of variability.

visualization Data-mining models can be viewed by representations displayed in a variety of graphs and charts. These tools are designed to eliminate some of the complexity surrounding the understanding of the model. For instance, a decision tree can be viewed as a series of interconnected nodes. A clustering model can be viewed using a scatter point chart to see the quantity and density of clusters.

W

windowing When training a model using time series data, the window refers to the period of time that will be used to make a subsequent prediction. To predict a value for next week, I may need to use a window of five weeks' worth of time-series data.

Index

Page numbers in italics refer to figures, tables, or illustrations.

A

ActiveX Scripting task, 166
algorithms. *See* data mining algorithms
Analysis Manager, 70–74, *70, 71, 73, 74*
Analysis Services. *See also* Microsoft Data
  Transformation Services (DTS); online
  analytical processing (OLAP)
    client architecture (*see also* Decision Support
      Objects (DSO); PivotTable Service; *OLE DB
      entries*)
      introduced, 21, *22*
      Multidimensional expressions (MDX), 25,
        129–30, *130, 131*
      prediction joins, 25
    connecting to
      using HTTP, 280, *280*
      using PivotTable Service, 276–77, *277–79*
    data-mining services within, 20–21, *21*
    defined, 15
    introduced, 15
    server architecture, 20–21, *21*
Analysis Services Processing task, 167
association, 13

B

bias, 54
bins, 96–97, *96*
Bulk Insert task, 163

C

C4.5 algorithm, 98
CART (Classification and Regression Trees), 97–98
CaseDimension property, *220*
case key columns, 45, 152, *152*
CaseLevel property, *220*
cases, 8, 24
case sets, 24

categorical values, 143
cause and effect analysis, 58–59
CHAID (Chi-Squared Automatic Interaction
  Detector), 98
chi-squared analysis, 62–64, *63*
Chi-Squared Automatic Interaction Detector
  (CHAID), 98
Classification and Regression Trees (CART), 97–98
ClassType property, 211
client (single-tier) architecture, 42, *42*
ClusterDistance function, 315, 316–17
Cluster function, 315
clustering
  analyzing the data, 156–58, *157*
  closeness concepts, 142
  conceptual attributes and, 142
  creating the model
    editing joins, 152
    finishing, 153
    introduced, 149, *149*
    selecting tables, 150, *151*
    selecting the case key column, 152, *152*
    selecting the data-mining technique, 151, *151*
    selecting the input and predictable columns,
      152–53, *153*
    selecting the source type, 150, *150*
  factors affecting, 142–43
  introduced, 12, *13*, 135–37, *136, 137*
  K-Means clustering algorithm
    cluster boundaries, 141, *141*
    finding the center of clusters, 140, *141*
    finding the clusters, 139, *139*
    introduced, 138–39
    known vs. unknown clusters, 140
    overview, 138
  measuring closeness
    distance between points, 144, *144*
    record overlap, 145, *146*
    vector angle similarity, 144–45, *145*

clustering, *continued*
  prediction queries with clustering models,
    315–17, *316*
  processing the model, 154, *154*
  as undirected data mining, 137, *138*
  viewing the model
    introduced, 154, *155*
    order of cluster nodes, 156
    organization of cluster nodes, 154, *155*, 156
  weaknesses of, 148
  when to use, 146–48, *147*
ClusterProbability function, 315, 316, *316*
columns
  case key, 45, 152, *152*
  choosing, 36–37
  columns to avoid, 38–39
  defined, 36
  input, 37, 45, 78, 79, *79*, 152–53, *153*
  key, 37, 78
  predictable, 45, 78–79, *79*, 152–53, *153*
  target, 37
  value, 37
COLUMNS rowset, 249
commit, 124
comparison analysis, 58
Connect method, 212
ContentType property, *220*
continuous data, 96
Copy SQL Server Objects task, 165
correlation, 57
CREATE MINING MODEL statement, 266, 280–81,
  284
cross validation, 64

D

Database object, 211, 219, 220, *220–21*, 233
database roles, 234–35
Databases collection, 211
Data Definition Language (DDL), 22
Data Driven Query task, 163–64
data granularity, 40–42, *41*
data islands, 35, *35*
data mining. *See also* data warehouses
  advantage over OLAP, 6
  current uses, 6–7
  defined, 3, 7

data mining, *continued*
  directed, 51–52
  introduced, 3–4
  methodology, 9–11, *9*
  OLAP vs., 11, 17
  overview, 11–14, *13*
  reasons for using, 4–6
  undirected
    clustering as, 137, *138*
    data mining vs. statistics, 52–53
    introduced, 52
    learning from historical data, 57–59
    predicting the future, 59–61
data-mining algorithms. *See also* clustering; *decision*
    tree entries
  association, 13
  defined, 8
  introduced, 12
  OLE DB for Data Mining, 13, 24, *24*
  regression analysis or sequencing, 13
Data-Mining Model Browser
  for Member Card RDBMS, 102–6, *102, 103, 104,*
    105, 106, 107
  for visualizing decision trees from relational data,
    88–94, *88, 89, 90–91, 91, 92, 93*
data-mining models
  defined, 8
  Document Type Definition (DTD), 290
  introduced, 11–12
  patterns vs., 12
  tables and, 237–38
  training, 61–64, *63*
  using code to browse, 238–43
data-mining model structure
  introduced, 237
  schema rowsets
    introduced, 243
    MINING_COLUMNS schema rowset, 249–59,
      251, 253–54, 256
    MINING_MODEL_CONSTANT schema rowset,
      259–62, *260*
    MINING_MODELS schema rowset, 243–49, *244,*
      283
    MINING_SERVICES schema rowset, 262–65, *265*
    MODEL_CONTENT_PMML schema rowset,
      268–69
    SERVICE_PARAMETERS schema rowset, 266–68

data-mining model structure, *continued*
  structure of the data-mining model case, 237–38
  using code to browse data-mining models, 238–43
Data-Mining Prediction Query task package, 167
Data Mining Prediction Query Task Wizard, 317–18,
    317, 320–21, *320, 321*
data models. *See also* data warehouses
  introduced, 27
  predictive vs. descriptive, 51
  preparing for testing, 64
DataPump task, 163
DataSource object, 232
DataSources collection, 232
Data Transformation Services. *See* Microsoft Data
    Transformation Services (DTS)
DataType property, *220*
data warehouses
  architecture for data mining
    creating warehouses from OLTP data, 33–36
    introduced, 33
    optimizing data for mining, 36–42, *39, 41*
    physical data-mining structure, 42–43, *42, 43*
  defined, 7–8
  introduced, 27
  maintaining data integrity, 28–31, *29, 30*
  problems encountered when creating, 34
  relational
    advantages of relational data storage, 44–45
    building supporting tables for data mining, 45
    introduced, 43–44
  reporting against OLTP data, 31–32
  when to discard data from, 36
DDL (Data Definition Language), 22
deadlocks, 32
Decision Support Objects (DSO)
  adding new data sources, 233–34
  analysis server roles, 234–35
  database roles, 234–35
  installing, 209
  introduced, 24–25, 209–10, *210*
  object model
    Database object, 211, 219, 220, *220–21*, 233
    DataSource object, 232
    introduced, 210, *210*
    MiningModel object, 221, 233
    Server object, 211–19

Decision Support Objects (DSO), *continued*
  OLAP data-mining model using, 230–33
  relational data-mining model using, 221–30
  scripting vs. Visual Basic, 210–11
decision trees
  introduced, 12
  when to use, 113
decision trees from OLAP data
  analyzing data with
    introduced, 126–28
    using the generated dimension, 129–30, *130,
        131*, 132, *132*
    using the generated virtual cube, 128–29, *128,
        129*
  creating the model
    completing the model, 123, *123*
    introduced, 115–16
    selecting the case, 118–19, *119*
    selecting the dimension and virtual cube,
        121–22, *122*
    selecting the predicted entity, 119–21, *120*
    selecting the source cube and data-mining
        technique, 116, *117*, 118, *118*
    selecting the source type, 116, *117*
    selecting the training data, 121, *121*
  introduced, 115
  OLAP Mining Model Editor, 125–26, *125*
  transactions and, 124–25, *124*
decision trees from relational data
  algorithms
    C4.5, 98
    Chi-squared Automatic Interaction Detector
        (CHAID), 98
    Classification and Regression Trees (CART),
        97–98
    Microsoft, 97
  bins in, 96–97, *96*
  creating the model
    Analysis Manager, 70–74, *70, 71, 73, 74*
    introduced, 69–70
    Mining Model Wizard, 74–80, *75, 76, 77, 78,
        79, 80*
    Relational Mining Model Editor, 81–86, *81, 82,
        83, 84–85, 86*
  dealing with numerical data, 96–97, *96*

decision trees from relational data, *continued*
  predictions with
    introduced, 109
    navigating trees, 109–10
    navigation vs. rules, 112–13
    problem trees, 110–12
  splits, 107–8
  structure and function
    introduced, 98–99, *99*
    Member Card RDBMS data-mining model,
      102–6, *102, 103, 104, 105, 106, 107*
    surfing conditions example, 99, *100–101,* 101
  visualizing the model
    Data-Mining Model Browser, 88–94, *88, 89,*
      90–91, 91, 92, 93
    Dependency Network Browser, 94–96, *94, 95*
    Relational Mining Model Editor, 87, *87*
  when to use, 113
denormalization, 30–31, *30*
Dependency Network Browser, 94–96, *94, 95*
Description property, *220*
descriptive vs. predictive data models, 51
deviation analysis, 59
dimensions, 121–22, *122,* 129–30, *130, 131,* 132, *132*
directed data mining, 51–52
Distribution property, *221*
distributions
  introduced, 56, *56*
  log-normal, 255
  normal, 255
  uniform, 256
diversity, 108
DLLSelfRegister function, 209, 273
Document Type Definition (DTD) for data-mining
  models, 290
DSO. *See* Decision Support Objects (DSO)
dsoServer object, 211
DTD (Document Type Definition) for data-mining
  models, 290
DTS. *See* Microsoft Data Transformation Services
  (DTS)
DTS Designer
  introduced, 170, 171
  opening, 171–72
  saving DTS packages, 172–74
dtsrun utility, 174–77, *176*
Dynamic Properties task, 165

E

evaluation set, 64
Execute Package task, 164
Execute Process task, 166
Execute SQL task, 166
Extensible Markup Language (XML), 20, 290–95

F

flat tables vs. multidimensional OLAP tables, 48–49
FLATTENED option, 305
flattened tables, 36
FromClause property, *220*
FROM PMML clause, 285
FTP task, 167

G

granularity, data, 40–42, *41*

H

HOLAP (hybrid online analytical processing), 19–20,
  20
HTTP, connecting to Analysis Services using, 280,
  280
hybrid online analytical processing (HOLAP), 19–20,
  20

I

influence analysis, 58
input columns, 37, 45, 78, 79, *79,* 152–53, *153*
INSERT INTO statement, 286–87, 288
interval values, 143
IsDisabled property, *221*
IsInput property, *221*
IsKey property, *221*
IsPredictable property, *221*

J

JoinClause property, *220*
joins, 78, 152

K

K variable, 139, 153
KD (Knowledge Discovery), 3. *See also* data mining
key columns, 37, 78
K-Means clustering algorithm
    cluster boundaries, 141, *141*
    finding the center of clusters, 140, *141*
    finding the clusters, 139, *139*
    introduced, 138–39
    known vs. unknown clusters, 140
    overview, 138
Knowledge Discovery (KD), 3. *See also* data mining

L

leaf nodes, 99
locking contention, 31–32
log-normal distribution, 255

M

MDStore object, 211
MDStores collection, 211, 219, 221, 233
MDX (Multidimensional Expressions), 25, 129–30,
    130, 131, 132, *132*
mean, 54, *55*
measures, 143
median, 55, *55*
Member Card RDBMS
    Data-Mining Model Browser, 102–6, *102, 103,*
        104, 105, 106, 107
    navigating trees, 109–10
    navigation vs. rules, 112–13
    problem trees and, 110–12
    splits, 107–8
Message Queue task, 166
metadata, 234
Microsoft Data Transformation Services (DTS)
    connections
        configuring, 168–69
        introduced, 167
        sources, 167–68
    defined, 162
    DTS Designer
        introduced, 170, 171
        opening, 171–72
        saving DTS packages, 172–74
    dtsrun utility, 174–77, *176*

Microsoft Data Transformation Services (DTS),
    continued
    introduced, 162
    package creation
        executing the package, 206–8, *206, 207, 208*
        first database connection, 189, *190*
        FTP task configuration, 184–86, *184, 185, 186*
        introduced, 177–78
        new package creation, 182–84, *183*
        preparing the SQL Server environment, 178–79,
            179–82
        processing task creation, 204–5, *204, 205*
        saving the package, 205, *206*
        scheduling runs, 207–8, *207, 208*
        text file connection, 186–88, *187, 188*
        transformation configuration, 195–203, *196,*
            197, 198, 199, 200, 201, 203
        transformation creation, 190–94, *191, 192, 193,*
            194
    package definition, 162
    package workflow
        introduced, 169
        precedence constraints, 170
        steps, 169–70
    tasks
        ActiveX Scripting, 166
        Analysis Services Processing, 167
        Bulk Insert, 163
        Copy SQL Server Objects, 165
        custom and third-party, 167
        Data Driven Query, 163–64
        Data-Mining Prediction Query, 167
        DataPump, 163
        defined, 162
        Dynamic Properties, 165
        Execute Package, 164
        Execute Process, 166
        Execute SQL, 166
        FTP, 167
        introduced, 162
        Message Queue, 166
        Send Mail, 166
        Transfer Databases, 164
        Transfer Error Messages, 164
        Transfer Jobs, 164
        Transfer Logins, 165
        Transfer Master Stored Procedure, 164
        Transform Data, 162–63

Microsoft Data Transformation Services (DTS),
  continued
  using DTS to run prediction queries, 317–22, *317,
    318, 319, 320, 321, 322*
Microsoft Repository, 234
Microsoft SQL Server. *See also* Analysis Services
  PREDICTION JOIN clause, 14, 24
  syntax to data mine, 14
MiningAlgorithm property, *220*
MINING_COLUMNS schema rowset, 249–59, *251,
    253–54, 256*
MINING_MODEL_CONSTANT schema rowset,
    259–62, *260*
MiningModel object, 221, 233
mining models. *See* data-mining models
MiningModels collection, 233
MINING_MODELS schema rowset, 243–49, *244*, 283
Mining Model Wizard
  for creating clustering models, 149–53, *149, 150,
    151, 152, 153*
  for creating decision trees
    from OLAP data, 115–16, *117*, 118–23, *118,
      119, 120, 121, 122, 123*
    from relational data, 74–80, *75, 76, 77, 78, 79,
      80*
MINING_SERVICES schema rowset, 262–65, *265*
mode, 56
MODEL_CONTENT_PMML schema rowset, 268–69
models. *See* data-mining models
MOLAP (multidimensional online analytical
    processing), 18, *18*
Msmddo80.dll, 209
Msmdlock.dll, 209
Msmdnet.dll, 209
Msmdso.rll, 209
Multidimensional Expressions (MDX), 25, 129–30,
    130, 131, 132, *132*
multidimensional online analytical processing
    (MOLAP), 18, *18*
mushrooms data-mining model
  color analysis, 92, *92*
  database, 73–74, *73, 74*
  Data Mining Model Browser, 88–94, *88, 89,
    90–91, 92, 93*
  Dependency Network Browser, 94–96, *94, 95*
  DTS package creation
    executing the package, 206–8, *206, 207, 208*

mushrooms data-mining model, DTS package
    creation, *continued*
  first database connection, 189, *190*
  FTP task configuration, 184–86, *184, 185, 186*
  introduced, 177–78
  new package creation, 182–84, *183*
  preparing the SQL Server environment, 178–79,
    179–82
  processing task creation, 204–5, *204, 205*
  saving the package, 205, *206*
  scheduling runs, 207–8, *207, 208*
  text file connection, 186–88, *187, 188*
  transformation configuration, 195–203, *196,
    197, 198, 199, 200, 201, 203*
  transformation creation, 190–94, *191, 192, 193,
    194*
  edible mushrooms, 88, *89*
  introduced, 72–73
  local data-mining model
    INSERT INTO statement, 286–87, *288*
    introduced, 280–83, *281–82*
    nested tables and the SHAPE statement, 289
    OPENROWSET function, 287–89
    SELECT INTO statement, 286
    storage of, 284–85
  Mining Model Wizard, 74–80, *75, 76, 77, 78, 79,
    80*
  odor analysis, 91, *91*
  poisonous mushrooms, *89*
  Relational Mining Model Editor
    for creating decision trees, 81–86, *81, 82, 83,
      84–85, 86*
    for visualizing decision trees, 87, *87*
  ring type analysis, 92, *93*
  stalk surface analysis, 92, *93*

N

NATURAL PREDICTION JOIN clause, 301
nested tables, 24, *24*, 238, 282, 289
normal distribution, 255
normalization, 28–30, *29*

O

OLAP. *See* online analytical processing (OLAP)
OLAP Mining Model Editor, 125–26, *125*

OLAP Services. *See* Analysis Services
OLE DB. *See also* PivotTable Service
  nested tables, 24, *24*
  providers, 23
OLE DB for Data Mining, 13, 24, *24*
OLE DB for OLAP, 23, *23*
OLTP. *See* online transaction processing (OLTP)
online analytical processing (OLAP). *See also*
     decision trees from OLAP data
  advantage of data mining over, 6
  cubes
    advantages, 47–49
    data mining uses, 46, *47*
    introduced, 46
    limitations for data mining, 49
    moving data from relational structures into, 44
  data mining vs., 11, 17
  flat tables vs. multidimensional OLAP tables,
    48–49
  highly-structured storage requirements, 48
  hybrid online analytical processing (HOLAP),
    19–20, *20*
  introduced, 16–17, *16*
  limitations for data mining, 49
  multidimensional online analytical processing
    (MOLAP), 18, *18*
  OLE DB for, 23, *23*
  relational online analytical processing (ROLAP),
    18–19, *19*
online transaction processing (OLTP)
  creating warehouses from OLTP data, 33–36
  reporting against OLTP data, 31–32
OPENROWSET function, 287–89, 298–99
overfitting, 62–64

P

patterns
  data-mining models vs., 12
  defined, 8
PivotTable Service
  architecture, *271*
  connecting to, introduced, 276
  connecting to Analysis Services
    using HTTP, 280, *280*
    using PivotTable Service, 276–77, *277–79*

PivotTable Service, *continued*
  installing and registering components
    file locations, 274, *274–75*
    installing registry settings, 275
    introduced, 273
    redistribution setup programs, 275–76
  introduced, 22–23, 271–72, *271*
  local data-mining model
    INSERT INTO statement, 286–87, 288
    introduced, 280–83, *281–82*
    nested tables and the SHAPE statement, 289
    OPENROWSET function, 287–89
    SELECT INTO statement, 286
    storage of, 284–85
  redistributing components, 272–73
PMML (Predictive Model Markup Language), 20,
    290–95
population, 53
predictable columns, 45, 78–79, *79*, 152–53, *153*
Predict function, 307, *307*
PredictHistogram function, 310–12, *312–13*, 315
PREDICTION JOIN clause, 14, 24, 300–304, *301, 303*
prediction joins, 25
prediction queries
  with clustering models, 315–17, *316*
  components of
    basic prediction queries, 298
    introduced, 297
    prediction functions, 307–15, *307, 309, 312–13*
    PREDICTION JOIN clause, 300–304, *301, 303*
    specifying columns, 300
    specifying the test case source, 298–99
    using functions as columns, 304
    using tabular values as columns, 304–5, *305–6*
    WHERE clause, 306
  introduced, 297
  singleton queries, 298–99
  using DTS to run, 317–22, *317, 318, 319, 320,*
    321, 322
Prediction Query Builder, 318–19, *319*
Prediction Query Editor, 320, *320*
predictive information, 4
Predictive Model Markup Language (PMML), 20,
    290–95
predictive vs. descriptive data models, 51
PredictNodeId function, 315
PredictProbability function, 308

PredictProbabilityStdev function, 309, 310
PredictProbabilityVariance function, 309, 310
PredictScore function, 314
PredictStdev function, 309, 310
PredictSupport function, 308, *309*
PredictVariance function, 309
providers in OLE DB, 23
pruning, 62, 111
pure leaf nodes, 99
pure trees, 99

Q

qualifiers, 304
queries. *See* prediction queries

R

range, 54
RangeMax function, 314
RangeMid function, 314
RangeMin function, 314
ranking, 143
record overlap, 145, *146*
regression, 13, 57
RELATED TO clause, 282
relational data warehouses
    advantages of relational data storage, 44–45
    building supporting tables for data mining, 45
    introduced, 43–44
Relational Mining Model Editor
    for creating decision trees from relational data,
        81–86, *81, 82, 83, 84–85, 86*
    for viewing cluster models, 154, *155*, 156
    for visualizing decision trees from relational data,
        87, *87*
relational online analytical processing (ROLAP),
    18–19, *19*
repository, 234
ROLAP (relational online analytical processing),
    18–19, *19*
rollback, 124
root nodes, 99
rows, selecting, 39, *39*

S

sample, 54
schema rowsets
    introduced, 243
    MINING_COLUMNS schema rowset, 249–59, *251,
        253–54, 256*
    MINING_MODEL_CONSTANT schema rowset,
        259–62, *260*
    MINING_MODELS schema rowset, 243–49, *244,*
        283
    MINING_SERVICES schema rowset, 262–65, *265*
    MODEL_CONTENT_PMML schema rowset,
        268–69
    SERVICE_PARAMETERS schema rowset, 266–68
segmentation, 92
SELECT INTO statement, 286
SELECT statement, 297, 298, 300, 305
Send Mail task, 166
Server object, 211–19
Service object, 212
SERVICE_PARAMETERS schema rowset, 266–68
SHAPE statement, 289
simulations and what-if scenarios, 61
single-tier (client) architecture, 42, *42*
SourceColumn property, *221*
SourceCube property, *220*
SourceOlapObject property, *221*
splits, 107–8
SQL Server. *See* Microsoft SQL Server
standard deviation, 57
statistics
    bias, 54
    cause and effect analysis, 58–59
    chi-squared analysis, 62–64, *63*
    comparison analysis, 58
    correlation, 57
    deviation analysis, 59
    distributions
        introduced, 56, *56*
        log-normal, 255
        normal, 255
        uniform, 256
    influence analysis, 58
    mean, 54, *55*
    median, 55, *55*
    mode, 56
    population, 53

statistics, *continued*
    range, 54
    regression, 57
    sample, 54
    standard deviation, 57
    trend analysis, 59
    undirected data mining vs., 52–53
    variance, 56–57
    variation analysis, 58
SubClassType property, *220*

T

target columns, 37
test set, 64
three-tier architecture, 43, *43*
TopCount function, 313
TopPercent function, 314
TopSum function, 313
training data, 61–64, *63*, 121, *121*
TrainingQuery property, *220*
training sets, 64, 109–10
transactions, 124–25, *124*
Transfer Databases task, 164
Transfer Error Messages task, 164
Transfer Jobs task, 164
Transfer Logins tasks, 165
Transfer Master Stored Procedure task, 164
Transform Data task, 162–63
tree operation restriction, 259
trend analysis, 59
two-tier architecture, 42–43, *43*

U

underfitting, 64
undirected data mining
    clustering as, 137, *138*

undirected data mining, *continued*
    introduced, 52
    learning from historical data, 57–59
    predicting the future, 59–61
    vs. statistics, 52–53
uniform distribution, 256
Update method, 234

V

value columns, 37
variance, 56–57
variation analysis, 58
vector angle similarity, 144–45, *145*
virtual cubes, 46, 121–22, *122*, 128–29, *128, 129*

W

what-if scenarios and simulations, 61
WHERE clause, 306, 308
Windows Scripting Host (WSH), 238
wizards
    Data Mining Prediction Query Task Wizard,
        317–18, *317*, 320–21, *320, 321*
    Mining Model Wizard
        for creating clustering models, 149–53, *149,*
            150, 151, 152, 153
        for creating decision trees from OLAP data,
            115–16, *117*, 118–23, *118, 119, 120, 121,*
            122, 123
        for creating decision trees from relational data,
            74–80, *75, 76, 77, 78, 79, 80*
WSH (Windows Scripting Host), 238

X

XML (Extensible Markup Language), 20, 290–95

Claude Seidman is an independent database developer, database administrator, and trainer who over the past fourteen years has designed and implemented numerous high-profile, mission-critical applications for some of the world's largest corporations. Claude specializes in database design and implementation, data warehousing, and OLAP. As often as possible, he writes articles on OLAP and on the management of Very Large Data Bases (VLDBs). On occasion, he teaches at various training centers and a university near his home. Claude holds the MCDBA. MCSE, MCSD, MCP+I, and MCT certifications from Microsoft. He can be reached at cseidman@dbflash.com.

The manuscript for this book was prepared and galleyed using Microsoft Word 2000. Pages were composed by Microsoft Press using Adobe PageMaker 6.52 for Windows, with text in Garamond and display type in Franklin Gothic. Composed pages were delivered to the printer as electronic prepress files.

Cover Designer:	Girvin | Strategic Branding & Design
Cover Illustrator:	Tom Draper Design
Interior Graphic Designer:	James D. Kramer
Electronic Artist	Rob Nance
Principal Compositor:	Carl Diltz
Principal Copy Editor:	Patricia Masserman
Indexer:	Hugh Maddocks

Get a **Free**
e-mail newsletter, updates,
special offers, links to related books,
and more when you

register on line!

Register your Microsoft Press® title on our Web site and you'll get a FREE subscription to our e-mail newsletter, *Microsoft Press Book Connections.* You'll find out about newly released and upcoming books and learning tools, online events, software downloads, special offers and coupons for Microsoft Press customers, and information about major Microsoft® product releases. You can also read useful additional information about all the titles we publish, such as detailed book descriptions, tables of contents and indexes, sample chapters, links to related books and book series, author biographies, and reviews by other customers.

Registration is easy. Just visit this Web page and fill in your information:

http://mspress.microsoft.com/register

Microsoft®
